LEAVING

BEFORE

THE RAINS

COME

ALSO BY ALEXANDRA FULLER

Cocktail Hour Under the Tree of Forgetfulness

The Legend of Colton H. Bryant

Scribbling the Cat: Travels with an African Soldier

Don't Let's Go to the Dogs Tonight: An African Childhood

LEAVING

BEFORE

THE RAINS

COME

|||||||||||||||||||||

Alexandra Fuller

The Penguin Press
New York
2015

PENGUIN PRESS
Published by the Penguin Group
Penguin Group (USA) LLC
375 Hudson Street
New York, New York 10014

USA · Canada · UK · Ireland · Australia
New Zealand · India · South Africa · China
penguin.com
A Penguin Random House Company

First published by Penguin Press,
a member of Penguin Group (USA) LLC, 2015

LIBRARY OF CONGRESS CATALOGING-IN-PUBLICATION DATA IS AVAILABLE
ISBN: 978-1-59420-586-6
978-1-59420-647-4 (International edition)

Printed in the United States of America
1   3   5   7   9   10   8   6   4   2

DESIGNED BY AMANDA DEWEY

Penguin is committed to publishing works of quality and integrity.
In that spirit, we are proud to offer this book to our readers; however,
the story, the experiences, and the words are the author's alone.

FOR THE SIX:

JOAN, BRYAN, SHARON, SUSIE, MELODIE, AND TERRY.

With my gratitude and love.

I and the world happened to have a slight difference of opinion; the world said I was mad, and I said the world was mad. I was outvoted, and here I am.

—RICHARD BROTHERS

We carry with us the wonders we seek without us: there is all Africa and her prodigies in us.

—SIR THOMAS BROWNE

CONTENTS

AND AWAY WE FLY

D ad says he's going to die next week," Vanessa said. The phone line from Zambia was good for once. No echoing, no hopping, no static. Still, I felt the distancing power of the whole of the Atlantic Ocean between us.

"Say that again," I said.

"Dad," repeated Vanessa loudly and slowly, as if she were an Englishwoman-on-vacation in the tropics. "He says he's not going to bat some other chap's innings. He says it's not cricket." I heard her light a cigarette: the scrape and hiss of a match; the singe of burning tobacco; the capacious inhale. I recognized we were in danger of doing things on Vanessa's indolent schedule. She would be there south of the equator cultivating nonchalance. I would be here north of it conscious of time-lapsing deadlines.

"Why?" I asked. "Of what?"

"The Bible," Vanessa said, calmly exhaling.

"Oh," I said. "Well, no one in their right mind takes the Bible literally."

"I do," Vanessa said.

"Exactly," I triumphed.

I pictured Vanessa at the picnic table on her veranda, a generous helping of South African white wine in front of her. Mosquitoes would be whining around her ankles poisonously. She'd be wiping sweat off her nose, pushing panting dogs away from her lap. I could also hear the rainy-season chorus of Southern Hemisphere woodland-living birds in the background. The tyranny of a Heuglin's robin, some chattering masked weavers, and a Sombre bulbul shouting over and over, *"Willie! Come out and fight! Willie! Come out and fight! Scaaared."*

Meanwhile the austerity of winter was still hanging on here. Outside my office window, there were tiny beams of frozen mud showing through tall snowbanks. The only birds I could see were an industrious banditry of black-capped chickadees at the suet feeder. They seemed robustly ascetic little creatures, like tiny chattering monks. I'd read they are able to lower their body temperature by up to a dozen degrees on cold winter nights to conserve energy. *Torpor* was the word the bird books used. Hummingbirds supposedly did the same thing, but they also had to eat sixty times their body weight a day just to stay alive, at least according to a fragment of a poem by Charles Wright I kept above my computer. "Now that's a life on the edge," the fragment concludes.

"I have to go," I said.

But Vanessa had begun to expand on her vision for Dad's funeral arrangements and she was in full voice now. Should there be an old Land Rover or a donkey cart for a hearse? And was that Polish priest from Old Mkushi still alive, the one who had been at my wedding? Because he had lived in the bush long enough not to blink if we asked him to have the service under a baobab tree instead of in a church, right? And perhaps we could get people from the villages to make a choir. "There are heaps of those Apostles all over the place," Vanessa pointed out. "But do they sing, or do they just sit around draped in white bedsheets, moaning?"

I said I didn't know, but I'd never forget the time Mum got in a dustup with the Apostle who had moved onto the edge of the farm with his several wives and his scores of children and whose vegetable plot had strayed onto her overflowing pet cemetery. Mum had yelled obscenities, planted her walking stick in the soil, and declared turf war. In return, the Apostle had thrown rocks at Mum's surviving dogs, brandished his staff, and recited bellicose passages from the Old Testament. "An apoplectic apostolic," Mum had reported with relish, although her neck had been out for weeks after the Apostle shook her, "just like Jack Russell with a rat."

Vanessa took another considered drag off her cigarette. "Oh right," she said. "I'd forgotten about that. Maybe Catholics might be better after all. They'll know proper hymns. Plus Catholics have wine at intermission, don't they? And Mum doesn't have a history of battling them, does she?"

"Not yet," I said.

"And what about entertainment for afterwards?" Vanessa asked. "People will have driven for days. They'll be expecting a thrash. It'll have to be a huge party from beginning to end, with a calypso band, Harry Belafonte, and buckets of rum punch. Perhaps we could organize boat races on the Zambezi in dugout canoes. That would be groovy. And what about a greasy pole over one of Mum's fishponds for the especially inebriated mourners, because you know it's going to be Alcoholics Unanimous from beginning to end? And maybe we could have a maze like the one we had at Mum and Dad's fortieth anniversary," Vanessa said. "Remember?"

I would never forget that either. There had been shots of

something fairly stiff at the entrance to the maze, and some guests got so drunk right off the bat they were stranded in dead ends until dawn. But I didn't bring this up, nor did I say that I thought Vanessa's suggestions were murderously bad. How many funerals did she want in one week? In the interests of time (mine, chiefly) I said I thought they were all ideas worth considering. "That is, when Dad is actually dead," I said. And then I added, in a way that I hoped suggested a signing off, "Okay, Van. I'm quite busy here."

But Vanessa wouldn't be deterred; she poured herself another glass of wine and rattled on. "No, no, no," she said. "We have to plan now, we'll be too distraught at the time." She reminded me she wouldn't be able to do any of the readings because she was illiterate, as well we all knew. Mum certainly couldn't do a reading, or much of anything, because she would be an inconsolable wreck. And Richard shouldn't be allowed anywhere near a pulpit. "He'll just grunt and growl and terrify the congregation," Vanessa said. "No, Al, when Dad dies, you're going to have to do the urology."

|||||||||

A week later, March 8, 2010, Dad turned seventy. The day came and went, and in spite of Psalm 90:10 my father didn't die. To prove the miracle of his continued corporal existence among us, Vanessa e-mailed me a photograph of his funeral party turned birthday bash. There he was on her veranda in the Kafue hills, his arm around Mum's shoulders. My parents were wearing matching straw hats and expressions of matching lopsided hilarity. Between them, they were holding a bouquet of beaten-up-looking yellow flowers. Daffodils, I thought, but I wasn't sure. For one thing—due to the camera shaking, or the subjects swaying—the photograph was a little blurry. And for another thing, Vanessa steals most of her flowers from Lusaka hotel gardens, and daffodils seemed unlikely for all sorts of reasons.

I felt a pang of jealous nostalgia, although *pang* is the wrong word because that suggests something satiable, like hunger. And nostalgia isn't quite right either, because that suggests a sentimental view of the past, like Artie Shaw or Doris Day was the soundtrack for my youth, but it wasn't. That was my parents' soundtrack. Vanessa and I listened to the Swedish pop group ABBA. We had Clem Tholet, the Rhodesian folksinger, ever a popular star at the annual *Bless 'Em All* Troop Shows. We learned to dance to Ipi Ntombi's "The Warrior." My family's history—with its very real, inevitable consequences—defied romantic longing.

Although Dad believes the only side you can reliably count on is your own, and Vanessa sometimes dispenses irrevocable threats to never talk to any of us again, and my mother carries an impressive grudge—"I sometimes forget, but I will never ever forgive"—my family mostly gets over it, whatever it is, and they move on. They have to be in the ever-replenishing present, partly because it is filled with ever-replenishing uncertainty; there are always fresh crises coming hot on the heels of the old ones.

"No rest for the beautiful," Dad says.

"Wicked," I correct him.

"Them too probably."

Over the years, there have been other phone calls. It is usually Vanessa: "Oh Al, nightmare! There was a black mamba in the kids' room," that was once. Another time, she reported that Mum had returned from her morning walk around the farm to find a rabid dog sitting weirdly placid under the Tree of Forgetfulness. "You know what Mum's like. Luckily she realized it wasn't acting normally and she didn't try to stroke it or invite it to sleep on the sofa or anything." Then there were the few surreal months when crocodiles flooded out of the Zambezi in unusual numbers and plagued my parents' farm. They were not only in Mum's fishponds as usual, but also in Dad's banana plantation; sunbathing outside Mr. Zulu's house in the morning; casually scraping their way past the watchman's hut toward the sheep pen at night.

I seldom told Charlie about the phone calls and I rarely shared with him the freshest dramas from Zambia in part because I had learned over time that the events we Fullers found hilarious or entertaining did not always amuse my American husband. Charlie was a gallant one-man intervention wanting to save us from our recklessness, quietly stepping in whenever he thought we were drinking excessively, ruining our health with cigarettes, or courting intestinal disaster with undercooked chicken. This made the Fullers howl with laughter and did nothing to make them behave differently. One year, in a fit of common sense, I sent a case of Off! insect repellent to the farm in the hope it would reduce the incidence of familial malaria. "Bobo sent us gallons of Bugger Off for Christmas," Dad told anyone who showed up under the Tree of Forgetfulness that year. "Go ahead, squirt yourself with as much as you like. Shower in it. Have a bath."

I still felt a little torn. For a long time, I had tried to be profoundly grateful to Charlie for his impulse of wanting to rescue us from our chaos, and I had even tried to believe in his systems of control and protection the way I had once tried to believe in God. But deep down I always knew there is no way to order chaos. It's the fundamental theory at the beginning and end of everything; it's the ultimate law of nature. There's no way to win against unpredictability, to suit up completely against accidents. Which isn't to say I didn't embrace the Western idea that it was possible—"Good God, you look as if you're about to shoot yourselves out of a cannon," Dad said when he saw Charlie and me dressed for a bicycle ride in Lycra, elbow pads, and crash helmets—but I understood that as much as it is craziness to court danger, disaster, and mishap, it is also craziness to believe that everything can be charted, ordered, and prevented. It's also more boring.

When I phoned home on Sunday mornings, Mum and Dad were usually at the pub below the banana plantation, overlooking the Zambezi River. It's evening for them, and they're taking a couple hours to put their feet up at the bar. Generally, a few drinks have imbued them with extra rations of optimism. Most often, Dad answers first, shouting even if the line is clear. "Fit as a flea," he usually says, or "Not bad for an old goat." He rarely elaborates, because in spite of an influx of competitively cheap talk time into Zambia (available for purchase at every intersection in Lusaka and in numerous kiosks all over Chirundu), Dad maintains the telegram-abrupt phone manners of someone for whom long-distance calls are a prohibitively expensive luxury. "I'll hand you over to Mum," he says as soon as the absolute preliminaries have been completed.

Then it's her turn to shout contagious enthusiasm at me from their noisy world to my habitually hushed one. She holds the receiver up so I can listen to the birds, the cicadas, and the frogs, and I can hear Dad objecting to this folly: "Bloody expensive conversation Bobo is having with a bunch of fresh air." But Mum shushes him and says, "Did you hear that?" And if the dogs begin barking she says, "Oh, the adorable little terrorists, can you hear them. Say hello to Bobo, Sprocket. Harry, say woof!" Sometimes she says, "And oh listen! The hippos are scolding us." And then she holds the phone up to the river, but all I can hear is Dad complaining: "Good Lord, Tub, we're not the bloody Rockefellers." But Mum ignores him and rattles on anyway.

"Big excitement this week," she was telling me now. "We got invited to a party in Lusaka. You know, those people with all the consonants in their names. Tiny blobs of caviar, well, trout eggs really, not sturgeon obviously, and scary amounts of vodka."

"Scary?"

"Yes, so by the time we were ready to leave the party, your father had already had far too much excitement. He climbed onto the roof of the pickup and refused to come down," Mum says.

"What?" I hold the receiver out from my ear and stare at it in delight. These are my late-middle-aged parents! They are grandparents nine times over. I put the phone back to my ear. "Then what?" I ask.

"I had to drive off with him like that," Mum says. "And you know what a terrible driver I am. Heaven only knows how we made it home. I was halfway to Makeni before it dawned on me that I might be driving on the wrong side of the road."

"Dawned on you?"

"Well, Bobo, you know what drivers are these days. I thought they were hooting at me because they wanted me to go faster."

"So?"

"I drove faster, of course," Mum says. "Dad was thumping on the roof but I assumed he was just singing the 'Hallelujah' chorus or Tchaikovsky's bells and cannons. How was I to know he wanted to come down? Oh, it was such a performance."

I shut my eyes and pictured the soft, hot world at the bottom of the farm, with the river lazily curling its way east to Mozambique, and my parents contributing to a general sense of easygoing mayhem in their inimitable way. By contrast, my days were amorphously mapped out with the repeating tasks of laundry and meals and deadlines. And I was more and more drained by an increasingly fraught effort to shore myself up against the belief system I had borrowed. "Well, situation normal here," I say. "Nothing new to report."

My parents pitied me the fact that—at least as far as they could tell—all my dramas had to be self-inflicted. They considered the acceptance of the certainty of pandemonium an essential ingredient to the enjoyment of life. "Don't yell so loudly or everyone will want them," Dad said when, on a visit home, a plague of insects and a couple of geckos rained out of the thatch roof of the spare bedroom onto my mosquito net. Nothing surprised him, not the rabid dogs, or the snakes, not the hippos and elephants. "Although the novelty's beginning to wear off a bit," he admitted.

It takes a kind of outrageous courage—recklessness even, I might have said once—to revel in the pattern of that much definite chaos. I had been raised in this way, and I had loved much of my early life, and of course I loved my family, but at some point I had lost the mettle and the imagination to surrender to the promise of perpetual insecurity. Instead I chose to believe in the possibility of a predictable, chartable future, and I had picked a life that I imagined would have certainties, safety nets, and assurances.

What I did not know then is that the assurances I needed couldn't be had. I did not know that for the things that unhorse you, for the things that wreck you, for the things that toy with your internal tide—against those things, there is no conventional guard. "The problem with most people," Dad said once, not necessarily implying that I counted as most people, but not discounting the possibility either, "is that they want to be alive for as long as possible without having any idea whatsoever how to live."

MADNESS IN

PRESCRIBED DOSES

B ut when I first met Charlie at the Marco Polo Club in Lusaka, Zambia, in June 1991, he seemed to me to have perfected the art of knowing how to live. He was nearly thirty-three, an American in Zambia, running rafting and canoe operations on the Zambezi and Luangwa rivers. We nominal foreigners—those who had lived in Africa for a few generations—usually gave actual foreigners a wide berth, especially Americans. They tended to wear socks with sandals and outsized safari hats, and they stood with legs akimbo, as if they needed a little more real estate than the rest of us just to stay upright. Also, we envied and disparaged them for their habit of bringing their own supplies with them; loo roll, candy bars, little bottles of hand sanitizer and sunscreen as if our rough lavatory paper, boiled sweets, germs, and ingrained sunburn were offensive to them, brands of an inferior way of being.

Charlie didn't look like the run-of-the-mill American-in-Africa, though. He seemed seasoned in the unruly, bearded way of an outdoorsman. Attracted to the country by our rivers, he had been living in Zambia on and off for years, camping out in a sweltering warehouse near Victoria Falls, subjected to the major inconveniences of malaria, crocodiles, and dysentery. I guessed he had long ago recovered from the minor inconveniences of our socialist-era toiletries, our dearth of Snickers bars, our cavalier attitude toward diarrhea and melanoma. And although he wore sandals, his were the sort worn to paddle a raft through whitewater, not the orthotic-support kind used by Bible-wielding Baptists to tramp through supposedly heathen villages.

I was barely twenty-two, in my last year at a Canadian college, majoring in English for a bachelor of arts. "BA stands for Bugger-All if you ask me," Dad said, before reconfirming his suspicion that education was wasted on women. "So is giving females the vote, while we're on the subject." But Charlie appeared to believe higher education wasn't wasted on women any more than it was on men. He seemed to take the cause of universal adult suffrage for granted. He declared himself genuinely impressed by my English major. "Have you read *The Vampire Chronicles*?" he asked, which I thought showed refreshingly eclectic taste. And, most endearingly of all, he genuinely believed—or pretended to believe—I could actually play polo, which I considered a gentlemanly disregard for my obvious shortcomings.

Charlie told me he had taken up polo for the adrenaline. I was fascinated and a little in awe. Most people I knew, myself included, had been saturated with enough of that hormone by early childhood to last a lifetime. Like whitewater rafting, it seemed noble and romantic to take up a sport for the sheer, pointless thrill of it. I thought it was, in a minor key, like Robert Falcon Scott slogging off to the South Pole, or Laurie Lee striking out for Spain on foot from England one midsummer morning. Although unlike Scott or Lee, Charlie's gestures toward adventure were grand without being necessarily death-defying, and they came with the understanding of built-in conclusions. Twenty-eight minutes of polo; a day, a week, a month of boating; a few weeks on a mountain, and then—"Cut!"—an end to the action and a helicopter or a Land Rover arrived, cold beers were served, wounds were salved. We Zambians, on the other hand, lurched from one unplanned, uncelebrated escapade to the next; misadventure without end.

Which was why we didn't need polo for the thrill of it, but for the contrary sense of normalcy we gained from the game. Under President Kaunda's nationalist-socialist ideology, polo was as close to robustly bourgeois as we could get without alerting the unwanted attentions of petty government spies and accountants. Most of us weren't very good at the game, or even at riding horses. Charlie was good at both. He was instantly put on a team with the few real players and his handicap went up. I was put on a lucky packet team with a combined handicap of an almost impossibly low minus eight. Besides myself, my team included an enthusiastically bumbling Zambian, a mad Irishman, and a wild Indian who terrified everyone, including himself, with his unpredictable and untrained mounts. "Make way! Coming through! Oh, God protect!"

When I told people in the States that Charlie and I met playing polo in Zambia, it took me a while to understand why they reacted the way they did. Then I went to a polo match in Jackson Hole, Wyoming, and saw the Texan patrons with their five-goal-apiece Argentinean professionals, riding their matching strings of ponies with their color-coordinated bandages and custom saddle blankets. After that, I would always add, "Which sounds more glamorous than it really was."

Because in those days—nearly three decades after the end of British rule—the polo grounds in Lusaka were little more than a dusty expanse in front of the Italian Club. The club itself had none of the aggrieved nostalgia of, say, Nairobi's Muthaiga Club, and none of the pioneering grandeur of the old Bulawayo Club in Zimbabwe. It was just a rather ordinary-looking socialist-era brick building with a large bar, a decent-sized veranda, and a dining room that local Italians had converted into a restaurant with a decidedly un-Mediterranean menu: slabs of tough salty meat, peanut oil, cabbage, and whatever else was in season.

During the week our polo ponies were exercised on the abandoned racetrack adjacent to the polo grounds. Aside from the narrow path the horses followed, the track was now mostly overgrown and used as an open-air latrine by pedestrians cutting through the agricultural grounds to and from the Great East Road. The whole place was still beautiful in a wounded sort of way, a Garden of Eden gone to seed; it wasn't uncommon to spot the odd snake in there, or a surprisingly fruit-laden tree, or an incongruous pair of discarded lacy knickers flung into the shrubbery. But it wasn't by anyone's definition glamorous.

It was Charlie who gave us cachet. While we lounged on rusty buckled bleachers between chukkas he told stories about whitewater rafting in Siberia, discussing Cold War politics with officers from the old Red Army, helicopter skiing in the Rockies. He had walked with gorillas in Rwanda, he had guided clients up Kilimanjaro, he had climbed in Yosemite. There had been a documentary made about his descent of the Bashkaus River for the Discovery Channel, *Bashkaus: Hard Labor in Siberia,* and an American magazine had featured him as its cover story: "Charlie Ross: Mr. Adventure."

By contrast, although we had all lived inarguably interesting lives, few of us could afford exotic travel, and, surrounded by enough unbidden chaos on a daily basis, we didn't go in search of it in our free time. No one had written much about us or made movies about our adventures, in part because there was no beginning or end to our undertakings, no way of knowing the arc of our narratives. We were less the authors of deliberate derring-do than victims of cosmic accidents, political mishaps, mistaken identities. "Must've thought they were someone else," Dad said by way of explaining the murder of an elderly farming couple found shot to death in their house on the Great North Road. What Dad really seemed to be saying was that none of us seemed important enough to kill on purpose.

|||||||||

Within hours of meeting him, I already imagined it might be safe to invite Charlie back to our farm; he seemed to have the experience to manage my family. So far, neither Vanessa nor I had had a potential boyfriend survive the ordeal. For a start, we lived hours of rough road from the nearest city, or even the nearest safari camp where eligible men might be found. Because of this, a trial cup of coffee or a test drive over dinner was out of the question. Anyone who showed any interest in us had to be prepared from their very first date to meet our parents and spend at least one night in our temperamental farmhouse with its rats in the ceiling and ill-behaved plumbing. Most men wisely balked and sought closer, easier, more conventional dates.

But even if we could lure men back to the farm—Peace Corps volunteers, Save the Children employees, and aid workers from Continental Europe—they would encounter first my unimpressed father, or sometimes our crazy, armed-to-the-teeth Yugoslav neighbor—"You take our women, we kill you!"—then they would be treated to Adamson's hit-or-miss cooking, and finally they would be subjected to my mother's military-tribunal-grade interrogation over a bottle or two of brandy. "When you say *old* American family, do you mean your people came over on the *Mayflower*, or do you mean you're a Red Indian?" Or she would pretend not to understand their perfectly intelligible Dutch or Danish or Norwegian accents and begin speaking to them like a Nazi prison officer out of the old war movies she had enjoyed as a child in Kenya. "Let me try that again. Sprechen Sie Englisch?"

My family was an undertaking, an endurance test, for which no person could be expected to train. Most of the men would flee a day after arriving, sunburned, alcohol-poisoned, savaged by the dogs, and crippled with stomach cramps. "Nerves," Mum said. "Weak constitutions. No wonder they lost the war."

"What war?"

Mum rolled her eyes. "Oh, you know what I mean."

The one man who had seemed a likely tough enough candidate—the Englishman with a proper accent, reasonable pedigree, and unwavering stiff upper lip who drove from Malawi to Zambia in a 1962 Land Rover—and who seemed able to endure any amount of undercooked chicken, flea bites, and cheap South African wine, ended up falling for my mother instead of for either of us. "Well, what do you expect, if you and Vanessa *will* sit around picking your spots and saying nothing interesting?" Mum said. Our father only shrugged unsympathetically and lit his pipe. "Your mother's boyfriends are no business of mine," he said. "Anyway, the chap has very good taste if you ask me."

I planned for a life of spinsterhood. Vanessa at least was working in England when she wasn't home on holiday, and she was magnetically beautiful. "The face of the eighties," a modeling consultant at her London finishing school had called her in her twentieth year. Plus, she had made an early decision to cultivate a demeanor of dumb acquiescence that had a devastating effect on men, although I knew her expression to be complete fakery. She was really just temporarily dormant, ready to blow up and smother everyone around her with ash and molten lava anytime the need arose. But London traffic screeched to a standstill if she floated into a busy street; men fell over themselves to carry her bags; if she put an unlit cigarette anywhere near her lips, a pyre of matches appeared; one of Dad's posh English relatives reported seeing her drifting aimlessly and barefoot up Elizabeth Street. "Smoking a cigarette and kicking up the leaves," Auntie Pammy said, and we could almost see the Vaseline on the lens of that image. We assumed she would marry early and well.

Meantime, I had inherited my maternal grandmother's timeless expression of Highland Scottish suspicion, my mother's startlingly unfiltered outspokenness, and my father's gift for easy profanity. "You were a pleasant enough child. Do *try* and make yourself more agreeable," my mother would occasionally plead, which I thought was rich coming from her.

For my sixteenth birthday, she bought me *The Official Sloane Ranger Handbook: How the British Upper Class Prepares Its Offspring for Life* by Ann Barr and Peter York. I was fairly certain that any other parent buying this book for a daughter had done so as a joke. Not so Mum. She had done so in lieu of responsible parenting. The cover instructed, "Why it really matters to: wear navy blue, eat jelly with a fork, read Dick Francis and the *FT,* giggle in bed, cry when you sing carols, not cry at funerals, kill salmon, drink seriously, put the 'Great' into Britain and the 'Hooray' into Henry, and live in the country."

I objected: I didn't want to put the "Great" into a nation I barely knew or the "Hooray" into some Eton-educated bon vivant; I wanted to live in the wild African bush, not in some denatured bucolic English field; I admired the full-throated Zambian way of mourning the dead with shaved heads and ululating lamentation; and pearls and navy blue were all wrong for a Southern Hemisphere summer. Also, *The Official Sloane Ranger Handbook* featured Princess Diana on the cover, the supposed epitome of Sloanedom, but she was a terrible advertisement for British upper-class insouciance. Even two short years into her marriage to Charles, she looked tragic and barely breathing, as if the killed salmon had got its revenge and a tiny nonfatal but obstructing fishbone had wedged in her throat. Mum agreed, "Yes, Di is a bit of a drip. They should have put someone outdoorsy and horsey on the cover." She paused and then added without any degree of subtlety, "Now you, for example, Bobo, are *very* outdoorsy and horsey."

But for me, there was no going back, no skipping the African years and reabsorbing into Britain as if Rhodesia's bush war and tough boarding schools and the giddy freedom of living on outsized ranches and the "whole of bloody Africa to play in" hadn't lodged like hardy parasites in my English/ Scottish blood. And regardless of my mother's idea that marriage to the proper person was an acceptable career choice, I was never going to marry a Tory aristocrat with deep pockets and a pile in the country. "I don't blame you, Bobo," Dad said, uncharacteristically taking sides. "I think all the decent chaps died out with Churchill and that other bloke."

"What other bloke?" I asked.

"I don't know, but there must have been at least one other."

No one thought to tell me that it was all right to make a career choice that didn't involve having a husband, although from the start Dad had been clear that I had to be able to stand on my own two feet. But the specifics of what that meant seemed to elude him—if I could change a flat tire, shoot a gun, and ride a horse, I think he thought it was enough. Also no one thought to let me know that my British passport, while a useful way to get off the continent, was no way to stay. And if anyone had asked what I wanted—if it had been my choice—I would have given up my British passport without a second thought and exchanged it for a Zambian one.

I was accidentally British, incidentally European—a coincidence of so many couplings. But I was deliberately southern African. Not in a good or easy way. There is no getting around the fact that there had been so much awful violence to get me here; my people had engaged in such terrible acts of denial and oppression; I so obviously did not look African; and yet here I still was. That seemed to me to prove a point. Someone had planted me in this soil and I had taken fierce hold. And although I had no illusions—this land wasn't mine to inherit, none of it belonged to me—I couldn't help knowing that I belonged to it.

When I was finally taken back to the UK on holiday, I felt panicked and unknowable and unknown there. I wasn't British. I didn't sound British. I didn't feel British. I sat at lunch with relatives and old family friends, miserable with the choice of utensils. Why invent such a test? Who needs so many ways to get food into their mouth? It made me want to eat with my fingers. It wasn't that my parents hadn't taught me what knife and fork to use in the event that more than one of each be presented, or that the correct response to "How do you do?" is not, "Fine, thanks," but rather a nod of the head. I knew what to do and say, but to me it was like a foreign language. The moment I was tested, all I could remember was that there were conjugations and rules, and beyond that I froze. I knew the vocabulary of British behavior, but its syntax often caught me out.

I was rooted in 1980s Zambia with its dearth of suitable men and zero birth control. The AIDS epidemic was burgeoning, our silent war; you could see the walking dead everywhere, smell disease on the rapidly diminishing bodies of the victims. And in spite of the foreign press dubbing it "the gay disease," we knew different. It would be a quarter of a century before we knew that twenty-five million people in Sub-Saharan Africa were living with the disease, but we could see it coming. Men, women, and children were struck down seemingly without discrimination, as if an odorless, invisible toxic gas had fallen over our world. One day a man would seem healthy and virile, and two weeks later he would present at the kitchen door with boils and lesions. In a month, he would be dead of malaria, or diarrhea, or a blood-spewing cough, and six months later his wife and mistresses and half their children would be dead too.

Since having a Zambian boyfriend seemed suicidal for all sorts of reasons, and overseas men had to run the life-threatening Fullers-of-Central-Africa gauntlet to get anywhere near me, I split the difference and took up for a while with a Zimbabwean woman. "Double ouzo, hold the Coke," Mum ordered at the Mkushi Country Club bar, during spanakopita night. "My daughter's a lesbian." The Greek farmers blinked at her uncomprehendingly. "Oh, don't pretend you don't know what I'm talking about. You bloody people invented it."

However, in spite of its built-in conveniences, lesbianism hadn't stuck with me. And although I had moved in with a Canadian boy at university—generous and caring from a steady middle-class family—I could not imagine Joey surviving afternoon tea with my family, let alone a summer vacation or a lifetime of get-togethers. Even from a distance, Mum reacted badly to the news that I was sharing not only a bed but also kitchen appliances with a man from the New World. "Double brandy, hold the water." Mum slapped the bar at the Mkushi Country Club again. "My daughter's gone off with a bloody Canadian."

But I couldn't see how anyone could object to Charlie. True, he wasn't British, but his other virtues more than offset this otherwise serious deficiency. He seemed accomplished in the manly arts, rubbing shoulders with Eastern Bloc military, powder skiing in remote European mountains, smoking cigars; Dad might at least think twice before setting the watchman on him. He could ride horses and he had moved to Zambia with his dog; that was likely to endear him to Mum. He seemed enthralled with me, finding me funny and clever; Vanessa would hate that. But before I could ask Charlie back to the farm, he asked me to go canoeing on the Zambezi River with him for a week.

"We can camp below the wall, after the bridge, at the confluence, in the park."

"One tent?" I clarified. "Just us?" And I thought about the way in which this would hop around the Zambian gossip circuit.

"Yes," he said.

I took a deep breath. "You should know my dad will wave a shotgun at you."

Charlie didn't flinch. "That's okay. I've spent every summer of my life on my grandmother's ranch in Wyoming and she waves her shotgun at everyone, especially after cocktail hour." Pressure I didn't even know had been there eased off my chest. I pictured a whisky-drinking, gun-toting woman propped up in the frame of a cabin door surrounded by swales of sagebrush and prowling wolves. Then Charlie said that although Wyoming was the land he loved best, he had been raised and schooled in Pennsylvania. His family, he told me, were Main Line Philadelphia on both sides, and having no idea that this implied bluestocking, old-money elite, I happily pictured heroin addicts, pale and thin, draped over souring bedclothes, their inner arms threaded blue with needle tracks.

We were both speaking in shorthand, assuming a shared language. But the way most Westerners immediately envisioned a sepia-charmed life of hunting trips, spectacular sunsets, and fez-donned, white-gloved servants when I mentioned I had grown up on farms in Zimbabwe and Zambia, I conjured a blighted inner-city life when Charlie mentioned mainlining and Philadelphia. And it fit perfectly with what I thought I knew of the place.

The United States of my youthful imagination was an impression created by our postcolonial, Maoist-socialist governments, who were forever warning against the debauched evils of capitalism. And where our governments left off scaring us about the West, the secretary at the farm agency in Mkushi enthusiastically took up. Waving one of her South African tabloid magazines at me, she said she had it on good authority: ruthless capitalist American drug dealers casually injected unsuspecting passing pedestrians with heroin just for the evil sake of creating more addicts. "No, Bobo," she said, speaking through an exhaled punctuation of cigarette smoke. "It's a terrifying place, I promise you."

The supposed fact that Charlie not only hailed from drug addicts but also had a trigger-happy grandmother who owned a ranch in Wyoming did not seem incongruous to me. After all, my family had owned a farm in Rhodesia and had worked on ranches and estates in Malawi and Zambia half the size of Rhode Island, and that did not preclude us from whole years of almost itinerant destitution. Also, having very little experience with drug addicts except the pot-smoking sons of a neighbor, and Adamson, our perpetually stoned cook, I didn't think of the unlikelihood that heroin-riddled parents could have produced someone as straight-limbed and clear-eyed as Charlie.

|||||||||

Now I said to Charlie, "I've never canoed before."

"That's okay. I'm a guide. I'll get us down."

And he sounded so unalarmed by me, so unconcerned about my lack of experience, so sure of his own prowess, that I fell there and then. And in my experience, once the falling has started, there are few options for recovery. To struggle one's way back to a pre-falling place, one would need to have planned in advance, to have packed parachutes, or ropes and harnesses, to have arranged for self-arrest. But, not seeing it coming, I had taken none of these precautions. And in any case, the falling was wondrous from this altitude, as if the whole world lay in miraculous miniature below us, too many miles to foresee the landing, and, gusted about by more or less comforting currents, the sensation was rather of flight than of anything plummeting.

Time took on a weird dimension too—eternity possessed in an instant. Having invented it, we tend to believe that everything happens over time, the way the seasons ease their way around the globe steady and measurable and relaxed. But the truth is, most of the things that change the course of our lives happen in fleeting unguarded moments; grief buckling us at the knees; fear shattering through us like buckshot; love pulling us out on an unseen tide. And finding ourselves in the grip of these overpowering emotions, we then invent reasons based on the flimsy evidence we have accrued why they have happened, trying to make sense of the insensible with armloads of self-justification, distortions, and deliberate mis-interpretations.

So I said, "Yes," knowing even then that this was no ordi-nary yes, no yes with a get-out clause, no penciled-in yes. It was a certain forever yes. It was the yes my Scottish grand-mother had given when she consented to go on a picnic with my grandfather in Kenya, certain the whole rest of her life would hinge on that single syllable. "Hodge's nose," she told me fifty-five years later. "It takes years of breeding to get a nose like that." And it was the yes my mother gave to my father, explaining afterward that she had approved of the length of his Bermuda shorts. It was the yes Auntie Glug had given to my uncle because he was the last man standing at the Royal Air Force bar at the end of every night. And afterward, when I was breaking down my reason for marrying Charlie to other people, I said, "He looked good on a horse."

But even if Charlie had looked like a sack of potatoes on a horse, I would have come up with some other reason for my having said, "Yes." I would have said it was his unkempt beard, or his long legs, or his uncompromising Romanesque profile like something off an ancient coin, that had drawn me to him. What I never would have confessed was the truth: at twenty-two, I was already exhausted, and what I projected onto Charlie's broad-shouldered frame was an embellished biography that made him both my sanctuary and my savior. I believed that if I moored myself to Charlie, I would know tranquility interspersed with organized adventure. He would stay in Zambia because he loved the romance of it. I could remain here, safely. Our lives would be the "three rifles, sup-plies for a month, and Mozart" of *Out of Africa* without the plane crashes, syphilis, and Danish accent.

DECISIONS BY DIONYSUS

Lacking practice, most people report making poor decisions while under the influence of alcohol, but in our family, we made almost no major decisions sober. We did as Herodotus wrote of the Persians: "It is also their general practice to deliberate upon affairs of weight when they are drunk, and then on the morrow when they are sober the decision to which they came the night before is put before the master of the house in which it was made, and if it is then approved they act on it; if it is not, they set it aside. Sometimes, however, they are sober at their first deliberation, but in this case they always reconsider the matter under the influence of wine."

Looking back, I suspect it was because our choices were often so limited, and required such outlandish courage to make, that the only possible way to plunge ahead was to be drunk at the time of the decision and hungover at the time of the execution. We seemed always to be on the move, crossing another more or less unfriendly southern or central African border with everything we owned stuffed into one Land Rover. But taken in the right, slightly drunken spirit of misadventure, the constant unraveling, the perpetual spinning away from the familiar, were made more bearable, wondrous even.

Mostly, though, I think my parents made major decisions drunk to avoid the possibility of ever doing anything either frugal or boring, which, of all the possible sins, are the only two they consider truly deadly. "Boring is number one," Dad says. "Absolutely the worst possible sin." All other offenses my parents excuse as merely venial. "Well, he who is without sin is likely to be a bit bloody boring, so there is that hitch," Dad argues.

In 1977, when I was eight, and had first been introduced to the itchy terror of Sunday school in the Umtali Anglican Church Hall, I came home with the Ten Commandments painstakingly hand drawn in bubble letters on poster board. "Show your parents," our Rhodesian Sunday school teacher had instructed, no doubt congratulating herself on subversively recruiting a dozen infiltrating little missionaries in one go. An enthusiastic if slightly confused convert, I considered my family could definitely use some holy guidance. "Putting a jewel in their crown in heaven," my maternal grandmother said of the proselytizers who came to her door in England, by which time I was old enough to detect the scorn in her voice.

Dad regarded my poster for a minute or two, eyebrows raised as if in surprise, then he tapped ash from his cigarette into the fireplace and said, "Some of the best chaps I know break all ten of those before breakfast." My father told me this with his gun stripped on newspaper at his feet, and a can of oil on the end table at his side, because in those war years, anytime he was sitting down, he was also cleaning his gun. I waited for him to elaborate, but that was clearly all he intended to say on the matter of the two stone tablets given to Moses on Mount Sinai.

Although like God, Dad had lots of inviolate Rules: never whine, talk less, eat moderately, walk more, work harder, don't waste water. Also like God, some of Dad's commandments seemed contradictory: for example, he insisted upon stoicism, asceticism, and clean fingernails, but he also celebrated immoderation, drunkenness, and recklessness. His overriding abhorrence of idleness had already led to some confusion. "God hates idol worship of any kind," our Sunday school teacher told us. And a flood of relieved recognition washed over me, my arm shot up, and I blurted out, "My father hates idle bastards too."

|||||||||||

I watched Dad twist a piece of cheesecloth onto a cleaning rod, shake a few drops of oil onto the cloth, and run it through the bore. He brushed and lubricated the action, polished the butt, reassembled the rifle, and held it to his shoulder, one eye closed. After that, he put the gun between his legs, propping it up with two fingers, as if the weight of it was as natural as balancing part of his own body. He dug into his ammo can and retrieved a flat rubbery object, like the otherworldly worms we sometimes found under the decomposing corpses of animals along the wild edges of the farm. He rolled it over the top of the barrel. "Stops water getting in," he explained of the condom's military use. Which made me think of the rainy season, and swollen rivers and the smell of Dad—bitter and musty like damp hessian sacks in the tobacco grading shed— when he came back from his two weeks' patrol in the Himalayas. He stood up and lit a cigarette, gun over his shoulder. "I'll tell you one thing, for what it's worth," he said. "All the heaven and hell a person's going to find is right now, right here, under our noses." Then he walked onto the veranda. "More than enough to be getting on with, I would have thought."

Vanessa was resting in our bedroom with a damp face-cloth over her eyes and a cat on her pillow. Olivia was under a mosquito net in her crib. Our two beds and Olivia's crib were clustered in the middle of the room. Dad had pushed them together away from the window in case we were mortared and the panes blew in. Olivia was naked but for a cloth nappy and a piece of muslin draped across her stomach. Years earlier, as a young man in the West Indies, Dad had awoken from a shirtless afternoon nap with a terrible gut ache. Subsequently, he believed that the exposure of one's midsection to air, even turgid equatorial air, was the cause of poor digestion, an incitement to malaria, and the reason for gout, insanity, and weak will. I bypassed the baby's crib and stood at the end of Vanessa's bed, breathing loudly until she could no longer deny my presence.

"What are you creeping around for?" she asked.

"Do you want to see my poster?" I whispered, so as not to wake Olivia, who was already making the kitten noises of a baby whose dreams are interrupted. "It's about God."

"No," Vanessa said, not lifting up the flannel.

"I made it myself," I said, by not much way of persuasion.

"No," Vanessa said again.

There was a long silence during which I attempted to make my breathing annoying and wounded, also very loud. Finally Vanessa, who had taken the average Rhodesian youth's obsession with ABBA to a new personal depth, lifted the corner of her damp facecloth and eyed me critically. "Who would you rather be?" she asked. "Agnetha or Anni-Frid."

"Which one's which, again?"

Vanessa sighed aggrievedly, as if I'd questioned the identifying characteristics of a close beloved relative. "Agnetha's the blonde one."

"Then Anni-Frid," I said.

"That's who I want to be, so you can't."

I retreated and made my way across the veranda to my parents' room. Mum was lying down, curtains drawn against the midday sun. I climbed onto the end of her bed with its green-and-red tropical flower cover and its pile of cats and dogs at her feet. I held up the poster for Mum's inspection. She looked at it impassively for a moment and then said, "But Bobo, there's no art. It's just lots of big bulgy writing." She sounded disappointed not to see graphic depictions of the Lord's name being taken in vain, or the committing of adultery, although honestly the mechanics of both sins had eluded me. I could, however, imagine drawing a picture of a man with a gun and a red line through it to signify Thou Shalt Not Kill, but that seemed too much like the sign we once saw being held on a street corner in Umtali by a long-haired man in a kaftan.

"Oh, groovy, man!" Vanessa had said.

But before I could think of something flower-powerish of my own to say, Dad had silenced us all. "Bloody hippie," he muttered. "Whole lot of them should be lined up and shot at dawn."

God, with all his wrath and constant references to war and patriarchal rules, seemed to me to show some very Rhodesian tendencies. But I was surprised, given the detailed instruction God offered to Noah and Abraham, that he had not been more specific with his ten commandments. Thou shalt not kill, except terrorists, commies, and hippies, surely. Also, thou shalt not covet thy neighbor's wife except if she was Mum dancing on the bar at the club on Wednesday nights. Mum and Dad both would have been very offended if everyone had averted their adoring gaze. As for keeping the Sabbath holy and praying twice a day, that was all very well if you didn't have cattle to feed, a calving cow, or tobacco to reap. Farm work didn't give a damn what day of the week it was.

I concluded then there were two kinds of people. There were black-and-white people who hung their faith on heavenly matters. They respected the Decalogue, and were like my Sunday school teacher with her mild stain of a mustache, her brimstone breath, and her pale, dappled, dairy-product skin. These people, I suspected, did not roll condoms over the barrels of guns, and I had a hard time picturing my Sunday school teacher dancing on any bar at any club around Umtali. I envied my Sunday school teacher her temperate life and her certainty she'd be blasted straight up to heaven if she was shot by terrorists, loved to death by a hippie, or bitten by a snake. Black-and-white people could afford to look placid.

And then there were colorful people who had no particular regard for rules as delivered by either God or man, and who were like Mum and Dad and everyone else I knew with their callused hands and their lithe hips and barbed-wire scratches on their arms. These people were soldiers because there was a war to be fought, and drinkers because there was tragedy to be endured, and farmers because there was food to be grown and tobacco to be smoked. These were the people whose lives were soil-stitched. They too knew what would happen to them if they were shot by terrorists or bitten by a snake, which is why they carried guns with them everywhere. They had the fraught, changeable expressions of those concerned with earthly business.

I had been born and bred of colorful people, but I had black-and-white leanings. I was certain that the relative absence of holy wonders in our lives—burning bushes and our many enemies smote by boils and pestilence—had more to do with a lack of faith and obedience in God than with his personal lack of interest in us. There was a clear biblical promise: if we observed God's rules and regulations, then we would dwell safely in our land, no sword would go through us, and we could lie down and not be afraid. Desperate to be one of the faithful, chosen, salvageable people, I determined to see God in hard-to-explain phenomena: rainbows, electric power, and Benny Andersson's womanly hair, for example.

Losing faith is not the same as losing belief, but it can break the fragile tether between a person and her innocence just the same. On the afternoon of January 9, 1978, when I was home from school for the Christmas holidays, my world as I had known it fell to pieces, and out of the devastation that remained I could never, ever again make anything whole. On that day, my sister Olivia drowned in a neighbor's pond. The sin of omission was mine; my eyes had turned from babysitting, my attention had been captured by the earthly wonders and temptations of a bright and alluring farm grocery store, my trustworthiness had been tested and found to be lacking. "It was one of those things, Bobo," Dad told me, trying to make it better. But I knew it wasn't a thing; it was a fault. Specifically, it was my fault.

That night and for months afterward, my prayers were so urgent, so clear, so grief-soaked and guilt-ridden, I was a nine-year-old vessel of Old Testament awe and superstition. I did not know then that suffering and grief are universal and that there would be a time, when I was older (although not much older), that I would know my own anguish to be nothing special or personal. All I knew back then is that God was our Father and that he could bring the dead back to life, I just wasn't sure exactly how to go about insisting that my miracle was worth his time. "Oh God, to whom vengeance belongeth, show thyself."

So like any child testing out the miracle-dealing propensities of an all-powerful God offered to her in church or in school, I conducted experiments. I held myself under bathwater, willing myself to take the breath that might resemble Olivia's last fatal inhalation of green duck water. Surely, if I had the faith and courage to drown myself on purpose, God might see my sacrifice and use his all-power to bring our sister back to life? And as penance for having allowed her death and to ensure that God knew of my serious commitment to him, I spent nights on the bare wooden floorboards of the dormitory, as I imagined monks and nuns must do. And I tried fasting, as Jesus had done for forty days in the wilderness, but by midmorning break on the first day, when we boarders were allowed a sandwich and the day scholars unpacked their tuck boxes of wondrous goodies, greed drove me to crimes of savagery and theft.

Then guilt heaped on guilt since God was ever-present, omniscient, and all-seeing. "Can any hide himself in secret places that I shall not see him? saith the Lord. Do not I fill heaven and earth?" In the black-and-white world of school, God was in all the rules about not talking after lights-out, not running the faucet for longer than a count of thirty, not taking more than one square of butter at supper. We were our surname, a number, accountable. "Be good. Our men and boys are out there dying for you," Mrs. Martingale told us every evening, and their deaths felt immediate, as if they were happening just outside the dormitory windows.

We, who were told to be good, were not like English or American children who were told to eat their spinach because of the remote specter of starving children in Africa. Unlike the vague benefits of vegetables, being good was a tangible imperative linked directly to the war and to all our dead whose number multiplied seemingly without end. At morning assembly, we were read the words of Cyprian of Carthage: "Let us on both sides of death always pray for one another." Then we bowed our heads and beseeched God to protect our troops, and to send us peace and plentiful rain, and to grant us an ample harvest. But God remained pretty meager with his miracles: the dead stayed dead, the war went on, the rain either came too early and too strong or not at all, and the harvest depended on whether or not we'd had eelworm and blight.

At last I concluded that if God existed, he was not my personal savior or a heavenly anything. He was, I thought, on the side of the anciently good and the contemporary mustachioed Bible-thumpers. He was for the people who were willing to get nailed to crosses or strapped to altars or to spend their lives wandering in the desert. I would have done any of these things if I had thought it would return Olivia to us, but I also doubted God would notice my sacrifice. I had a suspicion he was too busy taking care of the genuinely black-and-white people like my Sunday school teacher, not the fake faithless believers like me.

Then on the night of June 23, 1978, at the Emmanuel Mission School, a place roughly halfway between town and our farm, eight British missionaries and four of their children, ranging in age from six to three weeks old, were killed by liberation forces. I can't remember now how we came to see the photographs of the massacre at our school, but I have a memory of us students huddled over grainy images that had been published in a booklet by the Rhodesian Ministry of Information. What has remained vivid for me all these years later is a photo of Pamela Grace, the bayoneted newborn lying face up, her mouth open, arm outstretched to her bloody impaled mother.

Perhaps inevitably, the image of that dead missionary baby became conflated in my mind with the memory of Olivia's motionless corpse on the bed of our neighbor's spare room on the afternoon of her drowning. Death might give meaning to life, rendering it precious and fleeting and something not to be wasted, I already understood that, but the death of blameless babies seemed to me worse than senseless. It degraded life and rendered it cheap and pointless. My already shaky belief vaporized, leaving nothing but fear and a terrible sense of aloneness in its place.

I came to the only possible logical conclusion: God could not exist. Little Pamela, child of two missionaries, did not look as if she had been blasted directly to heaven. Like Olivia, she looked awfully and futilely dead. And if God hadn't been with those babies in their tiny innocence, or at least gathered them to him bodily at the moment of their demise, then he certainly wasn't with us, or with our soldiers, or even with the Sunday school teacher. God was nowhere. It was just all we Godless people—regardless of whether we were black-and-white people or colorful people—bashing up against one another on a lonely planet. None of us was going to be saved by anyone but each other.

My flawed but convincing calculations made mathematical leaps. Since God was nonexistent, the only thing that stood between oblivion and me was love. Unlovable people, I reasoned, were invisibly endangered. Lovable people were memorable. Lacking natural cuteness, I used the gift of volume I had been granted from birth and I became siren loud, deliberately unforgettable. Wanting to ensure a reliable exit from any catastrophe, I was careful to make every entrance count. I stage-managed my way into the center of my parents' boozy get-togethers by dressing up as a troopie, singing patriotic Rhodesian songs (of which we believed ABBA to be some of the leading writers), performing faux stripteasing acts behind bedsheets over which I flung my mother's underwear pilfered from her top drawer. I sang about not losing and having no regrets, layering an approximation of the Swedish accents of Anni-Frid and Agnetha over my Rhodesian nasal whine.

And in the absence of God, I transferred his authority to the next highest, visible, logical power: my father. After all, like God, Dad's rules were absolute, capricious, and patriarchal. "Don't argue with your father," he said, if we ever dared contradict him. Like God, Dad could seem remote and mysterious, by turns withholding and munificent. Like with God, you could talk to Dad without the expectation of reply or favor, and even if nothing happened, or the outcome was unfavorable, you could comfort yourself by arguing that he knew best. And as the man of the house, and, more important, the man with the FN rifle, he held in his gift the seeming power of life and death. I worshipped him.

MR. ADVENTURE'S
IMMUNITY

I had always thought it would be an impossibly tricky sideways maneuver to slip just far enough out of my father's haphazard but indisputable jurisdiction and under the influence of some other calmer control without eddying out of my life altogether. But Charlie seemed the perfect escort for such a move. He was capable and unflappable, and most important of all, he seemed naïve enough not to know whom he was truly up against. Or perhaps he was above it all. In either case, I was saved.

For starters, Charlie didn't appear enthralled or impressed by my father's suicide mission of a deliberately disordered life. While Charlie had a degree in international business and liked to discuss global finance and economic theory, Dad seemed so bored by money that he kept only mental accounts. "It'll come out in the wash," he said, by which I knew he meant he expected to be paid—just as he expected to pay—what was reasonable. Anything more than that didn't make sense, in part because having a theory about economics was predicated on a certain belief that the world wasn't a chaotic and surprising place. "You win some, you lose some," Dad always said, and didn't seem to mind on which side of that equation he landed.

Then the strong-arming to drink more than the sensible amount—a couple of beers, an aperitif, a glass of wine with supper—didn't impress Charlie at all. "What's the matter with you?" my father asked. "The Muslims get to you?" To which Charlie only smiled and walked away, his left shoulder cocked in a way that I later recognized as an attitude of irritated self-righteousness. "Bloody teetotalers should be shot at dawn," Dad muttered. "Anyway, half of them, turn your back for three seconds and they've siphoned you dry."

"Never trust anyone who doesn't drink," my mother said.

But in our very first evening alone together, Charlie defied my parents' fears and offered me a kamikaze. "Vodka with lime," he explained. "And there's supposed to be Triple Sec, but since this is Zambia, we'll have to make do with a splash of brandy and some orange peel." It was as if he was speaking an exotic foreign language. I wanted to shut my eyes and listen to him reeling off the ingredients of cocktails for the rest of the evening. Whisky and water was about as sophisticated as we got at the Mkushi Country Club unless it was Greek night. In that case, we always hoped for ouzo. This we drank weakly diluted with Coke until even my mother could understand the logic of lesbianism and the working-class lyricism of Nikos Kazantzakis. "Bouboulina," she called me then, to show not only her literary prowess but also to demonstrate that all was forgiven.

I said, "Sounds wonderful."

So Charlie mixed two drinks, scraping the skin of a fresh orange over the top of the oily concoctions, and led me into the garden. It was a bachelor setup, a couple of wire lawn chairs, a rickety table, a few straggling plants in pots straining against the enthusiastic but uneven watering regime of his employee, Mr. Sinazongwe. Charlie's Labrador retriever lay at our feet, panting in the heavy way of a large dog in the tropics. It was a good sign, I thought, that Charlie had brought Tank with him from Wyoming. It demonstrated he was committed to staying in Zambia, because whatever else I knew about him, I chose to believe he was someone who would never leave a dog behind. "I'll call all my Labradors Tank," Charlie said. "My grandmother always named her Labrador retrievers Sam."

"What if she had more than one dog at a time?" I asked, thinking of our pile of animals.

"She didn't."

"Oh." I let this demonstration of heroic restraint settle for a moment.

Charlie raised his glass, "Nostrovia," he said.

"Mud in your eye," I replied.

Then I swallowed my drink the way my mother does, as if marauding barbarians are bearing down on her to steal it away from her parched lips. But Charlie sipped his thoughtfully, relishing the clink of ice against the glass; ice made from bottled water, I noted, not like the Fullers who drank whatever they could find, lukewarm if need be, and had no compunction about using ice made from unboiled water. "A few germs never hurt anyone," Dad always said. And if a bout of diarrhea ensued, it simply proved his point. "See? Keeps you from getting all blocked up."

The sun went down and darkness happened with the abruptness of a curtain being drawn across the sky, and with it the temperature dropped. Charlie, seemingly immune to the cold, told me about Wyoming, and it seemed a land of fairytale proportions, the way Africa sounded to me when I heard foreigners speak about it. It was winter for seven months a year there, he said, snow piled up to the eaves of his grandmother's cabin (no wonder she drank). And when summer came, it descended like panic, everything happening at once. He gestured back to the chimneypiece in his house where he kept a sprig of sagebrush to remind him of home, and I understood this gesture like my mother's, a superstitious prophylactic against homesickness, her touching the four walls of any home to which she wished to return.

Half an hour passed and the complete blackness of a moonless southern African night covered us. We went inside and Charlie built a fire and we sat watching the flames in silence for a while. I waited expectantly for Charlie to make more kamikazes, but when he was finished with his drink, he took both our glasses into the kitchen and put them in the sink. I was astonished. By every measure, what we had just done could not be considered anything close to kamikaze, the divine wind of destruction. By my book, it barely counted as a feeble dip of the wing at an aircraft carrier. Still, it was a drink with a serious-sounding name and it reinforced my idea that Charlie was a colorful enough man with a reassuringly black-and-white foundation. I breathed.

Thirteen and a half years after Olivia drowned and thirteen years after the massacre of those missionaries, eleven years after the end of Zimbabwe's bush war and the death of another of my mother's infants; after a lifetime of seeing tragedies of the sort that seemed both accidental and continual—drought, the genocide of the Ndebele people in Matabeleland, the beginning of the AIDS epidemic—my mind knew that tragedy and violence weren't mine alone, but my body hadn't stopped knowing panic. I had run out of whatever chemical it is that resets to calm. But Charlie seemed to have none of my brokenness. Whole and undamaged to the naked eye,

Charlie's default was calm. Slightly concerned it might be a borrowed calm, I asked him if he was religious at all.

"Not really," Charlie told me. His God, he said, was in mountains and rivers. His church was big sky and deep water. His religion was the wilderness. He said he'd lost his heart to it long ago while summering on his grandmother's ranch in Wyoming. Instead of the Bible, he read whitewater and lines of rock. Instead of church, he summited peaks and fished pristine braids of unpeopled water. Instead of bowing down before any god, he submitted to the superior power of a class five rapid. It was worship, but it was rational worship. It did not involve the humility required to sink to one's knees in the presence of God and a congregation; there was no snake handling and babbling in tongues; there was no lamentation and rending of garments.

I too had lost my heart to the wilderness long ago, but it was the dangerously lost heart of a lover, not of a believer. We southern Africans had not thought to look for God in the wilderness because that was where we went to fight one another and to forget our separation from Him. It was also where the adrift and lawless among us journeyed after the war, staying beyond the reach of society until true hell could open up. Of the men I knew who had done this, ex-soldiers mostly, they seemed haplessly tugged back to the theater of their killings. "They've gone bush," we said, by which we meant they were no longer governed by the rules of society and had gone into a place of living suicide. "It can happen to anyone," Dad said, by which I knew he was really saying it might have happened to him.

No one wants to go truly mad. But the line from spectacularly eccentric to irreparably mind-lost is invisible, and easily crossed by accident. And when this happened, when someone tripped that wire and blew their mind beyond the reach of even our tolerance, we were in horrified awe. "Lost the plot," we said. "Benzi." "Penga." We cleared space for such people, as if wary of detonating their disorder, as if their madness was something we could trace back with cables, wires, and clips to a device hidden in a cake tin. We knew of men, fatally scorched by war-terror, who played Russian roulette in the bar at the Monomotapa Hotel in Harare; who attempted flight from the balcony of third-story buildings; who swam with crocodiles. "Crazy for real," we said.

It is a kind of madness to live in a place to which one does not subscribe to the prevailing natural religions and beliefs. I knew that some of the Shona liberation fighters, deranged after years of conflict and fighting, had expunged their demons in mhondoro ceremonies, calling on the lion spirit of ancient dynasties to remove from them the ngozis, the avenging spirits of those whom they had violated. Left intact, such ngozis precipitate madness, sudden death, awful luck. Spirit-possessed men ran from their horror and ran out of choices. They ended up stranded, wretchedly buried under yesterday, entering a kind of animal state from which the only return was a ritualized reunion of body and soul. Those who have an understanding of the mhondoro ceremony told me that all beings in a community are connected, that the madness of one is the madness of everyone, that there is no separation of minds and bodies between people. Healing of the afflicted and stricken and unhinged is imperative because rain cannot fall on a broken people; drought and an unstable economy will ensue. There'll be accidents and incidents and epidemics.

In his enviable Western guileless innocence, though, Charlie had made the world's wild a place of sanctuary and recreation, a reliable way to make a living. He could step into and out of it anytime he chose as if it were a church, because he had arranged for a Land Rover to meet him at the end of his adventures. He had a Plan B, a passport to elsewhere, a get-out clause. At least by our measure, he was unscathed by the wars of his own people—experienced only through television images, drills under his school desk, and the slightly burned-out druggy rebellion of people half a decade his senior. Charlie didn't burn through the present, or drown it out, or wash up against it, because his past had left him intact. He had a future to look forward to.

||||||||||

We left Lusaka the next morning just after dawn, and were launching our canoes below the Kariba Dam a few hours later. Looking up at the dam, I envisioned the massive crush of water above us, the fourth largest river in Africa contained behind the four-hundred-foot concrete wall. Given everything, it seemed unequal to the task. Nothing lasts forever, and yet here was this great gray curve of wall stanching the river between Zimbabwe and Zambia as if those two countries would always have stable governments, as if there would always be enough money in the national coffers to maintain a project of this magnitude, as if the climate would always be predictable and stable.

Who, back in the late 1950s and early 1960s when the dam was being built, could have envisioned weather unbound from nature? Who could have envisioned an independent country instead of Rhodesia? Who could have envisioned a murderous despot like Zimbabwe's infamous leader, Robert Mugabe, being in charge of half its upkeep? Well, actually, anyone paying attention could have seen a war, and him, coming. In April 1961, Mugabe was already publicly discussing guerrilla action to fight for the freedom of his people, going so far as to rashly declare to a Rhodesian policeman, "We are taking over this country and we will not put up with this nonsense." Whatever else Mugabe had done in the intervening years, I was fairly certain shoring up the dam to the largest man-made lake in the world wasn't one of his priorities.

But Charlie had chosen to launch here because even if he maintained a river runner's hatred of dams, it was close to the tarmac road and he was persuaded by an American's love of convenience. "It's easy to get the canoe down to the river from here," he explained, easily swinging the craft off the trailer and into the water. Then he steadied it while I lurched for the front seat. "You'll be okay," he said. But I knew this is where the local Tonga villagers say the Zambezi River god, Nyaminyami, has been separated from his mate by the dam and that he will one day break it down to get to her. "If we capsize, or you fall out, just remember, float downstream feet first," Charlie said. "Get to shore if you can. And wait for me."

I didn't say there would be no point because the villagers also said anyone falling into the river at this place, near the rock where the river god was purported to live, would be sucked down immediately, never to be seen again. Evidence suggested this couldn't be dismissed as mere folksy superstition: between October 1956 and February 1961, sixty-five southern Africans and twenty-one Italians died right here, building the dam. The Frenchman who designed it, André Coyne, said of his own profession, "De tous les ouvrages construits par la main humaine, les barrages sont les plus meurtriers."[1]

The rumor in Zambia was that Coyne had committed suicide after several dams he had engineered in Italy had

---

1. "Of all the works of mankind, dams are the most murderous."

collapsed. This turned out to be a typically Zambian almost-truth: in fact only one of the seventy dams designed by Coyne, the Malpasset in southern France, had ever collapsed. On December 2, 1959, that dam on the Reyran River breached and burst. In the ensuing flood, villages, roads, and railways were flooded and 423 people were killed. Coyne himself died six months later of natural causes, although it was said he never got over the heartbreaking guilt of that tragedy.

A pod of hippos snorted at us as we began our wobbling descent downstream. I closed my eyes and paddled as calmly as I could. Behind me, I could hear Charlie taking deliberate, sweeping strokes through the water. He was unafraid of what might happen, because he saw the hippos not as I did, as the most murderous of all African wildlife, but as fellow river dwellers. Charlie knew he was supposed to be here. I knew I was a trespasser. "Don't panic," Charlie said. We were wearing lifejackets, Charlie had a throw bag and a river runner's knife. He knew CPR and had taught river rescue on rivers in Wyoming and Colorado as well as on the Zambezi. But I understood; it's rarely the thing you prepare for that undoes you.

Still, I also had grasped enough of the West's views of such fatalism—that it made of us primitives, naïfs, and fools—to keep such beliefs to myself. In the West, it was believed that attitude and ambition saved you. In Africa, we had learned no one was immune to capricious tragedy. What I didn't know then was that ignoring my own southern African knowledge was its own kind of mischief: it rendered me speechless when I should have spoken, helpless when I was profoundly capable, and broken when in fact the very places inside me that had been damaged and snapped were their own kind of strength. I saw the landscape around us as tattooed with death, fraught with the possibility of unrecovered land mines and undetonated ordnance. Charlie, however, saw it as recreationally pristine and friendly. Instead of trusting my own experience, I wanted to borrow Charlie's vision and innocence, the way a visitor at a party walks away with a stranger's fortuitously fitting coat a universe away from her own taste or means.

We pulled away from the wall, away from the hippos, away from Nyaminyami's rock. The sun struck the water in burning silver threads and bounced back into our faces. I never really got the hang of canoeing, counterproductively dipping my paddle into the water just when Charlie had pulled his out. Still, he managed to compensate for my ineptitude, and by the early afternoon we had made enough progress to justify beaching the canoes for something to eat. After lunch, Charlie decided it would do us good to walk up a gully and "stretch our legs." If it had been up to me, I'd have stuck close to the river, drunk another beer, slept in the shade. The midday sun was at its most intense and the bush was at its most flat and unknowable this time of day, as well as being particularly dense just here. "Unless there's really no other choice, never walk where you can't see forty paces ahead of you," Dad had always warned us. Still, I followed Charlie.

"Mad dogs and Englishmen," I said.

"What's that?" Charlie said, turning back toward me.

But before I could repeat myself, the foliage in front of us exploded and an enraged elephant emerged, ears flapping, trunk raised, dust clouding at her feet. The dry-season jesse bush clattered. It was a classic mock charge, but on the ground, facing her, it seemed undeniably serious to me. Charlie, who had read his guidebooks and therefore knew not to run, turned implacably to face her; I scurried up the nearest anthill. The elephant stopped short of full attack, tossed her ears at Charlie, and then retreated, her tail straight up in the air.

When he had first told me his name—Charlie Ross—my mind had snagged on it, and then whirred backward, searching for the familiar reference. Charlie Ross had also been the name of a famous rogue elephant hunter in Zambia in the early part of the century. Eventually, sometime in the 1930s, he had been charged and killed by an elephant near Mpika and was buried under a tree there, and it's said that elephants came to visit his grave in the months and years that followed.

But when this elephant stopped short of this Charlie Ross—*my* Charlie Ross—I remember thinking in a superstitious way, "He's charmed. He's the Charlie Ross who walks away from an elephant charge." Which was silly, of course. The historic Charlie Ross must have been charged by elephants—and stood his ground—hundreds of times. Even he probably didn't think much of the elephant that killed him until it was too late; until his gun jammed, or his foot slipped, or whatever it was that caused a man who knew elephants with the intimacy of a person who hunts them to be destroyed by one.

MARITAL ADVICE FROM

A MILDLY STONED COOK

Six months later, Charlie and I were engaged. Six months after that, we were married on the farm. A day before the wedding, I sat out on the kitchen veranda with Adamson, our legs stretched toward the pale heat of an early June sun. Mum's scruffy flock of guinea fowl scratched in the flowerbeds, the horses cropped in the home paddocks, a couple of dogs flattened themselves at our sides. It was like it had always been with Adamson and me; as if tomorrow would always come around in more or less the same shape as yesterday, and time was meaningless, and we had nowhere else to go.

Except now, in recognition of my upcoming marriage, Adamson had brought me a rough, hand-carved wooden chalice as a gift. It had been wrapped in months-old newspaper on which Adamson had written, "Madam Bob." Until then, Adamson had always addressed me as "Miss Bob," or simply "Bob." I read that salutation, the weightiness of those two syllables—"Mad-am"—and I felt a new, unwelcome distance between us. It was evident my soon-to-be bride status had made time unnaturally solid; tomorrow was inevitable and it would change everything. Soon I would be a foreign man's wife, I would no longer live on this farm, or even on a farm in the district, and all of those things shoved me beyond the reach of Adamson and beyond the protection of our historic status as allies.

Until this moment, until that solemnizing "Mad-am," Adamson and I had always been coconspirators. I covered for him when cigarettes and brandy went missing from the pantry, and he protected me from all the ways life could go missing or awry on a Zambian farm. He had secretly tended my wounds with hydrogen peroxide the time I put Dad's motorbike through a barbed-wire fence. And when I ill-advisedly experimented with some nastily potent Malawi Gold—smuggled across the border and into our community by some pre-Eurotrash relatives of a Yugoslav neighbor—he ferried me tea and comfort until the worst of the hallucinations had worn off.

Now I asked, "Do you remember those soldiers, Abambo? The ones that came here for meat and beer."

Adamson laughed raucously.

"It wasn't funny," I said, reaching out my hand reflexively for his, closing the circuit on his humor.

"Too funny," Adamson said when his coughing fit abated.

||||||||||

It was during the Easter break of my sixteenth birthday—"I'm sixteen and I'm not ashamed of my body," my parents kept saying in awful Cockney accents whenever the subject of my age came up. Given that Vanessa was still wowing London with her face-of-the-eighties looks, and Mum and Dad had gone for the day to the Copperbelt to do the farm shopping,

Adamson and I were alone in the house. Although truthfully we were alone only in the ways Westerners speak of being alone in Africa, as if the few hundred locals by whom they are almost always surrounded are part of the landscape, instead of part of humanity.

I had spent the morning on horseback, riding the north fence checking for poachers' snares, keeping an eye on the clouds massing to the west. And after lunch I had taken the dogs for a walk up to the vlei, returning well before the threatening evening storm. Then as rain drummed on the roof, Adamson and I ate our supper in front of the television. The electricity sizzled off and on a few times until we eventually lost our nerve and unplugged the set so it wouldn't blow up. After that, Adamson took his time over an enormous leisurely joint on the back veranda and I settled into Dad's chair in the sitting room with a book.

The rain let up, and now there was the thick contentment that comes after a storm, everything tranquilized and heavy, the world freighted with dripping vegetation and buzzing with insects. I always reminded myself on these occasions never to leave Africa—as if terrified I might inadvertently forget and accidentally drift off the continent. I suppose I knew even then that if I did, an essential part of my connection with this earth would become forever detached, like a soulless body or a heartless lover. Africa had been my primary relationship for most of my life, defining, sustaining, and unequivocal in a way that no human relationship had ever been, with the exception of my parents, whom, in any case, I could never separate from this soil.

"Do you ever regret moving to Africa?" I asked Dad years later, when it was clear I might never return permanently.

Dad took his pipe out of his mouth and tapped the spent tobacco from it. "Regret's a waste of bloody time," he said.

"But still," I persisted. "After everything." And I recited a partial list of all that he had lost in his fifty years on the continent: several farms; miles of beautifully straight painstakingly laid fence; herds of pedigree cattle; tobacco barns; contoured fields; communities. I didn't mention his three lost children and the lost Rhodesian war, partly because he hardly ever did and partly because I hated to see his face cloud over.

"No, Bobo," Dad said. He made a gesture, like a magician blowing a silk scarf out of his clenched fist. "Pfff, there went your life. There's no time for regret. Get up, dust yourself off, shake a leg." Then he tapped more tobacco into his pipe and added, "Your mother and I will be here until it is time for lights-out. I wouldn't have it any other way."

He didn't ask me if I had regretted leaving Africa. Having no patience for regret, Dad has a hard time understanding why anyone else would bother wallowing in it. In any case, my leaving Zambia had been tied to my marriage to Charlie and to his nationality and life. It made sense to my father that a wife should follow her husband. Although it was Dad who had come from England and found Mum in Africa, and stayed on with her even when things got unwelcomingly rough because she would never leave the continent. "Loss is part of the game," he said. "What else are we going to do? Retire to some horrible semidetached hovel in England and die of rising damp?"

Most of the people we knew died in harness, usually of drink, or a car accident, or some tropical disease. "Of natural causes, in other words," Dad said. Whereas to die of old age, infirm of body and mind frittered away, this was something horrible and unnatural to him. "Malaria," Dad said when his bank manager asked him what contingencies he had made for his senior years. "A bloody good, permanently fatal dose of malaria."

||||||||||

Suddenly, the dogs lifted their heads and a few of them stiffened. I put down my book. A snake was always my first thought, but that usually got the Jack Russells going in a frenzy of hysterical, especially high-pitched barking, and now they were hackles up, low-throat growling. This was something else, something outside. A few of the dogs got up and went to the door; a couple of them began to bark. Then I heard it myself, the contralto whine of an engine powering a heavy vehicle through the sandy patch of road by the gum trees. Whatever it was, it wasn't supposed to be here this time of night on this road.

I turned out the lamp and stood beside the window, my body shielded by the wall, and strained to see into the darkness. In a short time, a single bumping headlight jiggled in dismembered confusion down our driveway, as if the eye of one of the Cyclopes had torn loose from the giant's forehead and was now on a mission to find its owner. In another half minute, by the farmyard floodlights, I could make out the unmistakable silhouette of a Zambian army lorry. It rumbled to a halt in front of the dairy. A couple dozen soldiers, some with guns shrugged over their shoulders, peeled out its back and a few more streamed out of the cab. Then, as if our house were some sort of enemy camp, they swarmed around the garden looking for an entrance, at last seeping in through every door.

Now the dogs set up a wall of barking fury that took some quelling, but at last order was restored, inasmuch as there can be order when there are a dozen or so armed, inebriated Zambian soldiers milling in your sitting room bringing with them the scents of campfires and gun oil released by rain. "We want rations," the man I took to be the commanding officer said.

"We've come for meat and beer." It was easy to see the soldiers were already bleary with drink. They clustered in front of me, as if I were an interesting exhibit at an agricultural show, peering over one another's shoulders to get a better look. The smell was of a collective souring, a bad night about to get worse. "Meat and beer," the commander repeated.

I said that we had not slaughtered a steer lately, and lied that there was no beer in the house, but that everyone was welcome to tea. So Adamson stoked the stove, boiled water, and made a fresh tray, and there was an awkward half hour while the soldiers lurched around the sitting room drinking sweet, milky tea they didn't want, and Adamson stationed himself behind my armchair reeking of marijuana. Then nothing else happened. The soldiers thanked me for my hospitality and I thanked them, not insincerely, for not shooting me, and we all laughed and they drove off, I assumed to harass the neighboring farmers.

Adamson and I stood for several minutes under the farmyard's floodlights that were now zinging with post-rain moths and sausage flies. We watched the Cyclops eye of the army lorry bob and weave searchingly back down the farm road until it got to the gum trees and vanished into the night. Then as we turned back to the house, I noticed that Adamson was holding behind his back the big butcher's knife Mum used to chop up the dogs' soup bones. "Abambo," I said, touched. "Were you going to stab them if they hurt me?"

Adamson looked down at the knife. "No, Bob," he said. "I was going to stab you if you said something stupid."

When I told Dad the story the next morning, he laughed and said, "Good for Adamson."

"It was very frightening," I objected.

"Oh Bobo, you were all right, as long as the soldiers weren't speaking French," Dad said.

"Then what?" I asked.

"Then you were in Zaire and in proper trouble."

||||||||||

That winter morning before the wedding, when I sat with Adamson's wedding gift in my lap, I had somehow not realized it would be my last morning with the old cook. I should have seen it coming, not just for all the obvious reasons, but also because of the wooden chalice. It was rough in my hands and smelled endangered and tinny like the freshly spilled blood of something magnificent and old. But I could already see the splitting thread in its grain where the first crack would form, and a few years from now cause the container to irreparably shatter on a Wyoming windowsill. By then, Adamson would be dead from the slow-boil tuberculosis that we had misdiagnosed as chronic bronchitis, and I would be nursing my second child, and Mum would be whirling her way into a madness so deep she'd end up restrained in a Zimbabwean asylum. Had I been more skilled, or perhaps more aware, I might have read all of our troubled futures into that single emerging flaw, but as it was that winter day, everything seemed to me to be perfect and, if it were possible, improving.

"This is very kind, Abambo," I said. "It's mukwa, isn't it?" I lifted it up. "I'll put it somewhere special so I can always remember you."

"Ah, you don't have to remember me," Adamson said. "You must forget all of this. You must go forward. Have children. You're getting too old." He rubbed his arms. Although it was already winter-cool in the mornings, he was still wearing his old summer shirt, short-sleeved and frayed at the cuffs. The vats and vats of curry Mum had ordered from an

Indian restaurant in Ndola for the two hundred expected
guests had putrefied on the way down to the farm.

"Well, that goes to show you, never put peas in food and
send it for a long drive," Mum said. She sighed. "And it hasn't
even fermented into anything interesting we can drink." So
Dad had gone over to the Yugoslav neighbor and ordered a
whole steer and a whole pig, both of which were to be roasted
over an open fire in the garden. The kitchen steamed the rest
of the wedding feast.

"I think you must have a child very soon." Adamson took
his left hand and cupped his right elbow, pointing to the sun
to measure the passage of time. "Before the next rains."

"No, I won't," I said. "I can't."

Adamson gave me a look as if I had cursed myself.
"Madam!" He appeared ready to snatch my careless blas-
phemy from the air and stuff it back into my mouth. "Don't
say such a thing. Your husband will go looking for another
woman. You will be without a small child. What is the matter with you?" Adamson had nine surviving children out of a
total of thirteen. I launched into a lecture on the pros of birth
control, but Adamson grew impatient. If I was going to damn
myself to a barren life and a straying husband, so be it, it
wasn't his lookout. He rolled one of his enormous marijuana
cigarettes, lit it, and stood up, cutting my discourse short. "I
have work," he announced and went back into the kitchen,
his cigarette stuck to his lower lip from which marijuana ash
dripped liberally into the pots.

I went in search of Mum. "Don't blame me if all the guests
get stoned," I told her. "Half of Adamson's pot crop is in the
creamed spinach."

"Just as well," Mum said. "It'll take the edge off." She
looked at me, her brows lowered meaningfully. "Some people
find weddings bring back the most unfortunate memories."

MARRIAGE VOWS IN

THE TIME OF MALARIA

The memories of my wedding are not unfortunate, although they are swimming and episodic because I had woken up with malaria, and in a frantic bid to get me well, my parents had overdosed me with their cures. First, Mum had treated me with chloroquine, and when that didn't work, she had made me swallow Halfan and then Fansidar. Then, on the morning of the wedding, Dad had given me a double gin with extra tonic, and a couple of aspirin. As I walked into the horse paddock where I had insisted Charlie and I exchange vows, the fever broke out of the bounds of the chemical straitjacket it had been in, and I could feel the tiny prickling explosions of what I imagined to be parasites in my blood. "That flushed, delirious look you have in all the wedding photos," Mum said. "In retrospect, it was probably just a temperature of a hundred and five."

When I reached Charlie's side, I looked behind me one last time, across the field where our guests sat on garden chairs and hay bales. It was standing room only because the entire farm and half the villagers from the surrounding area had showed up for the spectacle. Guests sat in order of their perceived importance: in the front sat family, close neighbors, and old friends; behind them were recent friends and distant neighbors; next came top farm staff and gatecrashers; last were the casual day laborers and people who had no particular business being there except that it was a Saturday morning at the beginning of winter and there was nothing else of much note going on in a fifty-mile radius.

I searched out Adamson with his two wives and several of his children. He caught my eye and, as if we were at an anti-apartheid political rally rather than an Anglo-African-American wedding, raised his fist in a Black Power salute. I smiled at him and held my bouquet of wild grasses a little higher. Then, as serene and confident as I have ever felt, I turned my back on the people who had seen me through a turbulent childhood and raised me through my happy adolescence and submitted myself to the bishop's proactive warnings. "Marriage," he said, "is not by any to be taken in hand unadvisedly, lightly, or wantonly, but reverently, discreetly, advisedly, soberly, and in the fear of God, duly considering the causes for which matrimony was ordained."

We exchanged vows, Charlie put a ring on my finger, and we were pronounced man and wife. I suppose there must have been music, because Mum had recruited the choir from a nearby boarding school, and I remember vividly that half the choristers got uproariously drunk and were violently sick in the canna lilies before the wedding speeches. I remember too Vanessa and her first husband, freshly married themselves but already looking as if they were on different boats in a choppy sea connected only by the rope of their frenzied toddler and the rising bump of their second child in her belly. Vanessa had refused to be my matron of honor and she avoided me at the wedding. "Oh Al, I just felt like I was bad luck," she said afterward. "Things were going so badly with me. I didn't want to pass it on to you."

But most vivid of all in my memory was the encounter with Dad's friend, the Polish father from the Catholic mission at Old Mkushi. He caught me by the shoulders just as I was making my way into the garden for the photographs, as if he had an urgent message to impart. "The first year is hard, and after that it gets worse," he said, his mouth so close to my ear that I could smell the red-dust-infused scent of his river-washed, sun-dried clothes. I laughed at him, excusing his sentiment as the meaningless words of a celibate East European who has lived too long in the Zambian bush. "No really, it's true," he insisted. "I should know. I've been married to God for fifty years."

||||||||||

The next day, we left Mkushi and honeymooned for a week, with a game scout and a cook, in a small fly camp on the edge of Luangwa National Park. We paddled a banana boat down the Luangwa River to our campsite. It was loaded with wine and food and a metal table on which we planned to put a white tablecloth and candles every night. The cook was a Malawian we'd picked up in Chirundu, a Muslim. He had frowned disapprovingly at our boxes of alcohol and at the skimpiness of my sundress. Then a female hippo defending her calf charged the boat. After that, the cook concentrated on his prayers until we pulled up on shore.

In the early mornings, we walked with the scout toward the hills, our backs to the river, skirting a small elephant herd, a matriarch with several younger females and two babies; tracking the night's journey of a resident leopard;

seeing where lions had stalked. In the heat of the day, we read in our tents until we fell into the uncompromising, near-death afternoon sleep that invites ghosts and visions into your dreams. In the late afternoon we walked down to the river and bathed in the shallow eddies, keeping a wary eye open for crocodiles. Then we dressed and walked again, following the river downstream to the open meadow by a grove of ebony trees where there were often zebras, and occasionally Cape buffalo, and once a spotted hyena. We didn't talk much, except occasionally in whispers to point out an unusual bird, or the fresh spoor of something interesting, or to marvel at our uncommon luck to be here now, with one another.

At night, we sat under the stars and drank wine—me chattering away in my usual fashion, Charlie listening indulgently in his—until the Muslim cook scurried out of the cooking tent with our supper. On our second day in camp, a boomslang had slain a pigeon in the tree under which we had dug our latrine. This, on top of the incident of the charging hippo, had put the cook off ablutions in particular and a life in the wild in general. Couldn't we cut this whole ridiculous honeymoon short? he wanted to know. Hadn't nuptials been sufficiently established? How long could two people stare into each other's eyes? Plus, he would like to be back in Chipata in time for Friday prayers.

So on Thursday afternoon we packed up camp and walked back across the river, pulling the banana boat behind us with what was left of our provisions. Was this the only way? What if we got into the boat? Couldn't we paddle back upstream? the cook wanted to know, now more afraid of crocodiles than charging hippos or murderous boomslangs. Charlie patiently explained the dynamics of a river's free-surface hydraulics. "It's not *impossible* to paddle against the current," he concluded. "But it's very hard." To be fair, I wasn't any less baffled by Charlie's explanation, or any more thrilled than the cook, at the prospect of wading across a crocodile-infested river. As the brown water came up to our thighs, and then our waists, the cook and I glued our bodies to the scout's side and to the comforting reassurance of his AK-47. "When I said, 'Until death do us part,' I didn't mean day five," I told Charlie. "The honeymoon's a bit early to bump me off, don't you think?"

But my own death wasn't my biggest fear. Charlie's death was my biggest fear. He seemed to be such an irreplaceable impossibility, so exactly the unlikely and correct combination of person for me—someone who wasn't a stranger to adventure, but yet who was not unpredictably, superfluously dangerous. For these reasons, it hadn't seemed rash and foolhardy to have married him at twenty-three. On the contrary, it seemed as if *not* marrying Charlie would have been a rash and foolhardy decision. My marrying him would mean I'd be all right forever. He'd be all right too. And our children would have double doses of all-rightness.

Plus, I was so in love I now understood the condition as a sickness. My physical self changed in Charlie's presence: my heart flipped; blood surged; nerves strayed out of their protective sheaths and misfired. The sudden shock of coming into such sharp focus—the sheer, unlikely, extraordinary luck of being loved by this man—was wonderful, but it was also slightly confusing. The few other men I had been with had found my intensity off-putting, unseemly, alarming, but Charlie calmly, fearlessly turned toward it, as if warmed by the heat I threw off.

Secretly, I couldn't help suspecting our courtship and marriage had all been a laughable misunderstanding. Surely Charlie would find out what my family had been saying all along, that I was none of the things he believed me to be—passionate and witty and articulate. Instead he would discover for himself that I was difficult and noisy and unpredictable. "Oh no," Mum said. "I *did* warn him you were impossible. He can't say I didn't warn him." She shook her head in the manner of a breeder who has pointed out the flaws of a filly, and managed to sell it anyway. "But that's the lucky thing about Americans. They're very susceptible to an accent." She dusted her hands victoriously. "Isn't it lucky we taught you how to enunciate properly?"

CONTINENTAL DRIFT

By the beginning of April 2010 in Wyoming, the earth's orbit had tipped enough to allow the sun's warmth to penetrate layers of tree bark and snow. Redwing blackbirds had returned to the willow bottoms along the river where I walked Dilly most days; our horses over in their field in Idaho had begun shedding their winter coats in salt-matted chunks; the snow was receding in a series of white high-tide marks from the south-facing wall of our house. Grape hyacinth and crocuses speared pioneering shoots out of the freshly thawed ground. Spring in the Rocky Mountains was a time of everything up and out and forward. Last month's winter, with its blizzards and below-zero wind chills and torporing chickadees, was something that seemed to have happened to other people in another world.

In late spring, I was scheduled to do a reading in Dallas where it was already ninety degrees. I flew south from Wyoming and talked about my Zimbabwean/Zambian childhood to Texans in a vigorously air-conditioned building filled with artifacts from Africa. It looked as if the closet of a continent had tipped into the place: Yoruba headdresses and Tuareg silver; Zulu beads and Ghanaian robes; Masai necklaces and Kuba cloth. The audience was well traveled, adventurously secure, university educated. They seemed to have formed strong opinions about Africa in the course of their studies and journeys. I had no such strength of opinion.

What did I know about the fifty-five (give or take) countries of Africa? I carried within me one deep personal thread of one small part of it, and it had changed and colored everything, but I'd lived in the States for sixteen years now. Plus, I didn't look or sound the way most people imagine a Zimbabwean or a Zambian should look or sound. I had a Wyoming-winter complexion and my accent had morphed transatlantic. Also, there had been too many things of the sort I couldn't have imagined or insured myself against—love and love's loss, a wide and rising ocean, an unexpected attachment to the high plains of the Rocky Mountains—between my childhood and now to have left me with much of a sense of certainty about anything. "Do you consider yourself African?" someone asked during the Q and A, as someone almost always does.

I thought about giving my usual accident-of-biology-and-geography answer. I thought about explaining that identity is fluid; it is not only the color of my skin, or my mother tongue, or where I was raised, or even a combination of all those things that makes me who I am, it's more complicated than that. I thought about appropriating a line from ex–South African president Thabo Mbeki's famous "I Am an African" speech: "I come from those . . . who taught me that we could both be at home and be foreign." But that seemed willfully naïve. Most Africans violently reject the label of foreign, and for good reason: not only are they usually several generations into a place, but it can also be unpleasant, even life-threatening, to be identified as (for example) Malawian in Zambia, Zimbabwean in South Africa, or British almost anywhere.

I thought about explaining that, technically speaking, in terms of passports and birthrights, I had only ever been African in the loosest sense of the word and even then for only a fraction of my life. For a few years in the 1970s, we had become Rhodesians, but the Rhodesia of those days was a pariah nation, an illegal republic unrecognized by the rest of the world. The Rhodesia of my blue passport embossed with two rampant sable antelope was a country at war with itself, out of step with social progress, and at vehement odds with prevailing global attitudes toward civil rights, racial equality, and black African independence.

And when my family could have become legitimate Africans, at the transition from Rhodesia to Zimbabwe in 1980, my parents relinquished our claims to Zimbabwean passports and opted to revert British. Thereafter, we continued to live in southern Africa as expatriates; "Poms," we were scornfully dubbed, as in "Prisoners of Mother England," or "soutpiel," as in one foot in Britain, one foot in southern Africa, and a salty penis in the sea between. And by the time Mum and Dad embraced the obvious fact that they could never be anything but Zambian, it turned out to be easier said than done.

It took scores of visits to the immigration office, mountains of paperwork, and years of waiting for the correct authority to recover from malaria or to return from a funeral and then to find the correct rubber stamp for Mum and Dad to be granted permanent residency in Zambia. But by that time, I had long since married Charlie, moved to Wyoming, and sworn allegiance to the Stars and Stripes. The fact that I felt more at home in southern Africa than I did anywhere else on earth, and that I missed the countries of my youth with a physical ache, didn't make me a legitimate citizen of Zimbabwe or Zambia any more than an amputee's cruel sensation of a missing limb renders them whole again.

Did I consider myself African? The truth is, I longed to say, "Yes," as I had years ago. Even, defensively, "Of course, yes." I longed to have an identity so solid, so obvious, and so unassailable that I, or anyone else, could dig all the way back into it for generations and generations and find nothing but more and further proof of the bedrock of my Africanness. I wanted to be like my fellow speaker. No one would have asked her if she considered herself African, because she looked and sounded exactly as anyone might imagine an African should. Although maybe, if challenged, she would have rejected the label of African, and instead insisted on her identity as Nigerian, or more specifically as Igbo, or less particularly as a citizen of the whole world, or more broadly as a feminist. Perhaps she would have said she was none of the above. But we would never know, because she wasn't the one whose identity was in question.

I said, "Not anymore. Not especially."

||||||||||

After the reading, I found my way up to the rooftop of my hotel and lay shoeless on a sun lounger until midnight. High, thin clouds were misted pink with city lights. Behind them, the stars were muted in a moonless sky (the moon—waning crescent—would be rising late). I knew without being able to see them that a few thousand feet up, there would be star-reading birds migrating north out of this heat toward our unrolling Wyoming mountain summer: owls, thrushes, orioles, sparrows. I knew that for some birds, migration is almost all they do, nonstop, hundreds of miles north, hundreds of miles south, back and forth, a ceaseless rustle of wings, years shaved off their wild lives with all the effort of near perpetual motion.

Once, twenty-five years ago, camping near a waterfall on the Zambian border with Zaire, I had caught a glimpse of a distant flock of birds traveling at night against a full moon, fleeting black cut-out shapes, intent on destination. Often since then, I've searched the night sky, and although I have caught the brief twist of bats flitting through currents of insects, I have never again seen that nighttime miracle of birds, secretly stitching together south and north with their hunger, with their collective, insistent, mounting realization of being in the wrong place at the wrong time.

"I am an African," I said aloud to myself now. It sounded ridiculous. To be honest, I had thought it sounded faintly ridiculous even when Thabo Mbeki had said it, like P. G. Wodehouse's Bertie Wooster assessing Shakespeare: "Sounds well, but doesn't mean anything." I knew I would never apply the label of African to myself again, and not only because it wasn't strictly correct (how can a person belong to a whole continent?), but also because it was something I would be called upon to defend endlessly. So, as long as the question continued to be asked, I would likely continue to respond as I had tonight: "Not anymore. Not especially." And in any case, what life had taught me is that where we come from is a point—not the starting point, not the defining point—just a point. It's where we are that really counts.

MARRIAGE ADVICE FROM
THE END OF THE WORLD

The next day, I caught the plane back from Texas to Wyoming, and two weeks later, I fell ill. I lay in bed with a fever, the windows thrown open, our brown velvet curtains billowing in an early June breeze. The fever evolved into a cough. The cough evolved into something that became all I was. I coughed until I lost my voice. I coughed until I felt as if my ribs might disconnect from my spine. I coughed until I was the sum of my biology. By night, I sat with my back against the cool tile of the bathroom, hot water running into clouds of steam, and I coughed until I was winded. I grew exhausted. Charlie grew exhausted too. Not only from being up nights listening to me but also from some nameless, deeper, more worrying weariness.

Then one late morning, in the middle of the illness—proving unseemly long—Charlie walked into our bedroom with his latest calculation of our finances and abruptly announced, "If something doesn't happen soon we're going to lose the house." In my drained, mildly hallucinatory state, I pictured the house lifting off its foundation and splintering to pieces in the sky. I pictured Carl Fredricksen, the retired balloon salesman from the movie *Up,* flying our house to Paradise Falls (or, more likely, Idaho Falls, Sioux Falls, Twin Falls). I pictured us coming home from the children's school one day and finding the house gone, the land reforested and wild-encroached.

I contemplated Charlie's profile, gray and shadowy in the darkened room. I wanted to ask him, "If you and I are not this house, then who are we?" But I said nothing partly because I didn't have the spare breath, and partly because I knew neither of us had the answer to that question. Without the house, Charlie and I were undone from one another, uprooted and uncoupled. We had reached the point of speaking past one another, as if in a code intended for someone else entirely. And yet the idea of not belonging under the same roof was unthinkable to both of us.

When my father spoke of his parents' divorce, which he did rarely, and then only when it sounded as if I was contemplating the same thing, he would not use that word. Instead, he would say, "When the house broke apart." And I knew what he meant. You hear about so-called good divorces, about amicable detachments, about houses morphing into two— holidays taken together, Christmas Days spent under one roof, children's graduations attended en masse. But ours would not be that kind of uncoupling. We'd come together with too much passion to break apart gently. We'd tried separations before and the trauma of the near-catastrophic implications of what our divorce would be had always pulled us together again. Ours would be a house breaking apart and that is a monumental, irreversible event, as if a geological eruption has occurred. Survivors will be scattered to the four corners of the earth; they will have the shocked, wounded expressions of people who have endured an explosion. It will be terrible and biblical. "And if a house is divided against itself, that house cannot stand."

A few more days passed. Friends phoned to say they had dropped off soup and flowers for me at the bottom of the stairs. Mum sent a care package of Epsom salts and aspirin from Zambia. Vanessa sent an e-mail that read like a fractured hallucinogenic neon sign pulsing over a midnight diner: "Hi Al, are you DYING? Mum says you're 'dying.' Do you have the BLACK plague? Leave me something juicy in YOUR WILL . . . 'Only joking.' Love you lots and lots, so please don't peg it. Xxxxxx Van." The kids pushed get-well notes under the door and shouted requests; could they eat this, play that, go there? Charlie ebbed in and out of the room, anxious and depressed. I felt restless with worry too, but helpless to do much about it.

My eyes, bloodshot with coughing, were too sore for reading or writing. The radio—hours of indifferent contemporary music and repeating loops of news for much of the day—only added to my sense of shiftlessness. Eventually, as much to reassure myself out of my unproductivity as anything else, I went up into my office and found my old tape recorder and the stack of tapes of the dozens of interviews I had done with my parents over the years. I brought the tape recorder down to our bed and put it on the pillow next to my head.

I had made the tapes in part because I had wanted some concrete way to reach back home; a way to tell my U.S.-raised children, "These are the other people you came from. Here are their stories. Here is how they sound." But I had never played the tapes for any of our three children because it turns out real children don't tend to work the way we imagine they might, as little vessels into which we can decant our own reconstituted pasts. In my experience, young children exist almost forcibly in the present; they have scant interest in their heritage. They little care if their ancestral histories are erased, or if the graves of their forebears and relatives have been untraceably overrun. To begin with, it's we who care and we try to make our children care too; we remind them to hold on to the idea we have created of ourselves; we tell them to remember where they come from. We are the ones who say, "This is your special identity." And by extension there is the implicit instruction, "Become violently attached to it."

Listening to the tapes now, I was struck by my younger voice asking the questions, the accent still purely colonial English so that it's almost indistinguishable from Mum's and certainly nothing like the accent I now have. I was struck too by how impatiently I spoke, how quickly I filled any silence, how little I appeared to be listening to my parents' answers. Not for the first time in my life, I wished I had spoken less and heard more. It had taken this illness—my own loss of voice, a mild fever, forced seclusion—for the quality of my listening to begin to change.

Mum's voice was firmer than Dad's. She painted life gilded, she skipped over the difficult bits, and she put a positive spin on Rhodesia's long and bloody civil war ("Best years of my life!"). She repeated her favorite stories over and over like church, and I think for the same reason: the more often you say something, the more likely it is to affirm itself, to become an accepted truth and to evolve into a communal memory. She was an upholder of myth, a creator of burnished image, a best-foot forwarder. "I know most people remember most vividly the horrible gruesome tragic bits of their lives," she said. "But I don't see things that way."

When Dad spoke, he said everything only once, and then quite clearly, which is the only way I have known him. "Those who talk the most, usually have the least to say," he said when I complained about the long silences he was leaving on my tapes. Perhaps it's his native British reticence, combined with years of war and common-or-garden trauma plus a few seriously uncommon tragedies that pared down his utterances to only the essentials. When he was not much younger than I am now, and we were living on a drought-prone farm in eastern Rhodesia, the workers gave my father the nickname "Boss Fuck-Off." With retrospect, I can see how intonation and context could render that phrase uniformly useful to a tobacco farmer of English origin turned reluctant, conscripted Rhodesian soldier.

But although Dad has a definite sense of delivery, he doesn't have Mum's definite sense of belonging. In fact, his most determining act seems to have been an early decision to go against generations of military tradition on his father's side of the family and not join the British navy. Unlike my mother, who has long defined herself as belonging to Africa, my father is defined not by place but by an unbelonging to anywhere. My father eschewed both the nation and the much-flaunted naval tradition of his British forefathers, it was the earth—*any* earth, as long as it was far from the madding crowd—that suited him.

"No, the sea wasn't really my strong suite," Dad admitted. And it is true I have seen him swimming in it only once, and then only reluctantly. Goaded by the rest of us on a rare vacation to the seaside, he finally agreed to paddle out with exaggerated laboriousness from the beach a little way, before splashing uneasily back to shore. He looked hapless and incompetent enough that some German tourists appeared seriously to be considering a rescue. "Bloody wet," Dad said, toweling himself dry with the urgent vigor of someone emerging from hours among deep ice floes rather than a brief warm tropical bath. "And some bastard's overseasoned it with salt."

As a little boy, Dad was occasionally dressed up in sailor suits that he loathed, the way most children hate the smart clothes imposed on them by their elders. He remembers posh regimental dinners, hours of dreaded stuffy nonsense and kowtowing. Once, when he was old enough to have such inspirations but not yet old enough to fully think through the consequences of his actions, he had the idea of putting an exploding cigar in the humidor to liven up the dreariness of after-dinner port. The effect on the nerves of elderly shell-shocked naval officers turned out to be spectacularly reward-ing. "I really got bollocked for that one," Dad said. "But it was worth it."

A few times his father took Dad out on a ship, and although the enormous, imposing battle-readiness of the thing was impressive, Dad doesn't remember feeling a thrill of wanting to be a part of it. "All that discipline," he confesses on the tapes. "Bit awkward with someone of my tempera-ment." So, in Dad's telling, he fled England ("An aunt and half a dozen cousins in every county") for a farm-laborer job in Canada, found it cold and alcoholically dry; tried a stint in the West Indies, where he stayed until his bar bill exceeded his salary; went to Kenya to see a giraffe and met my mother. And she, fresh from the confines of dreary finishing school in London ("Tweedy lesbians and boiled cabbage," she says), was ready for the sort of adventure he promised. "Tim Fuller of No Fixed Abode," he introduced himself. Which would have rung out as a warning to anyone else, but manifested as a mating cry to Mum.

Ten years into my own marriage, when it was becoming clear that Charlie had receded from me, or that I had flowed out beyond his reach, maybe irrevocably, I asked Mum if she had any advice about being married, or (more to the point) staying married. I was home on the farm from the States, it was early morning and we were a little hungover, inspecting the fishponds before the heat of the day could really pick up. The dogs, as usual, were spilling all around us, scaring up pigeons and grasshoppers.

Mum frowned at me and, thinking she hadn't heard, I repeated the question. "No, no, no, I heard you perfectly well the first time," she said. She dusted flies away from her ears. "Oh Bobo, I don't know. Marry the right chap to begin with, I suppose." And then she whistled for the dogs and marched on ahead. It occurred to me then that Mum had probably never thought of herself as *married*. She just sailed on with life as she saw fit, and Dad, smitten with her, more or less steered from the stern, occasionally shouting (usually unheeded) words of warning.

By all logic and by any standards, my parents should have spun away from one another years ago. Together they had lost three children, a war, a few farms, and for a while my mother had seriously lost her mind. And yet they incorporated these losses into their marriage along with what they had gained, assigning very little in the way of either blame or praise almost anywhere. They put no more weight on despair than they did on joy. The way they did love was also the way they did tragedy, as if it was all an inevitable part of the gift of being alive. It was rare for my parents to make a production out of their tragedies unless sometimes, drunk, the past eddied out in Mum's mind and she was caught in the circulation of her old grief for a day or a week or a season until the sorrow passed.

"I was just bloody lucky to find your mother," my father told me after breakfast when I asked him the same question.

"No one else would have put up with me." He thumbed some tobacco into his pipe and tapped it down. "Anyway, we've always given each other heaps of room." Then he added, as if this mattered more than anything, "Whole bloody acres of room." He clamped his pipe between his teeth and lit it. "Yep, that's it. Acres and acres of room." Dad set his cards out for a game of solitaire. "Now," he said. "Let's see what sort of day we're going to have." By Dad's questionable reckoning, if his game came out, the day would be good. If it didn't come out, Dad cheated and the day would still be good. "Win-win," he said.

I watched Dad's hands hovering over his old cards, sticky with spilled tea and dog hair. I remained confused: Charlie and I seemed to have nothing but acres of room between us, and my parents, who had the kind of marriage to which I thought it worth aspiring, had none. They had lived, worked, and played together for the better part of forty years. Their tastes have cleaved and overlapped; they share bathwater, silently conceding that the grubbiest person goes last; they sleep under the claustrophobic confines of a single mosquito net. I said, "That's absolute rubbish, Dad. You give each other no room whatsoever."

Dad looked up at me, his eyes crinkled against pipe smoke, eyebrows raised as if I had said something of surprising stupidity. He tapped his temple with a forefinger. "Ah, yes, but it's all in the head, Bobo. All in the head."

I had a glimmering of understanding then. No, my parents are not two solitudes, as Rainer Maria Rilke would have had it, protecting, touching, and greeting one another. To the contrary, they are indistinguishable from one another, inseparably connected; they have become a single recognizable culture with its own food, its own scents, and its own private language. Even the way they have annoyed one another over the years has become part of their shared culture, the way mosquitoes are a difficult but inevitable part of the Zambezi valley, or rain has become a standard joke in Scotland. Over time, they have learned to make their foibles part of the ties that bind them, their love is *everything* about them—not only the passion and humor and resilience, but also the aggravating habits, the quirks, the flaws.

When they were younger, Mum's excessive love of plastic bags made for one of those plaguing marital recurring arguments that are always about more than the subject at hand. As if terrified that they would run out in her lifetime, Mum collected bags, washed them, reused them, washed them and reused them again until eventually they disintegrated into little plastic dust atoms. Until then, like neurotically beloved pets, they came with her everywhere. "Just in case," she said.

Dad, more worried about broken-down lorries and armed bandits in the forest than he was about a dearth of petrochemical packaging, grew increasingly impatient. "Nicola, I am leaving now," he would suddenly declare, as if an invisible starting flag had been dropped. "We need to get back before dark." Then he roared off in the pickup while Mum still had only one leg in the car. Meanwhile, plastic bags were strewn like wind-buffeted reprimands all over the driveway. "And my poor limbs ripped off at the knee, arms severed at the elbow," Mum remembers.

Now, though, Dad sits behind the steering wheel calmly smoking his pipe while Mum has a last, protracted faff in the house. "She's getting together all her plastic bags, the bane of my existence," Dad says cheerfully. "Just you watch, she'll have about five hundred of them and she'll rifle through them all the way to Lusaka."

At last Mum emerges from the house and gets into the car clutching her treasured cache. Dad waits for her to swat the dogs away from the car. "Don't run over the terrorists," she says. "Go on, Harry. Off you go, Sprocket." Then she shuts the door and after that there's the lengthy performance of the seat belt. Finally she's ready, and she flashes Dad a victorious smile and a thumbs-up, like a Formula One racer leaving the pit.

"Got all your plastic bags, Tub?" Dad asks.

"Yup," Mum says. And after that for a hundred or more happy miles, Dad drives and Mum rustles around making small, satisfying discoveries—"Ooh look, I found my copper bracelet. I knew I had put it somewhere safe," or "Ah, there's my receipt for the fingerlings, Tim. See? It had to show up somewhere"—until we reach the Munda Wanga Botanical Gardens on the outskirts of Lusaka where there's always a chance the caged lions will be eyeing a bunch of children on their school outing. As soon as she catches sight of the huge trees that line the gardens' walls, Mum's attention is diverted from her plastic bags and is riveted instead on the enclosure. "Oh, no schoolchildren today," she says, disappointed.

"Mum can't wait to see a schoolchild being eaten by a lion," Dad says.

"I'VE TOLD BOBO THAT A HUNDRED TIMES ALREADY," Mum shouts. Then she turns back to me. "It's like living with a sheep," she says. "Every day's a fresh day for Dad."

SIGNAL FLAGS

By early July, I had been treated for swine flu, tested for pneumonia, and had subjected my lung meridian to acupuncture needles, but still my illness would not abate. A friend brought me flowers, soup, and bottles of eucalyptus oil. Then she sat on the end of the bed and watched me cough. "This won't do," she said at last, and had me phone a doctor who specialized in tropical diseases. He made a house call, listened to me for a few minutes, and diagnosed me with whooping cough. He prescribed steroids for me, and prophylactic antibiotics for the rest of the family. Even after I felt well, he cautioned that I should probably stay out of circulation for a while. Whooping cough, he warned, is very contagious.

I thought of a ship in harbor flying the international maritime signal flag Lima, also known as the Yellow Jack. It meant, "This ship is quarantined." I liked the word, *quarantine*, and all the protective cover it implied. I liked too the idea of signal flags. In a crisis of the sort that unlanguages a person, when there is no longer any possibility of intimate and complex communication, there is still the simple, dread symbol of two yellow squares juxtaposed with two black squares: "You should stop your vessel instantly."

After a few days, the fever subsided. I stopped coughing. Spinning from the steroids, I woke before dawn and started tidying the yard of its winter debris. "Sweat equity," Charlie called it, a phrase I hated for the way it took the joy out of labor, but one that had nonetheless stuck in my mind, reemerging every time I swept the driveway, weeded the flowerbeds, raked the lawn. After that, I went up to my office. Beginning that afternoon, and in the weeks that followed, I did the seventh draft of a frustratingly out-of-reach screenplay. I wrote eighty pages of a new book. I reviewed a couple of novels for newspapers, I accepted a magazine assignment on the Pine Ridge Indian Reservation for the following summer. I worked and worked as if so doing could tether our house to the earth; Charlie to me; our family to itself.

"It'll be okay," I said. "Won't it?" But Charlie's anxiety swelled and began to fill the room. Although he went into the office every day, and stayed there all nine or ten hours and sometimes late into the night, his real estate business was dead; there was nothing left now but the phantom labor of shuffling papers from one side of his desk to the other. The edges of other people's panic leaked into our lives. Charlie talked about clients who had lost their jobs, their homes, their savings. Then he said we would have to put our own house on the market and move into something smaller, downsize. "We're going to have to tighten our belts," he said. "Batten down the hatches. Save every penny we can." At night our sighs and exhaustion left our mouths and settled over our bodies; a cloud of unmet expectations, a threatening storm of broken promises, a low pressure system of the unsaid.

I thought of how it isn't impossible, but it's overwhelmingly daunting and perhaps even pointless to construct a viable future from an imperfect past. I thought of Charlie and me confined again to a little cottage; his brooding silence, my reactive chatter. It was too late. Fifteen years ago, I would have moved into a teepee or a hut or a tent with him. But we'd killed the very possibility of small air between us. We were a broken working relationship. Dread played a long, low note in my chest. We couldn't move into something smaller. If we were going to stay together, we needed a wing each, adjoining cottages with a drawbridge, two houses divided by state lines. We needed the kind of extraordinary space ordinary people could never afford.

Ours had contracted into a grocery-list relationship—finances, children, housekeeping. We concentrated on logistics, cautiously withholding, careful of what we said to one another in case it was used against us later. We were competitive with one another about the difficulties each of us faced in our everyday lives, as if to announce our individual happiness to one another was the final infidelity. And instead of disclosing our souls, we recounted complaints and kept score of the ways in which we had irritated one another or let each other down. After that we had nothing left to say.

I asked Charlie if he could imagine me dead, really wanting to know. He said, "What kind of question is that?"

"It doesn't have to be a tragic death," I pointed out. "I could be painlessly evaporated. Gently vaporized by a bunch of angels. Raptured into heaven."

Charlie was quiet for a bit. Then he said, "Yes, sometimes I do."

"Me too," I said.

Death is the great silencer into which people can pour their interpretations of love and loss and longing. But divorce is a choice, and it's hard to listen to the inevitable rancorous fallout and shaky insecurity it engenders. The social disease of a breakup threatens and destabilizes, and all but the closest of friends—and sometimes even they—recede from the threat it poses. Marriage, with all its fairy-tale promise, its allure of security, and its impression of superior morality, is something we hold up as a badge of honor. Politicians and sports stars rise on the borrowed capital of long and steady marriages; they fall on their discreditable failures.

We had made every effort. There had been the trial separations, the cultish weekend marriage seminars encouraging conjugal spirituality, a couple of disastrous vacations without the children when I missed them so much it only served to highlight that we were better parents than we were romantic partners. There had been dozens of couples' counseling sessions with the accompanying rules about holding a relationship together by using safe words, or by setting up date nights. But the suggestions filled me with dread. I couldn't grasp the concept of safe words—"There are no bad words," I've always taught my children. "Only bad ways to use good words." And our attempts at date nights had increasingly ended in silent standoffs or out-and-out fights.

I had begun to understand that neither of us was wrong, and neither was either of us right. But we saw the world so differently that it seemed to me as if Charlie was living in a different space and time than I was. He saw the world in concrete terms, rationally, and as if the place were solid and the systems set in place were dependable. Charlie never questioned his own sanity, although he sometimes questioned mine. I saw the world as something fluid; I expected irrationality and surprises. I could not tell the difference between inspiration and mild madness, and most of the time I did not think the gap between the two was important.

A month earlier I had gone to our local public library and

walked down the aisle of relationship-related books, piling
volume after volume into my arms. I made it as far as the help
desk with the books before I pictured myself running into an
acquaintance in the checkout line or in the parking lot. How
would I explain these titles? *The Emergency Divorce Handbook
for Women; Helping Your Kids Cope with Divorce the Sandcastles
Way; Too Good to Leave, Too Bad to Stay: A Step-by-Step Guide
to Help You Decide Whether to Stay In or Get Out of Your Relationship; Coming Apart: Why Relationships End and How to
Live Through the End of Yours.* My panic escalated. Even if I
managed to negotiate my way out of our small-town public
library parking lot without bumping into half a dozen people
I knew, how would I get the books into the house unob-
served? What if Charlie saw them? Worse, what if the children saw them?

I dumped the books on the shelving cart by the door and
hurried out of the library into the high-altitude sunshine,
inexplicit in its cheerful clarity. What I wanted more than
anything was a sign that told me unequivocally whether or
not to divorce Charlie—a thunderclap from the heavens,
maybe, words written in clouds, something as unambiguous
as the sensation in my whole shocked body the first time I
met him and knew without any doubt he was the love of
my life.

I drove home, and found myself walking into the house as
if it might hold the answer to that question. We'd built the
house together more than ten years earlier but even so it had
never really felt mine. Although I can't say it felt as if it
belonged to Charlie either. Domestically our two cultures
had come into opposition like participants in a nominally
friendly sports competition and clashed more aggressively
than was necessary. It turned out Charlie prefers clean, modern lines. My taste leans toward the sort of thing that would

not be out of place in a brimming African farmhouse. Now Charlie's low-slung, shiny leather sofa faced my canvas-covered, dog-stained, allergy-hot-zone sofa over the coffee table on which there was a buffer zone of shared interests: a book of Lee Miller's war photography; a biography of Paul Bowles; orange candles on Japanese-print-inspired holders; Charlie's weekly newspaper; a world atlas; bills; the children's homework.

The kids weren't home from school yet, Charlie was still at work. I went online and ordered a variety of books, from those that promised to rescue a rocky marriage to the sorts of fresh-from-the-fray divorcée memoirs I would ordinarily have avoided. I got used paperbacks because I knew I wouldn't want them on my shelves after I'd read them. If the marriage survived, they would be a threat—always suggestively wink-ing up from my shelves on the days our union reverted rocky. If the marriage didn't survive, I knew I wouldn't want to be reminded of this day forever afterward by their presence.

When they arrived, I stashed the books in their anony-mous brown packages behind my collection of obscure Afri-cana, where I knew they were unlikely to be discovered. Every time I went on assignment or to a speaking engagement I stuffed a few volumes into my carry-on. I was distressed to find that many came in the telltale, rippled condition of women on the brink; read in the bath, wept upon, or both. I imagined their previous owners propped on the edge of the steaming tub, taps running, tears streaming. I read them hur-riedly, in increasing dismay, and left them in the backs of air-plane seats, in airports, in hotel rooms—a guilty trail of contagion. *The Unexpected Legacy of Divorce: A Twenty-Five-Year Landmark Study* disturbed me so much I tore it into parts and discarded the fragments in separate gas station garbage bins across South Dakota and Nebraska.

Like alcoholic memoirs and their twelve steps to freedom and recovery, divorcée memoirs seem to follow a familiar path: the grim realization that the marriage is truly over; the reluctant acceptance that the unhappy liaison has an ungodly power over the couple; the terror and dislocation that preceded and followed the actual awful act of divorce; the new man and renewed belief in the old lies about love. I had begun to give up on these books at the first mention of a woman collapsing with grief on the kitchen or the bathroom floor. Why always these two rooms? Couldn't anyone fall over anywhere more comfortable? The sitting room perhaps, the bedroom even? It was only later I discovered that women dissolve in these two places for good reason: the kitchen because it is the place from which we have nurtured our soon-to-be devastated families, and the bathroom because it is private.

"I think it's over," I said, stopping Charlie at the front door one morning in mid-August. Even as I spoke, I could hear the mix of anxiety and finality in my voice, as if for several months we had both been watching over a dying relative whose time had finally come. It sounded to me as if I were warning Charlie: if he walked out the door now, he would miss what we had all been waiting for, the moment of death.

"What's over?" Charlie asked.

"This," I said, and I gestured us, and the house, and by implication everything we had collected and made together. Our family, the shelves of books, the rows of pills on the bathroom shelf, the boxes of old tax returns in the garage, the photo albums showing us on vacation in Central and South America, the Shona sculpture of a mother with child, the eccentrically beautiful pink-and-cream rug made from home-grown Zambian wool woven for us by Vanessa as a wedding present. "It's the beach," she had explained unhelpfully when I stared at the wavy design in puzzlement. "With rocks."

"Not now," Charlie said. "If you want to discuss this some other time, we can schedule a meeting."

"Schedule a meeting?" I said. "I'm not your business partner."

"Don't yell."

"I'm not yelling," I said.

"You are."

Then I was.

Cecily came down from the kitchen and stood between us, tiny and fragile-looking in her ready-for-preschool braids, her backpack seeming to double her size. For too long our children had done this, inserting themselves between us and the words that might finally blow us apart. "So right now?" Charlie asked. "You really want to do this right now?"

I didn't, but I couldn't help myself. Cecily was a burgeoning part of my hysteria. I wanted her world to be predictable, safe, and, above all, normal. I wanted all my children to be able to say of their childhoods that they were if not idyllic, then at least uneventful. I didn't want our children losing their house, or their sense of family. I wanted them swaddled in continuity and predictability. In other words, I wanted for my children what I'd never had and what I seemed unable and unwilling and far too unbelieving to create for myself: a solid, obvious, and unassailable sense of self attached to an immovable home, the same address for decades, routines and traditions. "Yes," I said. Then, "No. No, of course not."

I had broken the sacred six-word vow of silence: *Not in front of the children.* But I was keeping the sacred six-word vow of parenthood: *For the sake of the children.* For the sake of the children we wouldn't talk about this now, or maybe ever. For the sake of the children, there would be days made normal by after-school sports and by PTO meetings and by cupcakes on their birthdays. For the sake of the children we would pretend everything was okay until our marriage went from cold war to nuclear winter, and maybe even then.

Charlie scooped up Cecily. "I'm leaving," he said. "E-mail me with some times we can meet. When you're calmer."

They left, Cecily yelling, "Hearts and kisses! Hearts and kisses!" and waving as she always did until the corner in the driveway rendered her invisible to me. I went up to my office, a small room—more of a landing than anything else, a stage stop from which I could easily monitor the comings and goings of the home. It would have been, if the house had had a heart, exactly there, suspended over the belly of the kitchen, and the incubating warmth of the children's bedroom. I turned on my computer and started the day's writing. There had been a time, ten or fifteen years ago, that I had believed I could write my way out of anything. For years I had even kept a sticky note on my computer that said exactly that: "You can write your way out of this."

But I had written and written and here we still were. For the first time, I admitted this might be something I would not be able to write my way out of. I couldn't make words take the shape of an escape for either of us. This couldn't go on. On the other hand, what options did we have? Charlie and I were in this together, house lifting off its foundation or not, sweat equity and tears, thick and thin. We had children together, we had history together, we had dwindling bank accounts and accumulated debt together.

I looked around at the couples we knew and none of them seemed to be tripping the light fantastic either. Most people I knew complained more or less tirelessly about their spouses: they disagreed about how to spend their money, how to raise their children, and how often or seldom they should have sex. They complained of being bored, of their lives being habitual and careful, of feeling spied upon, of carrying with them a perpetual hangover of guilt. It seemed that no one felt good enough at being married. Maybe marriage wasn't supposed to be unfettered joy. Maybe this was it, coupledom as a slog with the reward being the comfort of believing you were doing your best, not for yourself, but for those to whom you had pledged your allegiance. Maybe marriage was a long exercise in compromise, and self-denial, and an increasingly furtive internal life. To aim for anything else seemed a fatal swim too far from shore in unknown waters.

There seemed nothing for it but to double down. Dig deeper. Work more and harder and longer. The Zulu signal flag is four triangles—black, yellow, blue, and red—making up a four-colored square. Ordinarily, it means, "I need a tug." But in 1905, when the Zulu flag was hoisted by Admiral Togo at the Battle of Tsushima, it meant, "The empire's fate depends on the result of this battle, let every man do his utmost duty."

THE MIDDAY SUN

Then in a kind of fin-de-siècle madness, we both planned working trips to Africa. Charlie said he would guide potential investors around Zambian safari camps. I said I'd go home and collect photographs for my new book. We planned our travel so as not to be in Zambia longer than a couple of nights together. I said I didn't want to leave the children home alone; Charlie said he would need to focus on the logistics of his clients' itineraries and wouldn't be able to deal with distractions. What neither of us said was that we couldn't bear to be together, that we couldn't breathe around each other any-more.

In their 1977 piece "Breathing In/Breathing Out (Death Itself)," the performance artists Marina Abramovic and Ulay kneel face-to-face, pressing their mouths together. Their noses are blocked with cigarette filters. The image is that of a passionate kiss, but it is in fact an intense, exhausting physical struggle. For the duration of the piece—nearly twenty minutes—the couple have no external access to air. Shortly after the performance starts, Marina's face grows shiny with exertion; she is audibly suffering. Soon, Ulay is gasping too. At last, they let go of one another's mouths—propelled backward by their need for oxygen and space.

Breath, *pneuma,* has also been understood since ancient times as soul, as the connection between the outer world and our inner beings, as our integrity. When we breathe deeply, we connect head and heart, and we are connected to the atmosphere. When we hold our breath, when our breath is forbidden, then we are isolated from all creation. Even if we can still function, we are not integral, we cannot be trusted, we are not whole, we have no hope of being authentic. We are dependent and immobile and fixed. In that way, the lack of breath between two people is an isolating, suffocating, limited contract. The couple, gasping, will eventually have to fall apart from one another.

|||||||||

In early September, I wrote letters to our three children, hid them under the cleaning products in the back of the bathroom cabinet where I was sure they would not be found until sufficiently long after my death, and flew to Zambia. By now, the hilarity of my father's seventieth birthday party had long worn off. A banana-leaf-ruining frost in July had left him with recurrent bouts of bronchitis. Then the rains returned and he came down with a particularly stubborn dose of malaria. Suspicious of medicine in general and of Western medicine in particular, Dad submitted himself to the care of a Chinese doctor, new to Lusaka.

Dr. Quek diagnosed him with polluted blood—"We could have told you that for free," the rest of us shrieked—and she prescribed inpatient injections of antimalarial medicine, intravenous infusions of antibiotics, and capsules of vitamins. Dad had to eat an egg a day, two servings of red meat, and a variety of green vegetables. He was to avoid drinking beer and water, he was prohibited the enervating effects of ice, but he was allowed as much red wine and tea as he liked. "You see?" Dad said. "Very sensible." I had my doubts but nonetheless offered to accompany him to town for his appointments.

Accordingly, we left the farm at dawn, hitting the edge of Lusaka just after rush hour. The city was barely recognizable from the one Charlie and I had left in the early nineties. The official end of the Cold War in 1992 meant the communist bloc no longer subsidized Zambia's social-humanist ideology. Decades of complacent economic stagnation had given way to a sudden proliferation of petty capitalism. Traffic lights and intersections were clogged with vendors hawking counterfeit perfume, pirated music, and plastic toys from China. Then the Chinese themselves arrived and instituted seriously consequential capitalism.

First they built roads. Then they took over mines and opened industrial plants. After that, they went onto the farms. Now they were in the shops, schools, and clinics. There were scores of Chinese restaurants, oddly empty and often bafflingly free of either menus or chefs. By 2006, there were more Chinese in Zambia than there had ever been British. Advertisements at the airport welcomed visitors in English and Chinese. Trucks and cars with Chinese characters on their doors teemed up and down Cha Cha Cha Road and disappeared into the compounds and suburbs loaded with gravel, bricks, cement. Hospitals, schools, and compounds with swooping double-eaved roofs sprung up all over Lusaka.

Suddenly time, which had never mattered before, had meaning. Nearly everyone seemed to have a cell phone, people could text, SMS, update their Facebook statuses. In kiosks and intersections across the country it was impossible to avoid vendors selling talk time. Until now, time was an abstract idea, possessing the languid pointlessness of all socialist-era states; striving was fruitless. Government clocks in post offices, hospitals, and police stations had rusted to a stop with dust and neglect. Waiting had been a national pastime. Now there were cell phones and time came in sheets of little scratch-off tickets, and people could make appointments. Unseemly speed was the new order of the delineated twenty-four-hour day.

"We're orphans of the empire," Mum lamented. "Our hour is over."

But Dad admired the Chinese workers he saw on the road over the Muchinga Escarpment on the way to and from the farm. They worked quickly and single-mindedly with the focus of a hungry people who have a historic understanding that things always could get worse. "Look at that," Dad said, indicating the men in their conical hats and their blue pajama uniforms toiling over steaming layers of freshly laid asphalt. "You wouldn't find a Brit or a Yank slogging so hard in this heat, would you?" He leaned out the window and waved his pipe at the surprised laborers. "Well done, chaps, well done! Good effort. Keep it up."

"Oh, don't encourage them, Tim," Mum said, lifting her head out of her book. "Or they'll never leave."

Then at the end of March 2009, toward the close of a particularly rainy season, a tanker-ship-sized chunk of the new Chinese-built road collapsed, leaving a massive hole between the hill on one side and a steep, high embankment on the other. Traffic was backed up for days; Mum and Dad were stranded on the farm. "Zhing-zhong construction," the regional press jeered. But Dad's support of the Chinese remained unwavering. "Very bad luck. Could have happened to anyone," he said.

"Not to the Romans, it couldn't," Mum countered.

|||||||||

Dr. Quek's clinic was in a little whitewashed house down an unmarked, refuse-lined lane in the eastern part of town. When we arrived, the doctor was relaxing in a bottomed-out chair, her legs thrown girlishly over one of its arms. She was watching a South African game show that seemed to involve very excitable contestants trying to gain the cooperation of profoundly perplexed chickens. "Ah, Mr. Fuller," the doctor said, glancing away from the screen. She waved her hands around her head where little explosions of white hair mushroomed. "Go lie down. Bed waiting. Nurse coming." I followed Dad down a short passage. Gray streaks on the walls showed where the roof had leaked during the rains. Floor tiles had peeled up. A few flies hung drowsily midair.

"Are you sure about this?" I asked.

"A hundred and ten percent," Dad said.

We went into a room in which there was an old single bed like the sort Vanessa and I had slept in at boarding school, and a gurney upholstered in heavy plastic. Dad stretched out on the bed, exposed his inner arm, and shut his eyes. A nurse came in and set up an IV. She said I could rest on the gurney if I liked. So I got up on the plastic mattress next to Dad's bed and lay down. Dad appeared to doze off. A colorless liquid fed into his veins. At the end of the hall I could hear the muffled rapture of the television set. Outside, starlings chattered in a droughty bougainvillea. Once in a while, the nurse came back into the room, fiddled with the IV, and killed a fly or two with her plastic swatter. It was all very serene. I felt a surge of affection for Dr. Quek.

It was rare for my father to admit to any illness bad enough to warrant a visit to a clinic. He believes most accidents and ailments—hangovers, heart attacks, and backaches, for example—can be fixed with a couple of aspirins and tea and/or brandy. My mother isn't much different. Aside from medicine for her bipolar ("mad pills, happy pills, panic pills, and sleeping pills") and inhalers for both my parents' asthma ("our puffers"), Mum believes Epsom salts will cure everything from constipation to a difficult labor. The shelf in their bathroom reflects my parents' medical austerity. Aside from aspirin and Epsom salts, there is Dettol for scrapes and scratches, and Andrews liver salts for indigestion. "Ninety-nine percent of what ails is all up here," Dad said, tapping his head.

"Unless there's actual blood," I argued.

"Even then," Dad said.

Several years ago, one late midweek morning, not so far from the farm, three armed men had jumped into the front of Dad's pickup and without much in the way of an overture began beating him with their fists and the butts of their guns. They took his watch, what little cash he had in his pockets, and then left him bleeding by the side of the road, having stolen his pickup. "Must've thought I was someone else," Dad said.

"Who else could you possibly have been?" I asked.

Everyone on the road between the Kafue confluence and the Chirundu turnoff knows my father. "He is most famous for five hundred miles," a Chirundu shopkeeper told me when I went to the market to get groceries and supplies for the farm. "Because of his good deeds and his kindness, his humanitarian acts."

"Good deeds?" I said, unconvinced. "Humanitarian acts? Are you sure you're not confusing my father with the Italian nuns?"

The shopkeeper became animatedly defensive then. He expounded on Dad's acts of service to the community. "He doesn't say anything," the shopkeeper insisted. "But he shows pity when there is a catastrophe." My father was there with fish and bananas when there were cholera epidemics, he told me. He arrived in the pickup to help clean up when a fire swept through the market. He ferried stranded villagers when the river breached its banks. "He is an angel of mercy," the shopkeeper concluded, hyperbolic with emotion.

"Well that's very nice for all of you," I said. "But I'm not sure he's ever been an angel of mercy to me."

"Then you must not have had a catastrophe yet," the shopkeeper said.

For some time after being thrown out of the pickup by the thieves, Dad sat under the lacy shade of a mopane tree by the side of the road thinking things through. He concluded that no one short of an East African Rally driving mechanic would get very far with his car because, like most vehicles he had owned, it was temperamental and required the loving understanding of a dedicated owner. Villagers, a crowd of children, and a man on a bike stopped and expressed concern. Dad, remembering his manners, stood up and mopped the blood off his face with his red-spotted handkerchief as best he could. "Bwanji?" he asked.

"Bwino," everyone replied.

Then, refusing the offers of help—the man with the bike suggested ferrying my father home on his handlebars—my father made shakily by foot for the nearest bar. The man with the bike and the other concerned villagers followed him, like supporters at the end of a marathon. Once at the bar, Dad ordered Cokes and beers for his new friend and eleven brandies for himself. "That's a medicinal quantity," Dad explained afterward.

As he had predicted, the pickup had stalled as soon as it reached the deep sand close to the Chirundu turnoff. The thieves had fled north on foot, into the millet fields that lined the road just there. Villagers near the market, seeing my father's vehicle veer wildly up the road, had given chase shouting, "Bwana Fuller! Bwana Fuller!" Two of the culprits had been caught, one already wearing my father's watch. The police put the thieves in custody, and indefinitely retained my father's watch as evidence. "So it all worked out in the end," Dad said. "Other than the watch."

But I couldn't get used to my father's new profile: his once straight nose buckled sideways in the center where it had been broken, a ribbon of pink in the middle of his scalp where it had been torn, a missing tooth where it had been shaken loose. Every time I caught myself being surprised by his altered appearance, I felt a flutter of anxiety. Now, lying there in the steamy calm of Dr. Quek's clinic with Dad dozing next to me, I recognized a common, irrational impulse. I wanted to stop what would happen next, whatever it was. We were okay here, now. Now. Now. Now. I watched the pulse in my father's temple beat time.

After twenty minutes or so, Dr. Quek came into the room. She felt Dad's wrist and made him show her his tongue; she broke needles out of sterile packets and gave him slow, fat injections of some sluggish liquids of various toxic-looking shades. She jiggled the emptying bag of IV fluids and said something neither of us could understand. After that, she left and the nurse came back in, this time without her flyswatter, and detached Dad from the lines leading into his veins. She told us we were welcome to lie where we were, in the clinic, until the sun wasn't so hot.

Dad sighed and lay back against the pillow, eyes closed again.

"You know if you read the whole verse of Psalm ninety ten, threescore year and ten isn't the end of the story," I said. "There's a whole other bit."

Dad opened his eyes and said, "I thought you were a Muslim."

"Lapsed vegetarian," I said.

"Oh. What do they believe again?"

A fly buzzed in through the open window and circled our heads in lazy figure eights. "I'm just saying, if you read past the first line, it says you can live till eighty. 'The days of our years are threescore years and ten; and if by reason of strength they be fourscore years, yet is their strength labor and sorrow; for it is soon cut off, and away we fly.'"

Dad swung his legs off the bed, stood up, and waggled his hips. "You mean I have another decade?"

"At least," I said.

"Well then, I should start misspending my youth. What do you think?" He lit his pipe and clouds of smoke filled the little room. "Hooray! How about I take Mum on holiday? The last tango to Paris!"

LAST CALL ON THE
AFRICAN QUEEN

L ike one of those dogs trained to sense low blood sugar in diabetics, or to detect an imminent seizure in epileptics, Vanessa has uncanny radar for trouble, knowing before any-one else when things are about to start falling apart. It was a skill developed partially out of self-preservation, partially from early if unintended training, and partially as a way to bypass suffering. If I had long ago run out of whatever chem-ical resets to calm, Vanessa had long ago run out of whatever tolerance she may once have had for upsets. So before I had even said anything about my marriage collapsing, Vanessa's supernatural powers had detected trouble and she set about fixing Charlie and me, attempting to cement us into each other by way of a family outing on the single day in which we overlapped on our trips to Zambia.

"Right, Al, we're all going on the river houseboat," she said. "As a treat. I've organized the whole thing." She glared at me. "The Kafue is a fabulous river, my absolute favorite. And you'll like the boat. There's a bar and a braai. We're going to have a fabulous time." It sounded more like a stern command than a happy promise.

I said, "Of course."

Dad demurred, citing an allergy to any body of water not sufficiently diluted by quantities of alcohol. And Richard fled for work, citing urgent business. The rest of us—Vanessa, her youngest three children, Mum, Charlie, and I—showed up on the banks of the Kafue River at midday. It was wide and brilliantly blue just here, covered with large swaths of dinner-plate-sized water lilies. Egrets, startlingly white, lifted and resettled in the grass along the river's edge. The boat—a double-decker with tables and barstools above and a smoking charcoal grill below—lurched gently on its moorings.

"This will be fun," Vanessa insisted again, and my heart broke a little bit because I knew she could feel trouble brewing, the way she always had, and I knew it was possible I was going to let her down.

Then some young women in impractically short skirts and impressively high heels teetered up the gangway ahead of us. "Look," Mum said. "How lucky, we even have our own prossies." Next a film crew showed up and a young cameraman, dressed, as if for war, in a flak jacket and a back-to-front baseball cap, flung himself on the bank, aiming a camera at us. Mum waved and smiled. The cameraman pushed his cap around impatiently. "You must move out of the way," he said, making a motion like he was trying to rid his eyes of a disturbing vision. "We're filming here."

"Oh please no, kissy-kissy one kwacha," Vanessa said.

But the alleged prostitutes turned out to be actresses for a South African soap opera. They walked up and down the gangway a few more times, stopping occasionally to stare moodily out into the middle distance. Meantime, Mum darted back and forth behind them, and encouraged Vanessa's children to do the same. "We'll be on tele, ek se," she said. "We'll be famous." She stopped occasionally to bestow well-aimed if terrifying grins at the cameraman. "What do you think? Which would you say is my best side?" which made her laugh so uncontrollably she collapsed into a wheezing asthma attack.

"Oh dear God please save us," Vanessa implored, really meaning it.

At last, the camera crew and the actresses left in an SUV with tinted windows—"What a pity, there goes the nightlife," Mum said, taking a few gasps on her inhaler—and we set ourselves up on tables on the top deck near the front. Mum bought a round of drinks. "Here's to us!" she cried, raising her sweating glass. We chugged upstream toward the gorge, into more and more lovely territory. Music piped out of speakers, and a fellow passenger with a poorly concealed pistol poking out the top of his shorts shouted approximate lyrics over the sound of the engine.

Charlie and I danced around the deck, relieved to be wordlessly in each other's arms, out of Wyoming, and away from the collapsing U.S. economy. The river appeared sparkling and perfect; the sky was blameless and forever, and Mum's gin and tonics lit us all young and hopeful again. Our nieces shrieked their embarrassment and covered their eyes. Vanessa put her hand over her mouth, as if she had suddenly happened upon locals behaving lewdly while in her Englishwoman-on-vacation-in-the-tropics guise. Charlie and I laughed.

Moments like this made it easier to be romantic, to feel in love, chosen, celebrated, alive. This vision of Zambia was the Africa of tourist brochures, with a smattering of wildlife, genuinely friendly people, and time oddly morphed to fill more than twenty-four hours on any given day. Here, from our slightly tipsy point of view, a kind of freedom blossomed around us, as if any miraculous thing were possible. "If you fall in love in Africa, don't trust it until you've gone back to the States," a Kenyan friend told me. "Because in Africa, none of it's real." By which he meant not only the passion two people might generate on the continent, but also the Africa that fostered that passion.

Anyone who knew what was behind the pleasant view of our Kafue River understood that things weren't nearly as perfect as they looked. By any number of reliable accounts, this water was among the most polluted in the country. Pulp-and-paper mills, fertilizer plants, abattoirs, and mines all disposed of their unprocessed waste in the river. Villagers reported that fish had developed strange and unpalatable flavors; diseases were appearing—blotchy skin, ulcers, stomach problems. And above the river, hidden by tall curtains of reeds and bulrushes, forests were being chopped down at the highest per capita rate in the world, second only to Indonesia. Unchecked topsoil bled red whenever it rained, leaving deep eroded gorges.

|||||||||

Later, on her veranda having wine before supper, Vanessa grilled me. "Are you and Charlie doing all right? Because I really can't handle it if you aren't." By the glare of the bare bulb hanging above the veranda door, I could see where a lifetime of grief, worry, and fear had accumulated in a web of fine lines around her eyes the way dreamcatchers are supposed to catch dreams. She ran her fingers along the lines now, counting her multitude of sorrows. "All I want is love and peace, and everyone getting along. No more war." Then she spelled it out: "P-E-A-C-E. Right?" She leaned forward as if she didn't want the space around us to hear what she was saying.

"Dancing in public's not natural," she said, her voice tight with suspicion. "People only dance in public when they're having problems."

"Or when they've just had a double gin and tonic," I pointed out.

Vanessa pursed her lips. When we were children, this expression usually heralded an imminent death threat as a way to divert me from real or imagined danger. "You'll die of a snakebite if you go in the bamboos," or "Terrorists will chop you to pieces if you leave the security fence," or "If I say you have to get in the cupboard then you have to jump in right away." Which isn't to say Vanessa was happy about her role as my protector-in-chief: there was her childhood broken, flooded with too much responsibility too soon, and there was annoying little me still alive and more or less well thanks to her. And instead of being grateful and well-behaved in exchange for Vanessa's caretaking, I used her hypervigilance as a wall from behind which to shout my discomfort and my alarming observations. "Shhh man," Vanessa said. "Why do you always have to be such a loudmouth?"

Now she sighed and lit two cigarettes. She handed me one. "Quick," she said. "You'd better smoke it before Charlie catches you." I took a few guilty puffs, and then wafted fresh air around my hair like we were teenagers again. In adolescence, Vanessa made up for her early years of caretaking and preemptive death threats by acting on all the sibling rivalry she had been thus far forced to suppress—"That was hilarious, Al. Remember when I tried to throw you out of the pickup in Malawi?" But finding it harder to bump me off than she had hoped, she decided to craft a shaky alliance between us using whatever pilfered contraband was at our disposal. "Let's have a fag, Al. And a beer." Since then, except when one or both of us has temporarily given up, we have passed cigarettes and alcohol to one another in the event words have failed us; they are our sealed pact, our memorandum of understanding, our truce.

"Anyway, you can't split up with him," Vanessa said. "You'll never find anyone else, will you? Who will look after you?" By which she meant, who would take over as my protector if I rejected the person who had replaced her in that role? As she spoke, I could hear Charlie playing with her children in the kitchen. He had bought them a toy helicopter that really flew, and was showing them how it worked. "Plus, see?" she said. "He's so good with my kids." But I wasn't soothed by the idea of Charlie as uncle, or even as father. On the contrary, the sight of us as a family—this supposedly impenetrable entity of self-containment—made my heart plunge with panic because our house was falling and I knew it was only a matter of time before we blew apart. "What were you hoping for, Al? This works, doesn't it? You've been good together, haven't you?"

It's true that for a while we had functioned well enough as a couple: me unconventional by Middle American standards, and too loud and outspoken for ordinary comfort; Charlie increasingly orthodox, containing us with his rational resoluteness. Both of us united in our love for our children. And then for years, even when kindness and trust between Charlie and me had eroded to the point of occasionally open hostility and days of silence, my mantra had remained, "But I'm in love with this unit." Now, though, I had begun to suspect that our uncoupled marriage was its own kind of violence, sure to hurt one of us, or our children, or everyone. Unit. United. Untied.

"Okay," I said to Vanessa, putting out my cigarette. "But if we do split up, can you at least be neutral this time? You know, impartial. Like Switzerland." Ten years ago, Charlie and I had separated for a six-month trial period, and while

Dad and Richard had stayed tight-lipped, Mum and Vanessa had supported me by taking Charlie's side, agreeing with him and with each other that he was far too good for me. It was their way, I understood later, of trying to keep the seas calm until I righted myself, came to my senses, and stayed safe and married. Vanessa spent hours on the phone from Zambia, consoling him. Mum came over to help me move out of the house, but ended up acting like emergency services, stabilizing things until someone who really knew what they were doing came on the scene. "I had such a nice lunch with Charlie today," she said, narrowing her eyes at me. "Are you sure this isn't just you being difficult?"

"I think this might be you," Vanessa said now, and there were tears starting in the corners of her eyes. And she said again, in case I had missed it all the other times, "He's too good for you, anyway." She sounded angry, bordering on scarily furious, but I knew from long experience that her anger came from somewhere old and not her fault, a defense mechanism with its fuse blown to hell. Me about to hurt myself, or about to get hurt, made Vanessa turn irrationally hostile, because protection and hostility had landed on the same place in her psyche. "Oh Al, I have this recurring nightmare," she told me recently. "We're being mortared and I can't get all the kids under the bed. Because that was always my job, right? I mean if we were getting bombed or whatever, I was supposed to get you all under the bed."

"I know," I said. "I'm sorry."

"Oh Al, me too," Vanessa said.

Then there was a long silence filled with all the things we knew, but could not say.

"It was confusing," I said at last.

It wasn't just the war and all the casual ways in which a sibling might die in southern Africa that melded the place

between love and anger in both of us. It was also the ways
some men used the cover of ubiquitous violence to turn into
casual violators of anyone weaker than themselves. Perhaps
the mechanism that allowed ordinary citizens to become kill-
ers also broke other basic codes of civil behavior. Or maybe
there was something about the power of having a gun, and
seeing behavior bend like gravity or magnetism at the end of
its barrel, that turned our protectors into predators. Or maybe
war and oppression and injustice had stolen the innocence of
those men, and it made them want to torment the innocence
out of the whole world around them.

Time and again, Vanessa stood between me and that
peculiar version of friendly fire, between me and the men we
had been told were fighting for our lives, our freedom, our
precious white skin. "Don't touch my sister!" she said, uncharacteristically loud and speaking out. Then, too often, she
stood in the path of whatever was coming my way, not will-
ingly, but with the flustered alarm of someone saving a life
not her own, human-shielding me from that common, blun-
dering, opportunistic ungodliness.

I suppose we were both more confused than hurt that at
least some adults in our midst had not protected us better
from those too-large, insistent hands; the wet, alcohol-
smelling mouths; the bodies too big and heavy pressed against
ours. At the time Vanessa and I didn't have the vocabulary for
what happened, since not only were our mouths too small
for the necessary words, but also such things are taboo and
unspoken and unspeakable. And anyway, it was so common,
and could something so common be so bad? Didn't it happen
to almost every little girl? The awful, silencing fingers? The
touch not brushed away? Crafty molestation disguised as
avuncular affection?

Decades afterward, Mum said, "But we didn't know it was

going on. We were so naïve and trusting." Which, by the way, are the other two things that this sort of casual abuse destroys in children, naïveté and trust. They lose too their sweetness and exchange it with unstable personal boundaries and irrational rage, unbecoming in a girl, unacceptable in a woman.

In the years that followed, Vanessa put her anger under a thin, beautiful veneer of calm, while I put mine, tempered with humor to make it more palatable, on the page. "I wish you wouldn't," Vanessa implored. But I didn't want to be her, keeping every broken thing inside. I wanted to break everything around me, especially the walls that had hidden what had happened to us. My noise wasn't a cure for what had happened, I knew that, nor would it be a preventative for what would happen in the future—the one in three women and girls in the world whose deepest, most private power would be forever stolen—but my silence wouldn't serve any purpose either. "There's really no such thing as the 'voiceless,'" Arundhati Roy has said. "There are only the deliberately silenced, or the preferably unheard."

Then Vanessa and I had both married men who looked like protectors; she, a soldier from our war, and I, a man who had stood up to the mock charge of an angry she-elephant. But it was unfair and unrealistic to expect we were completely salvageable. Neither of those men could protect us when we had both most needed it, twenty years earlier in some dark corridor on the way to the neighbor's lavatory, or in the spare bedroom of someone else's unfamiliar house. Which was why Vanessa's second marriage made so much sense to me. Richard had been raised in Malaysia and educated in English boarding schools; he was similar enough to us to know who we were without ever having been complicit in the ways in which violence slopped over and down through our collective memory to make us who we were now. For that, for his straightforwardness, for his gruff humor, for his irrational generosity, I adored him.

"Oh good heavens, have another glass of wine," Vanessa said, and sloshed more into my glass with a couple of ice cubes.

Then Richard came out onto the veranda and poured himself a drink. "All right, Sweetie?" Vanessa asked.

Richard nodded. "Yep." He talks so seldom and with such seeming reluctance, it's as if he's had to chisel his words from granite. A few years ago, visiting Mum and Dad on the farm, he came back from a morning's fishing on the Zambezi looking a little pale. "Hippo," he explained. "Chomped the boat." So the family trooped down to the riverbank to inspect the damage. The whole front of the boat had been spectacularly torn away, the hippo's teeth slicing easily through fiberglass.

"With you in it?" Vanessa wanted to know.

"Yep," Richard said.

"Did you see God, angels, and whatnot?" Vanessa asked. She likes to read books and magazine articles by people who have had near-death experiences, and who write subsequent moving accounts of the heaven they found beyond earth. She's always looking for proof of a peaceful, better life after this one. She wants to know there are shafts of sunlight and soft clouds like an illustration out of our Enid Blyton book of Children's Bible stories. "Did your life flash in front of your eyes?"

"Nope."

Vanessa sighed. "Oh, what a waste of nearly dying," she said. "You should pay more attention next time, Sweetie."

||||||||||

"Cheers," Richard said now, lifting his glass.

"Guess what?" Vanessa said. She blew out a cloud of

cigarette smoke and announced the end of my marriage. "Al's getting divorced."

"Ah," Richard said.

"And I have to be Sweden," Vanessa said.

Richard took a long sip of whisky and then appeared to consult his glass. "Well," he said at last. "KBO."

"What?" I asked.

"Churchill," Richard said. "Keep buggering on."

"Oh," I said. "Thanks."

Vanessa blocked her ears. "La la la la." Then she looked at Richard and me. "I'm not taking sides. I'm Sweden, remember?" Which must have reminded her of our beloved childhood anthems, because now she turned to me. "Hey Al, do your Swedish accent. It's so hilarious when you do it. I don't vant to talk about zings we've gone through . . ."

"Switzerland," I corrected her.

"Oh, Al-Bo." Vanessa sounded disappointed.

But I didn't want to make Vanessa laugh. I wanted her to take me seriously. I wanted her on my side, unequivocally. I wanted her to express her unassailable, unconditional, irrational love for me. Because of all the kinds of love there are out there—romantic, passionate, parental, spousal, brotherly—the love that is touted as most unassailable, complicit, and colluding is the love between sisters. But whatever she felt about me deep down, Vanessa wasn't going to offer her unconditional support right now.

For one thing, she couldn't stand a rocking boat coming anywhere near her vessel's berth. She was a ship carrying the signal flag Delta. A thick blue stripe sandwiched between two yellow stripes, it means, "Keep clear of me; I am maneuvering with difficulty." And for another thing, perhaps more fundamental than that, Vanessa and I are so dissimilar it is hard to imagine we are related at all; there is barely a cousinly resemblance, much less a sisterly one. We look nothing alike, we think nothing alike, we share few of the same beliefs. We don't share a common vocabulary. If we had passed one another in the street, we would have seen nothing at all in common. There would have been no second glance of surprised recognition.

For that, we need to look back into the spiral of our families. Only then you can see peripheral glimpses of each of us; the hint of something shared about the mouth, a similar way of standing, sloped with one bent knee, like a resting horse. Unbraid each of us back, strand over strand, and only then you can see where we begin. Follow the sinewy rope of our cores and you can see how tenaciously we're knotted. So forever and always, whatever irrationality comes out of our mouths, whatever we've said and done to one another, it's preemptively forgiven. Because in the end, we have blood in common, and we have history in common, and we have coping mechanisms in common—the way we throw up dust clouds of laughter or anger as a mock charge, the way our deadly serious defense is all ways of surviving at once. "You're sink *and* swim; fight *and* flight," my friend Bryan said of me once. "I didn't know that was biologically possible."

THIS GRAND INHERITANCE

From my earliest memory of her, Mum spoke longingly of her childhood in Kenya, and of her own parents. She unequivocally adored her English father, his love of horses and dogs, his impressive ability to build and repair almost anything, his deeply honed knowledge of earth and farming. She also took definite pride in coming from mad, savage Scottish stock on her mother's side and she warned us of our likely inherited Celtic inclinations, none of which sounded good, but she was unable to keep the satisfaction out of her voice. "Irritability," she said. "Intolerance. Irascibility."

By contrast, I knew almost nothing of my English father or his people. He seemed airdropped upon us, formed from soil and water, like Adam. And if he was sprung from earth, there was nothing of his smell or behavior or look that suggested otherwise. He was elemental, eternal, as if a version of him had always existed in perpetual adulthood, as I had always known him. But gradually with the instinctive impulse of a girl-child trying to feel her way forward by look-ing back, I created the parameters of my father's family and heritage from the habits and adages that had slipped out of his Englishness and into our African lives, their peculiarities made more vivid by their inappropriateness for either our cli-mate or lifestyle. "Bath and dress before dinner," Dad always insisted.

"For whom?" I wanted to know, looking out into the unpeopled farmyards around us, the empty dirt roads leading all the way into the deep bush beyond our cultivated fields or to our neighbors some miles distant.

"It's just the rule," Dad said.

Our days were mostly open, without rules. "You've got the whole of bloody Africa to play in," Dad told Vanessa and me, as if that were instruction enough, and we were supposed to disappear into as many hours of self-entertainment as it took until the gardener stoked the boiler at the back of the house to provide hot water for our mandatory evening baths. Also, while I had to exercise my horse like religion, Vanessa—who had been bitten and kicked too often, thrown off and bolted with one too many times—was expected to paint. "After that, as long as you don't shoot each other above the knees, it's your own lookout," Dad said.

But Dad couldn't fully explain why we all had to arrive at the dinner table every evening, washed and freshly clothed, napkins on laps, fingernails scrubbed. "Madness," he offered. "Weak minds."

"What?"

"It's the beginning of every end, Bobo. Let your socks sag and the spine will follow." I pictured a wax figure, drooping under the tropical sun, stiff upper lip warping into a fearful grimace. "Present and correct at the appointed hour. Pass inspection. Excellent company until dismissed."

||||||||||

So we came to dinner at eight, dressed as if for the captain's table, although I knew, without knowing why I knew I knew it, that ours was really a lifeboat flung out onto the high sea of disorder. "Bloody dogs," Dad said, kicking indiscriminately under the table. He put his revolver next to his side-plate. Mum put her Uzi on an empty chair beside her. "Safety on?" Dad always asked. "Those things are liable to go off at the touch of a gnat's testicle."

Then Dad asked for us to pass the green beans, or the chicken, and we helped ourselves to supper—"Footmen's night off," Dad said every night—and that was the signal that we were now expected to be charming and entertaining, making light of the day's hardships, engaging in competitive banter, flinging words back and forth at one another like deck tennis. And regardless of reality—Mum occasionally sliding off her chair, the dogs always squabbling at our ankles, the odd distant explosion of a land mine in the hills behind the house—we kept up the banter, as if practicing for a time we might be called upon to sing slightly off-color sea shanties as the ship went down.

Until an undertow of anguish pulled her out beyond the reach of reason—too far for our agile little leaking lifeboat to reach her—it was a game at which Mum excelled and at which Vanessa and I could hope only to be also-rans because, for one thing, my father could hardly take his eyes off her, and for another, neither of us could match her wit, her poetry, and her vocabulary colored by whatever book she was reading at that moment. "There were picanins laying snares in the dairy paddock today, naughty blighters. I chased them all the way to the road and one of them hopped right out of his little blue jersey with fright." That was her Beatrix Potter phase.

It took a fluid mind to navigate the choppy waters of my father's unwritten rules, to be properly improper, to see just how far we could sail into the wind of the required amount of jocularity and poor taste before my father's fork lowered, the mast went down, and we were cast into the doldrums. Because beyond the usual strictures of acceptable and unacceptable vocabulary (some swearing was fine, overrefined use of language was not), basic table manners (it was okay to lob a bread roll at someone, not okay to cut a bread roll with a knife, it had to be dismantled by hand), and codes of conduct (dancing on the table was encouraged, elbows on the table were not), the rules weren't clear. They weren't supposed to be.

I gradually came to understand that in my father's view, those who needed clear rules revealed a forbidden degree of self-doubt, exposed a fatal lack of confidence. "You either know what to do, or you don't. It's either cricket, or it's not." The same went for anyone caught praying publicly beyond the sacred confines of a church. Dad blinked in bewildered noncompliance if anyone stretched out a hand to be held before a meal in preparation for saying grace. "I don't mind having my knee groped between courses, or a little footsie-footsie during port, but what's this peculiar bloody thing of clutching one another before you even get offered a glass of wine?" Dad asked.

I can only imagine the energy and discipline it took to get us all together at our table every night. This wasn't a directive from some instruction booklet on how to get closer to one's overscheduled children through the mandate of family nights. It was more like a survival tip from the equivalent of D. H. Grainger's 1967 *Don't Die in the Bundu*, a book Mum kept in the loo, the pages dog-eared to the chapter on way-finding. Somehow, if we kept showing up for dinner, dressed and bathed, we were keeping madness and fatal dishevelment at bay. We would not, God forbid, "Go native."

It was only much later that I was able to trace the root of my father's uncompromising insistence that we be vitally present at dinner not just to a blind desire to hold on to what was left of his English upbringing in the remotest reaches of southern Africa, but also to his own mother's chronic inability to make it to the table at night. Because as far as he was concerned, you weren't irrevocably off course and permanently lost at sea until you could no longer steer your way toward the evening meal, properly attired.

|||||||||

While my mother's family was mentally ill in ways that should have had a wing of the local hospital dedicated to their memory—a great-uncle who tried to murder his own mother with a poker at the precocious age of three; another ancestor who kept two Tasmanian Palawa Aborigines as pets in his garden on the Isle of Skye; shell-shocked Uncle Allan who kept up a secret marriage to the postmistress's daughter for decades, too timid to admit to his mother that he had married below their class—my father's side of the family seemed to put most of their genetic energy into producing at least one seriously impressive drunk every other generation or so.

It was as if all the stirrup cups, Pimm's, and a snifter before dinner, all the genteel drinking that went along with their masked dances, regimental balls, and polo matches, occasionally tidal-pooled into a tragic, dipsomaniacal disaster. And although this exterminating birthright very likely goes back further, the first record of a bona fide alcoholic on my father's side of the family is also one of the most spectacularly awful. My great-great-grandmother, Mary Mortimer

Garrard, fell backward into a fireplace, drunk as a lord, and died. "Well, she was Australian," Dad explained. "And also probably pretty flammable by then."

Possibly to make up for his catastrophically intoxicated mother, my great-grandfather, Sebastian Henry Garrard, married May Eleanor Cazenove, a woman of such God-fearing, sober habits, and of such fearsome maternal proclivity, that she not only gave birth to half a dozen daughters (including, finally, a set of twins, of whom my father's mother was one) but also immersed herself in what can only be described as a life-threatening amount of do-gooding: hosting mothers' meetings, presiding over gatherings of the Primrose Society, giving out annual prizes for handiwork at the village school, holding elaborate children's parties, organizing fetes, securing the vice presidency of the Northamptonshire Red Cross, fund-raising for the workhouse, discreetly assisting pregnant village teens, training Maypole dancers, arranging flowers for church functions, and becoming president of the Women's Institute and chairwoman of the Women's Voluntary Service.

My great-grandmother is still widely praised in the family—"a very upstanding old lady," Dad insists—but she sounds awful to me, overbearing, inflexible, and domineering. It's an otherwise unfounded suspicion only circumstantially confirmed by the discovery that her children's nickname for her was "Mugger." Although it's an affectionate-sounding moniker, I think it's also worth noting that mugger is the common name of the Indian crocodile, *Crocodylus palustris*, made famous as the fearsome monster in Helen Bannerman's popular 1904 children's book *Little Black Mingo*, part of the series that included *Little Black Sambo*, quietly bigoted fodder for the impressionable imperialistic mind. Meanwhile, all my great-grandmother's daughters—Phyllis, Marjorie, Barbara, Joyce, Pamela, and Ruth—had their names shortened or spoofed in childhood to sound like heritage chickens or juicy little hamsters—Phil, Mar, Bar, Joy, Pammy, and Boofy.

"A waste of valuable time," Mugger said of reading and learning from books. So that by the time the twins—my grandmother and her sister—were of school age any idea there ever may have been of educating the girls was more or less abandoned. A series of governesses were employed—their focus was to be on instructing their wards on the arts of handicrafts and gardening—but Pammy and Boofy seemed to balk at structure and organized learning. Hosts of exasperated nannies and instructors fled Welton Place, citing the twins' trickster ways and their perpetual pranking.

So Pammy and Boofy—two girls too many in a family already riddled with daughters, a double disappointment in their parents' final attempt to sire an heir—became little pantomimes, beautifully attired pastiches. Most of the time, they were relegated to the nursery, or allowed the run of Welton Place, more or less unsupervised. But when Mugger did turn her attention on them, it was in the service of ratcheting up her own Good Samaritan act to ever-giddier heights. Accordingly, almost as soon as they could fit a tutu on their hips, Mugger had the twins tap-dancing in the wards, or performing a wounded soldier/caring nurse double act to actually wounded soldiers and caring nurses.

|||||||||

On our first visit back to England from Africa, when I was fifteen and Vanessa was eighteen—with Boofy long gone— we were taken to meet her twin, Auntie Pammy. On the morning of our visit, Mum attempted a crash course in posh manners, trying to cram a decade and a half of English niceties into her colonially accented daughters. "Your vowels," she pleaded. "Keep them short. You don't want Lady Wilmot to think you can't speak properly, do you?" My brain short-circuited with panic, instantly struck with what I now know to be my first migraine.

So I remember only two things from that otherwise indistinct, headachingly nauseous visit to whatever Mews it was in London. The first is that Auntie Pammy—self-contained, gracious, and precise—seemed as apologetic about the tininess of her guest lavatory, to which I had to repair almost immediately to be sick, as I was about my accent. "No, no, no, you have a beautiful speaking voice," she lied when I preapologized for whatever else might come out of my mouth. "Very musical." My second appalling recollection is that I emitted a bark of horribly loud laughter when she told us that almost a decade earlier her son, Sir Robert Arthur Wilmot, Eighth Baronet of Chaddesden, had been killed in a hit-and-run accident moments after his divorce had become final. He had been barely thirty-five; his children were both under ten at the time.

"Bobo!" Mum said, blanching with embarrassment.

"I'm sorry," I hiccuped, covering my mouth.

But something about that awful story, told over tea in the quiet, cigarette-smoke-filled flat, while my head spluttered and sparkled with exquisite pain, had shocked me into an inappropriate hoot, not of mirth but of recognition. Until that moment, I had imagined my father's English family as coddled and protected by their titles and money. They went to the first night at the Proms, they were on first-name basis with royalty, they swanked it up on champagne and strawberries on opening day at Wimbledon. They would live for decades in splendid comfort to become affable old geezers at the Army and Navy Club, or handbag-swinging dowagers at the counter at Harrods where they kept accounts.

I didn't envy them necessarily. Yes, it was unlikely they

had parasites, and I knew they didn't have civil war, or much in the way of malaria and rabies, but they also didn't have leopards stalking in the home paddocks, or nights under the southern sky scented with mopane woodsmoke from a campfire, or the thrilling terror of roaring through the lowveld clinging to the roof of an ancient Land Rover. But I assumed that as a trade-off to our adventures, they had comfort and security, and they had the certainty that they were protected and worth protecting.

However, on that warm summer London afternoon, in the revelation of Pammy's prolonged mourning for her son, I saw that our English relatives were just as vulnerable and broken as we were. Except their tragedies and grief were magnified by the loneliness of the experience, by the shocking singularity of the accidents, by the almost religious belief that keeping one's vowels short provided adequate protection against the world. We, at least, could see clearly the ways in which we might die—Mozambique spitting cobras in the pantry, an ambush on a lonely road south of the equator, bored drunken soldiers at a checkpoint. We knew too with a certainty born of long experience that luck was capricious and life was fleeting, no one was too special to avoid suffering. We could tell that bad things happened all the time, to everyone, regardless of who you thought you were. On the other hand, it seemed to me, our English relatives couldn't see their own oblivion coming.

||||||||||

As the six Garrard sisters grew up and war loomed, the field days and garden fetes turned into weekends of entertaining cavalry officers. While suitable boyfriends courted the older sisters, the twins were left to run amok. The future actor David Niven lived nearby and was often asked to keep an eye on Boofy and Pammy. When he left for America, he wrote to them frequently, in the cheerful, deliberately careless style of P. G. Wodehouse. "Then came a lapse in activities while I had my tonsils jerked out by the local vet. He does the job for five dollars when sober and for nothing when tight. As a result of his drunken excavations I developed a neat little thing in hemorrhages and as near as a toucher passed away from loss of blood (or was it alcohol) before they could get me to a hospital and operate again."[2]

But there was a cost to the casual boozing. Five of the six sisters seemed able to steer out of the incessant rounds of revelry and into marriage, grand weddings in Calcutta, where the Garrards kept shops to bejewel the Indian maharajas and English civil servants, and at Welton Place. Something swamped in Boofy, though, and while everyone around her was joking about intoxication, she was a sopping mess on the floor of the bathroom, draped helplessly over the banisters, flopped unfixed across her dressing table before dinner. It was a relief when she too could be married off. "I suppose they just had to keep her upright long enough to get her down the aisle," Dad said of his mother. "And then she was someone else's problem."

Boofy married a man who looked so like her own father— the very blue eyes, the sharp nose, the high cheekbones, the country estate manners—that it's easy to see how, in a thick gin haze, she might have mistaken the life she was stepping out of for the life she was stepping into. They were soldiers of a type too, both the man who bred her and the man who claimed her. Her father—nicknamed "the Major"—had taken time off from the crown jeweler business to fight in the First World War; her husband was a career naval officer. Both men were

---

2. From Annie McCaffry, *The Family Behind the Firm: Garrard and Co., 1834–1952.*

used to giving orders, and they were accustomed to having those orders instantly obeyed. "Absolutely fatal for my mother," Dad said. "She was completely allergic to rules of any sort."

Meantime, with all her daughters married off, Mugger did not slip quietly under the pond water. Instead, her sense of noblesse oblige went into overdrive. As if in a grand conservative attempt to preempt Clement Attlee's radical Labour government of the late 1940s, with its slew of nationalization and social engineering, and having achieved the heights of philanthropy herself—she was mentioned by the secretary of war for her "devoted war service as Commandant of the Auxiliary Hospital in Daventry" and awarded the Order of St. John of Jerusalem for her work in Northamptonshire—she turned her not inconsiderable energy into cultivating good works in her three eldest grandchildren. Per her instruction, they were each to "adopt" a needy village child. Accordingly, after family lunch on Sundays, the three cousins had to troop down to the village to fetch up their little wards and return with them to play games on the lawn at Welton Place. Things went so far that the girls even undertook to have one of the children christened, putting themselves in the role of godmothers.

"Perhaps it was overcompensation," I suggested.

"For what?" Dad asked.

"Well, wasn't your grandmother also the alleged Armenian?" I asked.

"Oh, supposedly," Dad said. "But actually, I think I saw somewhere she was descended from Hottentots. There's that very nice book my cousin Annie wrote. *The Family Behind the Firm*. Have you read it? *Very* good book."

"Not Hottentots," Mum said. "HUGUENOTS."

"You should read that book," Dad persisted.

So I read Cousin Annie's book and decided that while it was informative and interesting, it was tactful to the point of misleading. For example, she wrote that my grandmother Boofy "always suffered from bad health and . . . died quite young."

"Exactly," Dad said. "Half the people who read that book will know what it means, and the other half don't need to know."

"Well, I think it's best to write things the way they are," I said. "I mean, the plain truth."

Dad regretfully offered me a cigarette. "I suppose the Hottentot blood had to come out *somewhere*," he said.

But I think of how unhappy Boofy must have been, so soddenly drunk all day that she manifested to my father and his younger brother only as a kind of washed-out absence, a vaporous essence of anger during breakfast, a specter of backwashed misery in her bedroom by lunch, surging and china throwing behind closed doors by dinner. And I think of how a family's shame at her fatal addiction ultimately euphemized her into nothing, hushed her into an early death of which I know very little except that it was poorly attended and painful. Throat cancer is what finally got her, the flagons of gin she drank every day accompanied by a perpetual ribbon of cigarettes. "Terrible waste of a life," Dad says. "No life at all, really."

From the start, Boofy could not even be trusted to hold her own children—a Norland nurse was hired for that—and although she made an effort to attend sports day and school plays, Boofy was always so mortifyingly drunk, her children wished her gone. And gone she is, negated, vanished, her epitaph—all that can truly be known of her—summed up in three words. She Drank Gin.

Nothing survives of Boofy's thoughts and creativity; no letters, no watercolors, no needlepoint cushions. Although she's heartbreakingly there in the early photos at Welton Place—indistinguishable from Auntie Pammy—startlingly innocent looking, smug in her privilege, playing bicycle polo, draped over the church wall in a white flapper dress, winged as a fairy. The twins weren't beautiful—a little jowly, with jumbles of bad teeth and thick ankles—but they had good figures, full lips, and thick hair, and they appear blithe and expensive, as if they expected to make an impression without ever having to make an effort.

There's one more photo of Boofy laughing a little breathlessly behind a veil on the arm of her father, being led down the aisle toward her future husband, and then she is gone from family photos, washed out of the frame and out of life. I think of her marriage, the shock of coldness in the navy family to which she had been relegated. And I imagine her pregnancies, an alcohol-soaked vessel for her two sons, whom she had no way of nurturing.

The Norland nurse, Nu, who was hired to take on the care and keeping of Boofy's sons, was the most solid presence in my father's early life. "To be one up on the Joneses—the royal Joneses that is—get a Norland nanny," wrote Nadeane Walker from London for the *Sarasota Herald-Tribune* in a 1967 article. "A genuine Norland nurse, brown-hatted, white-gloved, and impeccably accented, is a treasure to be prized above pearls." Norland nurses, the article goes on, are not allowed to spank their charges. "But she must be firm not only with the children, but with the Madame in any disputes over authority."

The principal of the Norland Institute, Miss L. Keymer, deplored any mention of the royal and aristocratic employers who snapped up most of her graduates. "Why harp on that?" she asked. "What gives me more pleasure than anything is sending a good nurse where she is badly needed, such as to a motherless family." Which described my father's family with unintended precision to a T.

"Nu was very dutiful," Dad remembers. "Very professional.

Very fond of her cat, Blackie." Caped, with a hat and white gloves, she took the boys on improving daily walks through the countryside and taught them to recognize birds, birdsongs, and wild plants. She worked on their elocution. She read to them before lights-out at seven. And when my father left for boarding school, Nu wrote him a letter every Sunday, and every Sunday he replied. Decades later when she eventually died, an early letter from Dad was found among Nu's possessions. It is a crayoned imaginary self-portrait, a little boy standing next to a giraffe below which my father, improbably prescient and perhaps wishing himself away from the domestic ache of his family life, has written, "Dear Nu. I am going to Africa to see a giraffe. Yours sincerely, Timothy Fuller."

It was the emotional iciness of England my father could not stand, not the actual climate with its famously drenching, low skies. As an added attraction to the supposed Dark Continent, no one from either side of his family had ever been to Africa, except his grandfather, in a naval ship, to Nigeria. "But I didn't know about him until much later. I think he won some sort of medal for blowing up a bunch of revolutionaries," Dad said. "Anyway, it didn't make much of an impression on me. No, I left England like my arse was on fire. I suppose I always wanted to see a giraffe, don't ask me why. But still, ending up in Africa was a bit of an accident. I just wanted to get the hell out of Britain. It was the pity I couldn't bear. After the house broke up, I mean, everyone felt sorry for us."

Boofy moved into a grim little cottage in Sussex. "Good address, horrible dark little hovel." And although my father and his brother were by then in their early teens and at boarding school, and therefore long beyond the need of a nanny, Boofy took the Norland nurse with her. "I suppose someone paid for Nu to stay on and look after my mother," Dad told me recently. "Well, it was terrible, but my mother couldn't cope on her own. She wasn't raised for that. Self-sufficiency, I mean. She was raised to be coddled and spoiled by some rich bloke, and when that fell through, well, she had nothing to prop her up."

|||||||||||

All six Garrard sisters divorced at least once, and most of them were wedded twice. "In those days women married for money and a title," Dad explained. "And it wasn't always easy to find a chap who had both, so it sometimes took a couple of rounds." My favorite divorce story is Auntie Bar's, whose husband, Lieutenant Colonel Sir Roland Findlay, was so overwhelmed with what he had married that he finally took off with a barmaid. "I don't think Uncle Roly minded the flocks of loose doves in the bedroom so much," Dad said. "But he drew the line at half a dozen Pekingese at the dining room table, all with gut rot from eating too much rich food."

For a while I was slightly stunned. Even by my high standards, this was eccentricity on an impressive level. I imagined breakfasts, a snuffling harass of little dogs with their squashed noses and dripping bottoms rooting about the marmalade, black pudding, and kippers. And Uncle Roly surreptitiously swatting them with his *Financial Times,* although perhaps by then he was reading *Beelzebub Jones* in the *Daily Mirror,* already dreaming of quieter breakfasts with the barmaid: soft eggs and the perfect Bloody Mary.

And meantime, there was Auntie Bar enthroned in the bedroom, a dule of doves clattering among the drapes of her four-poster bed and cooing restfully from their perches along the moldings. I think of her bedroom walls gray-dripping, the air downy and pungent with breast feathers. Still, Uncle Roly must have waded through the dogs and risked the fallout of the birds at least once, because there was, as they say, issue—a daughter, Jane.

Auntie Bar was apparently adored by children for her outspoken ways, her wit, and no doubt the menagerie she kept, although it's hard to know if Jane was as delighted with her mother's eccentricities as were non–family members. "She always collected around her people of diverse interests and origins who lived colorful lives," Cousin Annie wrote of her. Which I decode to imagine a fabulous collection of arty comrades of the sort who would be thrown out of most established social clubs in the mid-1900s: Jews and homosexuals; immigrants and socialists. There would have been champagne and music, odd ideas, and radical tolerance, because art comes from a loosening of the mind, not its damming up.

But in spite of it all—or maybe because of it all—Uncle Roly and Auntie Bar's only child ended up rewarding all Mugger's exhausting social climbing in spectacular measure: by the time of her death, in 2009 at the age of eighty-one, Cousin Jane was one of the queen's oldest friends, and widow of her majesty's master of horses, David Anthony Thomas Fane, Fifteenth Earl of Westmorland. "You see?" Mum said, as if this proved a point she had been trying to make ever since handing me *The Official Sloane Ranger Handbook* more than two decades earlier. "Having a barmy mother is a veritable bonus in the proper circles."

"Well, it hasn't always worked out for me," I said.

"No," Mum agreed, but I could tell she was trying to think her way out of a tight spot. "Although it seems worth the risk, doesn't it? I mean, better to err on the side of insanity than total boredom, isn't it?" Then Mum started flapping her hand in front of her face in delighted panic. "Or to be descended from Hottentots," she managed to wheeze before lurching for her asthma inhaler. "Oh Bobo, don't make me laugh!"

|||||||||||

To say someone has lost her mind does not do justice to what madness looks like. It's not as if a person's mind rolls out of her head, lodges under the carpet or between the cracks of the sofa, and is therefore retrievable by some logical search. A person whose mind has gone is lost to herself as well as to the world; she becomes a shell of terror in search of what is missing. What is confusing, from the outside, is that a madwoman might still have relatively long periods when her mind is restored to her, or times when muscle memory allows her body to behave as if she is coherent and all here, present and correct.

I watched my mother go mad. Afterward, when I tried to put a time on it I would have said her mind left her when I was around eleven and she did not conjure, or will, it back in a robust and enduring way until I was in my late twenties. But my mother's absence wasn't anything like a solid washout, a Boofy-like obliteration. It was drier than that, more as if an internal current had shorted, and flickering outages would occur, only to suddenly trip on again. And in those times, as if to make up for her gone days, my mother was a prism of creative clarity: compassionate, witty, capable, and fierce. I could feel myself slipping into the deep grooves of her influence; her passion for books, her appreciation for art, her addiction to the BBC, her obsessive love of dogs inherited in turn from her own parents.

Meantime, Vanessa cleaved to the Garrards. Photos of my great-grandfather, my grandfather, the six Garrard sisters, and their children put her firmly on that side of the family. She has their enormous blue eyes, their slightly disapproving look of torpid detachment, the dreamy artistic temperament of Auntie Bar, the Welton Place addiction to an appearance of perpetual childhood, and the spiritual susceptibility that led a couple of the Garrard sisters to become Christian Scientists. She has, too, Boofy's fatal aversion to pain. I can see why Auntie Pammy took one look at Vanessa on that unfortunate visit to her in London and recognized disappearing versions of her lost twin. "Such a lovely, *love*-ly, child," Auntie Pammy said of my sister. "So utterly, so completely one-of-us."

And I had cringed, knowing that I was not completely one-of-them. Instead, like my mother's side of the family, I am small-framed and intense and anything but languorous. My creativity wasn't the enchanting landscapes and innocent vibrancy of Vanessa's William Morris–inspired pastels. My creativity was the madness of all that Scottish passion and fiery tribalism, barely contained. While Vanessa refused to paint unless the mood was perfect or her studio allowed the right light, I wrote because the urge to do so collected the fuel of too much left unsaid, and sparked onto the page almost unbidden.

I have the shape of my mother's face, her thick hands, her short torso, her thin, long legs—"Wonderful leg for a riding boot," Dad always said charitably of our underpinnings—and her unswaying, staccato walk. I had her sense of humor too, finding delight in the absurd, the deliberately provocative, the ridiculous understatement. In the way of all daughters, I watched my mother for clues to my future. Her madness terrified me in part because it was too easy for me to see that if I had inherited her small ankles and her oversized laugh, how could I have skipped the place where her ingenuity and passion sat too close to insanity on the spiraling legacy of heritage? Add to this the fuel from all that alcohol on my father's side of the family, my star sign, and half a dozen other physical and metaphysical facts, and I figured I was probably an inferno waiting to happen. Stop, drop, and roll.

MARRIAGE IN THE TIME
OF CHOLERA

t is the perpetuating tragedy of all families: each of us believing our congenital pathologies and singular pains end with us. We think of ourselves as individual dammed rivers, the blood of generations stopped up in our veins, the accumulated habits of a lifetime ceasing at the border of our skins. We don't think of our present, our current conditions, and our immediate decisions as incurable infections or persisting gifts that will cross through the porous vectors of inheritance and time and blossom into the future. In spite of biblically ancient warnings, we don't think of our choices—our decision to wake up each morning and be free, or remain in the thrall of some visible or invisible jail, for example—as contaminating or blessing not only ourselves but also our children, their children unto the third and to the fourth generations.

But here I was. Look back into the double mirror images of my history, past my mother to my grandmothers, and to their mothers before them, and regardless of their true talents and ambitions, the women whose blood rushed directly into mine were basically glorified housekeepers, their fates inextricably tied to the men they married. There's the tragically drunk Australian, understandably homesick perhaps, immolated in the fireplace of one of England's grand homes. There's Mugger, all her ambition going powerfully sideways into ever-greater and more extreme acts of charity. There's Boofy, all her joie de vivre horribly funneled into self-destruction. And there's my mother's mother, reading late into the night through all the histories of England and Scotland, memorizing clans and battles and chiefs and kings and queens until she could have earned a double doctorate in the subject, but still rising at dawn to make oats porridge, weed the vegetable garden, and do the laundry.

"When we were first married, I kept the chamber pot within reach at all times," my grandmother confided to me when I was over in England as a teenager. "Otherwise you never get any sleep, or any time to read, or any time to yourself." She sighed and sank back against her pillows, Antonia Fraser's *Mary Queen of Scots* resting on her chest. "You need to empty it over their heads only once. They won't pester you without your permission after that."

Out my grandmother's bedroom window that warm English summer, I could hear my grandfather in the garden removing the suckers off his small crop of tobacco. "If I could do it all again," Granny said, "I'd do more of it my way." Then she closed her eyes and with that went whatever she might have said next. What was bewildering to me then was that my grandparents seemed to have the sort of marriage anyone might think of as sound. They synched perfectly, their habits and addictions, their passion for Kenya and Cairn terriers, their love of books, strong tea, and rough midmorning martinis. They shared secret languages, speaking Gaelic or Swahili to one another so they could gossip about fellow passengers on trains and planes. And yet at least once a week in the time I spent with them that holiday from Africa, Granny would say, "Marriage is the workhouse, Bobo. Don't do it."

But like all newlyweds I thought I had made a contract of a different sort with my spouse, a fresh pact, distinct and separate from all the ways my grandmothers and great-grandmothers had done marriage. I thought that Charlie and I would operate out of our own unique and complete love, as if boredom, thwarted ambition, petty sulking, and the tiny ways in which we deliberately or accidentally misunderstand one another could not happen to us because we alone had fallen in love, as it had never been done before. Ours was a love across seas, between cultures, and against all the odds. Charlie was the perfect rescuer, and I the most relieved and grateful rescue victim. "Wahini," he called me. "Chica," he said. Or "Mamacita." I didn't know the meaning of Charlie's terms of endearment, but their foreignness only served to prove to me that ours would be a new and different connection.

Still, the Polish priest at our wedding had been right. The first year was hard, and after that, well, it didn't get worse immediately, but it got more and more silent, and silence frightened me more than almost anything else. What was confusing is that I had wanted to be saved from the uncertainty and the noise of my childhood, but beyond a definite idea that I would feel safe docked to the steady command center that was Charlie, I hadn't thought it all the way through. I hadn't figured that what had terrified me had also defined me; without the exuberant crazy-in-a-good-way and the disturbing crazy-in-a-bad-way pendulum that had been all I had ever known, I wasn't sure how to be. I turned the music up, and Charlie turned it down.

"How about somewhere in the middle?" he suggested.

But I wasn't good at the middle. I was good at the

extremes; I had been trained for that. Loud was my specialty, although if I needed to—in the bush when surrounded by wildlife, in the hours and hours of chapel at boarding school under the gaze of unforgiving teachers, when the business of war turned serious and deadly—I could outsilence anyone. Still, a silent marriage—a house without banter, without one person shouting and another screaming opera, without the occasional all-out drunken brawl—was going to take some getting used to. "Marriage takes work," I had heard over and over again, but I hadn't believed that would be *our* marriage.

To begin with, we rented a sterile house on the outskirts of Lusaka. The main attraction was the land, seven walled acres, large enough to keep our four ponies and to maintain a small vegetable garden. But the house was a dismaying thing, long and dark and bricked up, clinical in its aspect. An Indian businessman had built it during the 1980s when the city was becoming increasingly violent, and it embodied his stifling paranoia: bars on the tiny windows, a metal door with a huge padlock to separate the bedrooms from the rest of the house, the yard cleared of shrubs and trees to dissuade snakes and robbers. I threw rugs on the floor, smothered the walls in bright African-print cloths, and planted scores of trees in the garden, but I couldn't shrug the feeling that we had been institutionalized by someone else's fear.

As far as I was concerned, the chief flaw of the Indian's security system was the massive black gate at the entrance of the property, which could not be opened from the outside. Charlie had brought Mr. Sinazongwe with him—an officious, hostile, supernaturally silent man with the creeping aspect of a spy—whom I avoided the way a junior consort might avoid the senior wife. Mr. Sinazongwe said he would be happy to open the gate, hover under the bougainvillea whenever I left the property in readiness for my return, but I wasn't taken in by his obsequious eagerness. "I think he just wants to know when I am coming and going," I told Dad. "He's such a snoop."

"When the wife walks in the front door, the gentleman's personal gentleman leaves out the back," Dad said.

"Oh good heavens," I said. "This isn't Jeeves and Wooster. It's Charlie's old cook."

"Lot of wisdom in that stuff," Dad persisted. "Take it or leave it."

I left it. But if I was going to have a jailkeeper, I thought I should hire him myself. I put out word at the kiosk down the road that I was looking for a gardener, whose other task would be to guard and man the padlocked gate. Among the potential candidates who came forward was an elderly man who appeared so blank and feeble I hired him on the spot.

"Have you done much gardening?" I asked.

Mr. Njovu made a face and I knew that whatever was about to come out of his mouth next was unlikely to be entirely true. "Plenty," he said.

I showed Mr. Njovu the gate, gave him a key, and begged him to listen for me when I returned from any outing. Mr. Njovu nodded and started work right away. After that, he stayed at work, regardless of how much I offered, and then begged, for him to take days off. After a couple of weeks, it finally dawned on me he had nowhere else to go, and after that, I let him drift around the seven acres as he wished. He mostly kicked around the rear of the property, and then he acted so wounded and exhausted from his long walk to the gate from whatever he was doing back there, I put out word I needed a groom, whose secondary job would be to open the gate. So Freddy Mapulonga arrived, arrogant and full of swagger, and I felt too hapless and inadequate not to hire him.

My mother would never have hired servants the way I

did—out of pity, intimidation, or habit—and allow them to run roughshod all over her and her property. She had learned her servant-managing skills from her mother, who had been sent away to a college for young ladies in Inverness specifically to learn how to run a grand home. And even after the world changed in the 1940s, war-wearied into rations and the great houses emptied of all but the most needy and least able-bodied servants, my grandmother's notes from that college survived, ledgers containing instructions on how to pay household bills, how to adjudicate the inevitable rivalries and tensions between a butler, the housekeeper, and the cook; when to order leg of mutton and how to best prepare shoulder of lamb. And Mugger, I knew, had been raised to the task. "She kept a beautiful house," my father said. "It ran like clockwork."

I, on the other hand, constitutionally opposed to the idea of servants in the first place, seemed unable to manage my modest household at all. I could not prevent the staff from fighting with each other and brazenly stealing from us, and then spreading blame all around. I had no control over when anyone came to work, or when, if ever, they left. I could not even persuade Mr. Sinazongwe not to scrub the floors outside our bedroom door at midnight. "I'll clean them myself," I offered finally. But Mr. Sinazongwe simply smiled enigmatically and was back the following night, the scent of Cobra floor polish wafting under the threshold and into the tangle of our mosquito net.

"I think he's spying on us," I told Charlie.

"No, he's just diligent," Charlie said.

Then Dad came to visit from the farm and kicked the soil in my vegetable garden around. "Oh, you've got this awful red stuff, haven't you?" he said. The soil dusted up and settled on his shoe like dried blood. "You're going to want a lot of manure in here, tobacco scraps would be good. I'll bring you some from the farm." He marched around to the back of the house and disparaged my pasture. "Your horses aren't going to get very fat on this," he said. Then he found Mr. Njovu's nascent marijuana crop. He pursed his lips. "Well, your gardener has done a good job with this at least."

Charlie's days were full of dreary government meetings and business plans and putting together safari itineraries for clients. My days stretched ahead of me interminably. With a British passport and nothing but a bachelor of arts to my name, I was both foreign and underqualified and I had been denied a work permit by the Zambian government. I gave free aerobics lessons to overweight government officials' wives. I wrote letters to the freshly appointed and woefully careless minister of environment lamenting deforestation and pollution. After that, I hardly knew what to do with myself.

"Routine," Dad counseled. "If all else fails, have a routine."

So in the mornings, I exercised the ponies with Freddy, and afterward gave him driving lessons, which terrified both of us. "Brake! Brake!" I yelled, as the garden wall loomed toward us. In the afternoon, I tried to persuade Mr. Njovu to put half the effort into growing our vegetables that he put into cultivating his drugs, and I took Tank and our new puppy, Lizzie, for walks toward the army camp at the top of our road. Then I stared at the clock and waited for Charlie to come home.

It was as if, marrying Charlie, I had stepped across some invisible membrane into another country. This wasn't my Zambia—days of unstructured freedom on the farm, chaos at the dinner table with Adamson's undercooked chickens. This was someone else's idea of Zambia. In the evenings, Charlie came home exhausted after a day of wrangling with ministers and government officials and exuded an air of wearied disappointment. We sat in near silence over dinner, no dancing on the table, no dogs churning at our feet, moderation, bloodless poultry. On the few occasions Mum and Dad came up from the farm to stay they too were subdued and orderly, especially after Charlie expressed his understandable opinion that we all drank too much. It was what I had wanted, a ticket out of disorder and into calm, but now that I was here I felt imprisoned, suffocated. "You should volunteer somewhere," Charlie suggested.

But in the early nineties, with the collapse of socialism and a new culture of anything goes, Lusaka was already awash with highly skilled foreign volunteers—"Bloody missionaries are always the first to arrive," Dad had said. "You mark my words, Bibles then bulldozers." There were the English hydrologists saving the water, the Canadian engineers rebuilding the sewage systems, and Irish actresses teaching self-expression and theater to abused and/or fallen women. No one needed an underqualified undergraduate in their aid programs, and in any case, that kind of do-gooding only made me feel more alien, as if I too were a visiting two-year wonder with no history in the country and no real intention of creating a future in it of my own. I'd be Mugger-lite, transposed to Zambia, ineffective. I'd mess it up.

I stayed home and continued with my thankless domestic round: Charlie's territory-seizing cook, Mr. Njovu's increasingly skillful rejection of our vegetables, and Freddy's death-defying driving lessons. Imbued with groundless confidence, Freddy became worse each time he got behind the wheel. In September, I decided to brave the back roads with him, hoping to encounter no other traffic. Freddy celebrated his newfound freedom with the purchase of a pair of exceedingly dark glasses and a portable radio that he put on the seat between us, the volume turned up to the maximum.

"How about somewhere in the middle?" I shouted.

"What?" Freddy said.

"Can you even see out of those things?" I yelled, as we rollicked over a culvert.

In October, the heat was fierce for everyone, but especially for big, elderly dogs. Tank labored to keep cool. We made a bed for him next to a fan in the kitchen—the coolest room in the house—and tried to get him to drink more water, but every day it became harder and harder for him to get up, and finally too hard for him to lift his head. His breathing became rasping and gurgling, as if his lungs were filling up. Charlie stayed up at nights next to Tank's bed, massaging his chest, stroking his back. At last, we decided to ask the vet to come out to the house and put the dog down.

In November, the rains came, obliterating and heavy. Gardening—what little there had been of it—stopped. Mr. Njovu spent happy days in the horses' shelter sampling his marijuana. The electricity surged, spluttered, and went dead, and with it went the fans. The house swelled and swamped with torpid humidity. Mold grew on shoes and saddles, our laundry stayed damp. We gave the horses their rainy-season vaccinations and turned them out.

With little else to do, Freddy and I spent the mornings in the kitchen watching the rain through the bars on the window, drinking tea and gossiping. Because our talk was mostly blather, small talk and little indiscretions, I can't remember now the specifics of our conversations, except that we were united in our dislike of Mr. Sinazongwe, and in our fascination with magic and the new music coming out of Zaire. Also, Freddy hated Lusaka as much as I did. He had been raised by his grandfather on a marijuana farm close to a river in Zambia's northeast. His grandfather apparently had healing and magical powers. Freddy told me of hearing animals that spoke in human tongues, seeing sunsets that went on for three days, and of women so beautiful and beguiling that men lost their minds. Listening to him, I felt homesick for a country I hadn't even left.

Once a week, Freddy and I embarked on our marketing; bran mash for the horses, bones for the dogs, fresh vegetables and meat for the house. Freddy got behind the wheel with his especially dark glasses, turned the portable radio up to somewhere in the middle, and we ventured into town. It gave us something new to talk about—the homeless madwoman who made a living off the garbage pile in the second-class district, the pig we saw being hauled backward across Addis Ababa Avenue by its hind legs, the effect on the city of the incessant rain. Major thoroughfares in the heart of the city were flooded, and in the waterlogged compounds on the outskirts there were rumors that cholera had broken out.

"Have you heard of this?" I asked Freddy.

"Oh yes. People are dying like chickens," he said.

So a few mornings later, Freddy drove me into George Compound and, following a funeral lorry, we found a humid, makeshift clinic in what had until recently been a small school, its classrooms and verandas converted into damp, crowded wards. There were a few cholera beds—plastic stretchers with holes in them, under which a bucket could catch the rice-water diarrhea that streamed from people's bodies—but most of the victims lay on pieces of soggy cardboard, helplessly swamped by their own leaking selves. I got out of the pickup. Freddy wound up the windows and frantically swatted flies. "You're going to die of cholera if you go out there," he predicted.

I walked toward a man in a white coat stirring a huge drum of yellow liquid at the foot of the stairs leading up to the veranda. A pervasive, sweet-rotten smell hung over the place. "Can I help you?" the man asked.

I had no good answer. I said something about wanting to write an article for the papers. "Don't you think people should know what is happening here?"

"What people?"

"I mean people who read the papers."

"People who read the papers already know what is going on," the man said, turning back to his drum.

"What's in there?" I asked.

"Disinfectant," the man replied. "Contaminated clothes. We are supposed to burn them. But how can you burn clothes if they are all somebody has to wear?"

On the drive home, Freddy occupied himself hunting down and killing flies. "Cholera flies, cholera flies, cholera flies," he muttered.

"Keep your eyes on the road," I said. "Never mind the flies."

"If a fly lands on you, you'll die," he replied.

"I don't know where you get your information."

Freddy waved his trump card. "My grandfather was a doctor."

"Your grandfather was a drug dealer," I said, waving mine.

After that, until the epidemic abated in late January, Freddy and I drove into George Compound at least once a week. Sometimes there was an army lorry parked outside the cholera clinic, or another government vehicle, and then we turned back, trying as much as possible to look as if we had somehow innocently taken a wrong turn into the deep heart of this decidedly accidental-feeling place. "You should try to look like one of those Dutch," Freddy advised. "They are only here for good reasons. You see them even digging latrines with their own hands."

After that, I gave up the idea of writing anything about the epidemic. Instead, I brought towels and blankets from home for the patients and food for the medical orderlies. Every few days, a few more corpses were added to the morgue tent next to the clinic. Some of the bodies were so tiny they looked like punctuation marks, damp little commas, a brief pause between life and death. The invisible membrane between my old life and the one I had married into solidified into a wall. There was the dank, dying world of George Compound, and there was us—Charlie and me—in our clinical if humid bunker on Lilayi Road.

"Where are the bath towels?" Charlie asked, dripping on the threshold of the bathroom.

"Oh," I said. My mind spun through all the possible answers I could give. Then I said, "We're having a hard time drying them because of the rain." It was a little lie, the first I remember telling in the marriage, and completely unnecessary because Charlie didn't have a temper. He had disappointment, yes, and disapproval, and he felt understandably entitled to one of his own towels. But he would never have been angry with me for giving a few of them away to the cholera clinic.

"They're not really lying. They're just saying what they think you want to hear," Charlie said of the Zambians he employed to work for him in his safari business. But I understood we had learned from experience, if you tell a fellow Zambian the truth, she is likely to laugh at the absurdity of it. Tell the truth to a foreigner, he is likely to yell. Except Charlie didn't yell, or very rarely, and he didn't view me as a Zambian. He viewed me as a wild version of himself, a Westerner in the raw. But now that he had married me, and I was out of my natural habitat, my plumage was less shiny, my skills less useful, my constant noise less charming. Instead of looking like a survivor of a tough and wondrous life, I looked like a damaged and broken survivor of sordid, violent, and undisciplined excess.

"Can you smell it?" I asked late at night, sitting up suddenly in bed, overwhelmed by the cholera scents of disinfectant and diarrhea and bodies.

Charlie put his hand out to me. "It's okay," he said. "Go back to sleep."

But I couldn't sleep. Not because I found the clinic awful and otherworldly but because it felt more knowable to me than did my new husband. The clinic disturbed me, it was life-and-death, it was tragic and unnecessary—like war and drowning and famine—and I felt at home there in a way that I knew I might never feel in this safe bed. No one in their right mind could say they prefer trauma, no one in their right mind could want injustice, no one in their right mind could like cholera. And I did hate it fiercely: the damp hopelessness of those bodies on the cardboard mats, the horror of that awful makeshift tent-morgue, the disgusting refusal of the government to acknowledge that anything bad was happening. But it was an old rut into which I could easily groove without missing a beat.

I told Dad about the clinic on one of his trips into town. "Awful," he agreed. "Poor bastards." Then he lit a cigarette and stared at its burning tip for a moment. "That's the whole problem, though. How we die is how we live."

"But no one lives like that," I said.

"No, Bobo, no one *wants* to live like that. That's a different story."

In late January, Charlie found me temporary, illegal work with an architect whose secretary was on vacation. I was bad at being a housewife, but worse at being a secretary: I accidentally cut off my boss's phone conversations, threw away duplicates of letters I didn't know were supposed to be filed, lost architectural drawings, and forgot crucial lunch appointments. My boss didn't fire me, but he sounded relieved when one morning in mid-February I felt too sick to go to work. It began with a wave of nausea at breakfast, spread to a headache by lunch, and finished with overwhelming exhaustion by dinner. The next day was just as bad, and the day after that an unwelcome repetition. By the end of the week, the sight of butter, the smell of coffee, the mere thought of alcohol made me retch. Walking made me retch. So did sunlight, exhaust fumes, and perfumed soap.

I took to my bed, the curtains drawn. Lizzie lay on the floor next to me, panting in the steamy heat. "You have cholera," Freddy told me with satisfied authority. He stood at the end of my bed covering his mouth and nose with a shopping bag. "If a fly comes to you, and afterwards he visits me, I also will have cholera."

"Can you fetch me a Coke from the kiosk?" I begged.

Freddy hesitated.

"Please," I implored. "You can take the car."

I went to the doctor and he tested my blood for malaria, hepatitis, and HIV/AIDS. He was unimpressed with my results. "There's nothing wrong with you," he announced, waving the paper at me. "All in your head." So I went home and tried to carry on as normal, but my body refused to work. I went back to bed, too enervated and queasy even to read. In the mornings, I begged Charlie to come home early, imagining the foods he could bring me that might quell my unstoppable biliousness: pickles, strawberries, salsa, none of which were readily available except at vast expense in one of the new South African stores. Charlie was dismayed by my depression and my sudden tearful neediness. He suggested exercise, a diet, getting out more.

"I'm dying," I said, only half joking and wondering if years of smoke, first- and secondhand, were already catching up to me. "Isn't this how cancer starts?"

Then Mum came up from the farm, took one look at me, and announced her diagnosis. "You're pregnant."

"I can't be," I said. "I have an IUD in."

Mum sighed and shut her eyes. "Oh, don't go into the gory details, Bobo. Just take my word for it."

|||||||||

In July, Auntie Glug phoned from Scotland to say that my grandmother seemed irreversibly unwell. "I don't know if she's had a stroke, or what's going on," she said. "But she's definitely lost the plot." My parents had recently left the farm in Mkushi and were camping in a scruffy farmhouse in the district while Dad figured out what to do next. The upheaval had sent Mum into a deep depression. In part to save her mind further shock, we decided I should fly over to see Granny and report back with my findings. "And you can buy nappy rash cream while you're at it," Dad said. "Or whatever it is babies go in for."

By then I appeared so hugely pregnant I brought a forged doctor's note to the airport to prove that I was only seven months gone and therefore unlikely to give birth on the soon-to-be liquidated Zambia Airways—motto: "A Pleasure in the Skies." The Zambian ticketing officers and the air stewardesses doubted the note and several of them put knowing hands on my belly. "Are you sure this date is correct?" they asked, waving the forgery at me. Frankly, I was beginning to doubt the calculations myself.

"Of course," I said.

I landed in London, caught a train to Scotland, and took a bus to the village where Auntie Glug lived. My grandparents had been moved from their cottage in England to a bungalow here several years earlier when it became clear that they were becoming too vague to remember to eat regularly, or make sure the woodstove wasn't smoldering before they went to bed. I dropped my bags at the door and followed Auntie Glug into the bedroom. The radiators blasted equatorial warmth. "All right," Auntie Glug said, pointing to Granny's bed. "Your turn to keep an eye on the madhouse. I'm going to put my feet up and have a cup of tea."

"Hello there," I said to the shape under the bedclothes.

"Nicola?" Granny pushed herself up on her elbows, her face alight with expectation. It was obvious Granny's mind was taking its final shaky flight; it flittered around like an elderly butterfly, perhaps still capable of fancy and beauty, but mostly notable for landing without conviction and taking off with unsteadiness. Her work-worn hands, permanently curled to the shape of a milkmaid's grip, fretted the bedclothes.

"No," I said. "It's Bobo."

"Oh." It wasn't me Granny wanted. She sank back into her pillows, disappointed. "Where's Nicola?" she demanded. "Where is she? Has she taken the horses out?"

"Yes," I said. I pictured Mum depressed in her borrowed shack near our old farm. I knew her pattern well: she wouldn't be riding, or taking the dogs for their afternoon walk, or much of anything. Her eyes would have lost their focus. "Yes, she's out riding," I said.

"I thought so," Granny said, satisfied. After that, she rambled on for a while as if I were a potentially helpful stranger: Could I fix the oven? Someone had fiddled with the dial on her radio; did I know how to tune in to *The Archers*? Where were her slippers? Then she suddenly struggled to sit up against the gravity of her soft bed and fixed her dark, Highland eyes on me for a long time. "You look pregnant," she said at last, her voice full of accusation.

"I know."

"I hope you're married."

"I am."

My grandmother's eyelids fluttered and she sank against her pillows again. "Well, that's something." Then her mind reeled back through all the eligible men who would have been living in Kenya at around the time my mother was meeting my father. I explained that Charlie Ross was no one she had ever seen before, and from no family she had ever known or heard of. "I met him in Zambia," I said.

"Ross," my grandmother muttered. Then her mind skipped centuries and seized on Scottish history circa the brief, shaky reign of Mary Queen of Scots. "Chief Alexander Ross," she said.

"No," I said.

"The ninth of Balnagowan," Granny insisted. "A very violent and unpleasant man. Wild and lawless. He's given to land raiding. *Land* raiding. Ardmore, Aird Mhor. You can't be too careful, you know. These tendencies are very strong. Very."

I said, "Charlie's from a very old Philadelphia family."

"That's not possible," Granny argued.

"He's American," I explained. "From the United States."

"Well then." My grandmother looked out the window. My grandfather was making his way slowly down a row of potatoes, weeding. His pipe clamped in the lower left corner of his mouth emitted tiny blue clouds of smoke. "There will be mildew, of course," Granny said. Then she respired in that way of the elderly, her cheeks sucking in, as if great sadness had overtaken her. We sat in silence for a while. On the wall above the dresser was a portrait of Mum as she'd been in her late thirties. She looked radiant, but also a little surprised, as if startled to find herself in a picture frame in this Scottish bedroom. The baby turned mercilessly, pushing feet into ribs. I shifted my weight.

Then Granny turned back to me and with sudden, ferocious clarity she said, "You know, you will be terribly lonely, Bobo."

I smiled, thinking of Charlie in Lusaka, and of the family we would have, and of the ways in which our house would soon be filled with noise and life and urgency. We'd get more dogs; there would be cats and horses. We'd settle into one another and a culture would grow around us, the way culture had grown around my parents and grandparents. Mum and Dad's house was salty with dogs and horses and sweat. My grandparents' house was redolent with old books, pipe tobacco, and dust—as if Kenya was something that had never shaken out of the furniture. They had overcome the early days of Granny threatening Grandpa with her chamber pot. They had survived Granny's hatred of the matrimonial state. Now, even with Granny's mind in full flight, they were like a tiny, unassailable sovereign nation. Charlie and I would do the same.

"No I won't," I said. "We won't be lonely."

But later that evening, in the spare bedroom where I was sleeping, I noticed the end of the bed was dented, as if a dog had habitually nested there. I settled myself into the hollow and looked up. On the wall opposite the bed there was a painting my mother had done as a teenager in Kenya. It showed giraffes cruising across the grasslands of the Uasin Gishu plateau. I knew then that I was sitting where my grandmother must have sat for hours, staring at her history, remembering the irrational decades in Africa, when she had most belonged to a land that would never have her. I knew then that there was a terrible possibility Granny knew everything there was to know about loneliness and that she'd seen my likely future in her own unlikely past.

BABIES IN THE TIME
OF YELLOW FEVER

By August Charlie's work wasn't going well. His investors in the safari company decided the government-issued permits were taking too long to procure. The canoe and walking safaris were canceled; Charlie needed to move closer to the whitewater rafting operations below Victoria Falls and concentrate his energies on that part of the business. So we packed up the house, sold two ponies, and rented a cottage in Livingstone on the banks of the Zambezi River.

Before we left Lusaka, I invented a reference for Mr. Njovu that might help him get work elsewhere. Freddy waved me away like a cholera fly, insisting the last thing he needed was a reference from me. His uncle, he assured me, had a car and a good nose for business. "I am going to be a taxi driver," he announced. Then he invited me to see the house he had been building near the Great East Road.

I was astonished. "You've been building a house?" I thought I knew Freddy and that I had been on friendly enough terms that I would have known something this monumental. "When?"

"On my days off," Freddy said. "You should see it."

So Freddy and I took one last terrifying drive together through town, over the bridge that spanned the railway line, past the Anglican cathedral, and out toward the airport. Then we turned down a jumble of dirt roads and stopped at a small house, redolent with fresh cement. Freddy negotiated the cluster of padlocks on the door and let me in. My eyes adjusted to the light and I saw that not all our belongings had made it down to our new house in Livingstone. Freddy's new house was furnished almost entirely from what he had gleaned from ours: a couple of small tables, two garden chairs, some pots and pans, plates and cups, cushions, a few vases, photo frames.

It took me a while to know what to say. "It's very nice," I said at last.

Freddy smiled. "We like the same things," he agreed.

Charlie and I moved south with the two remaining horses and the puppy. At the end of the month, when my belly had stretched far beyond the limit of what it seemed possible my skin could contain, we drove across the border into Zimbabwe and found lodgings on a farm next to a clinic in Marondera. I worried about being alone for the delivery, by which I meant I was worried about being beyond the reach of anyone related to me by blood. I phoned Dad and asked for Mum, even as I feared that her latest depression compounded with her own mother's precipitous final decline had put her out of the running as a potential helpmeet. "I'll have a word with her," Dad said. "She'll pull her socks up for you, Bobo. She always does."

So Mum joined us—her hair slightly askew, her eyes paled to yellow, and her hands more unsteady than normal. I could tell it was a great effort of will for her to stay on the surface of

her mind, to keep her madness at bay. She had difficulty con-
centrating, she drank a little too much too early, her sentences
sometimes came out of sequence, slurred and breaking the
bounds of customary logic. I could tell she felt my watchful-
ness, anxiety, and wariness and she wanted to compensate
with a level of caring she was barely capable of giving to herself. "Come on, Bobo," she said. "Isn't it time for your afternoon nap?" Or, "Here's a nice cup of tea," by which I knew
everything she had left unspoken.

In the mornings, we went for walks around the lodge. In
the afternoons, we drank tea under the flamboyant trees
in the yard and read. In the evenings, we ate an early supper
on the veranda and listened to the sounds of a southern African spring: bush babies, crickets, and frogs. About once every
three hours, Mum looked at her watch and said, "This has
been a biblically long pregnancy, Bobo. Why don't you drink
some Epsom salts and hop up and down?" Then, early on the
morning of September 15, 1993, the slight contractions I had
been having all week tugged stronger. We drove to the little
clinic nearby and the midwife declared the baby ready for
arrival. "First we give you an enema," she said, snapping rubber gloves onto her hands.

I looked at Mum in terror.

"Oh sorry, Bobo. I forgot to tell you about this bit." But
the truth is, no one had told me about any bit, or at least not
in any way that might now be helpful. Anything I knew
about childbirth I had gleaned from my *Where There Is No
Doctor* book, from high school biology, and from Vanessa
who had closed her eyes when I asked her what to expect.
"Oh Al, it's not the *most* fun I've ever had."

I labored hard for eight hours. And then, at two in the
afternoon, I suddenly felt the baby insisting itself into the
world, its head crashing against my pelvis. But as hard as I

strained, nothing would change. The baby stayed inside me, and I stayed helplessly beetle-turned-up, my spine buckling with the pressure of this unproductive heaving. I searched for Mum. "Is this bad?" I asked.

"You're fine," Mum said, which I didn't think I was, but if she sounded calm, almost bored, then I reasoned we were probably still okay. "Just keep doing what you're doing."

Charlie told me not to panic. Then he said something about the difficulty he'd sometimes faced breathing thin air near the summit of Kilimanjaro back when he'd guided it for American clients. I glared at him. A cigar poked preemptively out of his shirt pocket. Another wave of agony surged through me. Another hour passed. I pushed and breathed and pushed and breathed. Yet another hour came and went. Then Mum said, "Oh, do get a move on, Bobo. It's jolly nearly time for tea." Which is how I knew even she was beginning to worry, seriously.

So I redoubled my efforts, and still nothing happened. More time passed. Then the doctor made an impatient noise. She brought out a scalpel, made an incision in what felt like the epicenter of my pain, sank her arms between my legs, attached something to the baby's head, and began pulling. Charlie put his foot on the end of the bed to stop it skidding across the room, Mum held on to my shoulders. I pushed and breathed and told myself I'd never do this again. Then there was an abrupt release, and there she was: a long-limbed, waxy, blood-smeared baby unfurling on my chest, her lips a perfect rosebud of query, and everything I had ever thought I knew about pain and love and fear of death raced out of me and was replaced by a fierce, murderous adoration. I looked at Mum in astonishment.

"I know," she said, and for a moment something swam between us that had to do with the children she had lost, although it wasn't anything I was prepared to put into words. Then before I could try, Mum cleared her throat. "Don't worry, Bobo. They all look like that when they're born. Chinless and a bit squashed." The baby closed her mouth over my nipple. Mum pulled the sheet back off my stomach with careful apprehension, as if expecting to unearth a small but vicious animal, and allowed herself a proper inspection of her first granddaughter. "Well at least she has a nice leg for a riding boot," she said at last.

|||||||||

Our new cottage, several miles upstream from Victoria Falls, had seemed romantic and charmingly eccentric when I was pregnant. But now that Sarah was here, I could tell it was not suitable for a newborn. Our landlady, a Belgian of White Russian descent, had come out from the gloom of postwar Brussels to the violently bright promise of the Belgian Congo. In subsequent decades, divorce, war, and her own restlessness had kicked her about the African continent and even for brief stints to Pakistan and England. But in the 1970s she had ended up in Zambia, teaching French in a Catholic mission school. When she retired, she bought this dry little farm at a bend in the river and named it Quiet Waters.

Out of rocks harvested from the farm, she built a house for herself and cottages for potential renters. We were the only takers. The buildings were picturesque enough from a distance. Up close, however, the concrete floors were cracked and seeped colonies of stinging guinea-fowl ants. The small, uneven rooms were stiflingly hot, absorbing heat all day and exhaling it at night. Electricity was sporadic; there was no running water. I became frantic and tearful, holding Charlie up on his way to work in the morning to plead my case.

"Nappies," I argued, pointing to the washing line. "The baby," I implored. "And it's so hot."

I wanted the luxury of running water, a fan, and reliable refrigeration. And more than at any other time since leaving for boarding school at the age of seven, I needed my mother. But one morning, not long after Sarah was born, Granny had refused her morning cup of tea, turned her face to the wall, and closed her eyes in the final Highland gesture. So in early October, Mum flew to Scotland and stayed in the antiseptic hum of a Scottish hospital for weeks, watching her mother gradually let go. Granny had already relinquished most of her mind, at least in the conventional sense of the word. Now she went about losing her appetite, her worldly attachments, and her will to live.

Her final words were, "I don't want to be a nuisance." Then Granny closed her eyes and seemed to hold her breath until everything stilled and she was gone. After that, Mum left the Dundee Infirmary and went back to the bungalow with its tropical-setting radiators and its radio forever statically lost beyond the reaches of *The Archers*. She found her father in his garden, bent over his potato bed, preemptively turning the hard winter soil for next year's crop, as if grief could be stanched as long as there was the promise of seasonal vegetables. Mum stood, cocooned in the sheepskin jacket she had kept in her parents' spare room since she had left England in the early 1970s. The wide collar had come and gone out of fashion at least twice in that time.

My grandfather saw my mother watching him, straightened up, and tapped his pipe out against his corduroy pants. "It's eleven," Mum said. My grandfather confirmed this fact with a glance to the soupy sky. Wordlessly, he propped his hoe against the shed wall, broke the clods of clay off his shoes, and went inside. Mum followed him into the kitchen.

They had their aperitifs—a couple of rough martinis—then Mum set the table with her mother's cracked or chipped china plates and with the old silver cutlery worn with the teeth of their ancestors. My grandfather took the food out of the oven and brought it to the dining room.

They sat down to lunch. My grandfather poured them both a Guinness stout. "She's gone, you know," Mum said. My grandfather nodded and a few huge tears rolled down his impressive nose. Then he carved the reheated mutton and handed her a plate. The green beans had been boiled gray, which was one of those details you notice after someone has died, and then can never stop noticing. My grandmother always blanched beans to perfection; salted water to a boil, the beans added and cooked for no longer than four minutes, rinsed in a shock of cold water, and served within minutes of coming off the stove. These colorless, limp things were the beans that would forever more come to this table now she was gone.

A week after her death there was a small memorial service for my grandmother at the village kirk, but there turned out to be remarkably little to say about a woman who had been born on the Isle of Skye, found her way to Kenya to raise her two daughters, and had come home to Britain for the last decades of her life. The fact of her having taken safaris in the shadow of Mount Elgon, or of her having been fluent in both Gaelic and Swahili, and of her ability to kill a rabbit with a single well-placed chop to the back of its neck did not seem worth recounting to a group of mostly dutiful, slightly doddering parishioners attending the service. They had known her only as the old woman in the Second World War cottage on the edge of the village, the owner of a sweet dog, the wife of the chivalrous, absentminded English gentleman who spent most of his days in his vegetable garden.

"Well, that's the thing. There's never very much to say at the end," Dad said. "Or there shouldn't be. Someone's born, does the bit in the middle, and then they die. It doesn't change all that much from one bloke to the next."

In the New Year, Mum flew back to Zambia and surrendered completely to that old undertow of grief. Although this time she went so deep that looking down even we—her daughters and husband—couldn't see much more than the waving shadow of her limbs. We missed her as much for who she was in particular—irreverent, intelligent, capable of surprising surges of compassion—as we did for who she represented for us: the mother ship.

Perhaps most of us never stop needing a person from whom we can fledge and return repeatedly, continually trying out our independence in the knowledge that there is somewhere and someone to which and to whom we can return. Vanessa and I had learned the beginning of this universal truth piecemeal and early in the sinkholes of our mother's periodic depressions and manic attacks, but what we didn't know then was the whole of that truth: the only way to stop needing a mother ship was to become the mother ship yourself.

Mum spent most of her days in bed, refusing to notice anything around her. She didn't notice mealtimes come and go, she didn't notice Vanessa or Vanessa's two young sons, she didn't notice Sarah or me when we came up to visit. She drank mostly brandy, and often she took pills, and the combination of the two caused her days to bleed into one long deferment. She had taken our family lifeboat—the one in which I had vaguely expected us all to reconvene and reunite from time to time—and she had wobbled off alone on her own compelling current. She was now impossible to reach by either ordinary or extraordinary means.

"She'll be all right," my father said.

"But what about us?" I wanted to ask. "What about Vanessa and me? What about you?"

I wanted someone—a mother to be precise, our mother to be exact—to see us, to feel what we were feeling, or even to acknowledge that we existed, but we were motherless in the most literal sense of the word. It was nothing new. It's not as if Mum hadn't taken long solo voyages into her dark, grief-disturbed interior before, but now Vanessa and I were mothers ourselves, and there is nothing like the profound loneliness of early motherhood to make a person ache to be embraced by their person of origin.

"Your mother was very good with all of you when you were little," Dad said. He frowned as if trying to remember back. "Which is just as well because I certainly wasn't getting anywhere near the business end of a baby." He shuddered. "Babies will do *anything*," he said. "Lots of hollering and buckets of nappies, that's what I remember. Good God, if I'd been left alone with any of you lot, I'd have called an ambulance."

But I recall Olivia's childhood as a time of uncharacteristic tranquility, our house redolent with comfort: Woodward's Gripe Water, Fortris juice, Germolene. I think of Mum as happy then, her tuneless singing as she danced the baby into the garden. I remember feeling jealous and proud all at once. Jealous of the attention the baby was getting, proud that this was our mother. She was so good with her infant, so practical and capable but also so smitten and joyful.

There is a reason women become a version of their own mothers when babies are born: having lost themselves in the moment of their child's birth, it is a way of anchoring themselves back to the habits—the smells and foods and rituals—of their own childhood. So I soaked Sarah's soiled nappies in bleach before boiling them in a huge vat over a woodstove. I rubbed her head, feet, and elbows with Vaseline. I kept a basin of Dettol handy to swab the stump of her umbilical cord. I bathed her prickly heat in calamine lotion.

Motherhood—the way too many of us do it alone now—without an exaltation of female relatives, without a heft of knowing matrons to buoy us up, is unnatural. But all the women I had anticipated being here at this stage in my life—my sister, my mother, my grandmother—had been tied off from me with a vast, invisible tourniquet. Granny was dead. I couldn't ax my way through the deep, frozen sea of Mum's sorrow to beg for help. And Vanessa was two toddling sons and one bad marriage under deep water of her own. When she did resurface it was only to gesture distress. The signal flag Victor is a no-nonsense, unambiguous red X on a white flag. It means, "I require assistance." We all did.

I found our Belgian landlady as sympathetic and helpful as a woman in her position could be—Grand'Mere, she had asked me to call her, as if that might bridge the distance between my youthful need and her elderly inability to supply it—but she'd had her own difficult and wearying journey. She had been a young mother herself when she had first left Europe for the brilliant white hope of the Belgian Congo: "Allez-Y & Faites Comme Eux"[3] was the tagline of a propaganda poster from the colony that showed a European man, dandyish in a white linen suit, lording it over half a dozen robust oxen and several industriously slaving black men. But our landlady's luck had been more equivocal than the colonial marketing poster had suggested it would be. And she had added even more uncertainty to her already uncertain future on an upheaving continent, her choices spurred more by

---

3. Go, and be like them.

romance than by rationality. Perhaps, like most of us, she believed time would circle back and catch up with her quixotic notions of how the world would treat her. But instead of a long, slow African sunset cooling into night surrounded by certainty and grandchildren and promise, she was ending her life alone on a bend on the Zambezi River, her body flooded by an array of known and unknowable parasites.

Her skin was yellow and she felt cold most of the time. More or less permanent malaria had thinned her blood to a watery chill. She kept a fire stoked in her bedroom, even in steaming midsummer, and at night she warmed her feet in tubs of river water brought to a boil over a fire in the kitchen. Dust and smoke covered everything she owned: a portrait of herself as a young woman in Brussels; books and maps and letters; a cuckoo clock that had long ceased working but that carried with it a fading aura of European concern for timetables and deadlines.

"No, don't bring the baby near me," she begged. "Perhaps I am contagious. You see how yellow I am? What if I have the fever?" She could no more reach out to help me than she could force disease out of her blood, or conjure crocodiles out of the Zambezi to inhale her collection of horrible village dogs. So we sat on opposite ends of her table on the veranda, Sarah curved in a heat-drugged sleep on my lap, Grand'Mere's two bad-tempered African gray parrots singing "La Marseillaise" and cursing complainingly in French, the troop of monkeys she had adopted clattering on the asbestos-sheeting roof. "Have a lemon cream," she offered.

I knew I had come from women who had done much better with a lot less, but there was also the closed-circuit cautionary tale of the women in my history who had done a lot worse with very much more, and who was to say how childbirth and mothering and isolation would catalyze in my mind? "I suppose it was after her mother died that my mother went completely to pieces," Dad told me. "Before that, it was just practice. Soaked through, but probably not beyond repair." And I pictured Mugger like the moon to Boofy's tide, pulling her back into the shallows every time she got too deep.

Exhausted and more than a little scared, I acknowledged I needed help to get me through Sarah's baby months. So I hired a villager, Jamie Nkomo, to bring buckets of water up from the river and help me with my struggling attempt at a heatstroked vegetable garden. I hired Mildred Tembo—the daughter of one of the supervisors at a nearby safari camp—to help me with the housework. Then one afternoon, as I lay nursing Sarah in the heat of the day, a woman suddenly materialized in the bedroom outside my mosquito net. I sat up, startled, holding the milk-drowsy baby against myself.

"I'm Josephine," the woman announced, crouching down next to the bed. She smelled of uncured tobacco and carbolic soap, smells so familiar to me I was instantly transported back to my own early childhood and the no-nonsense slightly impatient nannies of my youth who had allowed me onto their laps and in times of pain and distress had lowered their shirts to let me rest against their skin.

I fell back onto the pillows, and Sarah began to nurse again. Josephine slipped her hands under the mosquito net and reached for Sarah's head. She said she had recently lost her own infant to the yellow fever outbreak in the village. So many children were dying around here, she said, hadn't I heard? "You are too thin to take care of this baby alone," she told me. "Babies aren't safe."

"I know," I said.

Grand'Mere had told me about the yellow fever epidemic when Sarah was just eight days old. But at the little clinic in

Livingstone, the Indian doctor—whom I visited frequently and with increasing discomfort in the weeks after Sarah's birth—had equivocated and added to my fear by expanding the list of possible pathogens. "Maybe yellow fever, maybe just malaria. Who knows with these people? They say yellow fever, they mean hepatitis. They say malaria, they mean meningitis. Are they doctors? No. Are you doctor? No. Am I doctor? Yes."

Then I explained I was still in considerable pain from the delivery, but before I could expound further or attempt to show him my aching rear end, the doctor threw up his hands preemptively. "No titties, no bottoms," he cried. So I went home to Quiet Waters and treated myself as best I could from my copy of *Where There Is No Doctor,* misdiagnosing hemorrhoids coupled with mild malaria as an infection from childbirth. The book said nothing about yellow fever, but sometimes if the wind picked up from the river I could hear village women on the way to their little funerals, ululating their limitless grief. So when Josephine emerged that hot afternoon and her capable hands spoke hungry sorrow for her lost child, I hired her on the spot.

I also found a local tailor and had myself measured for a wearable mosquito-net cloud under which I could keep Sarah while I was nursing her anytime between four in the afternoon and sunrise, when the mosquitoes would be out to feed. And all the rest of the time—even in the supposedly mosquito-free middle of the day—I watched her soft skin for the slightest passing shadow of a drifting parasite. Her white terrycloth diapers hung on a washing line above our heads in the sitting room and kitchen, like strings of white flags requesting cease-fire or signaling surrender.

Most days, Josephine and I took turns walking Sarah along the banks of the Zambezi, while inside the cottage

Mildred sweated over piles of cloth diapers with a charcoal-heated iron—unironed clothes risked carrying the eggs of putzi flies, which hatched as maggots under the skin and produced squirming boils. I also insisted that drinking water and water for bathing the baby be boiled to avoid bilharzia. From dawn to dusk, the kitchen was thick with vapor and mopane-wood smoke. But now I was not alone. The voices of the two women filled the house. Josephine sang Congolese kwasa kwasa; Mildred competed with mournful religious dirges. Jamie sat on the veranda between chores and chatted to the women with cups of tea and slabs of white-bread sandwiches.

By February the heat had become so unbearable that I moved our bed outside under a Bohemia tree and brought Sarah from her crib to sleep with us: a shared being between Charlie and me, sweetly sweating, her arms flung above her head in capitulation to the temperature. If rain threatened, we would drag the bed back inside, but at least on dry nights the breeze from the river could reach us. And, lying under the mosquito net with my child and my husband next to me, listening to the shouting hippos, the pulsing night insects, the shrieking bush babies, I fell deeply back in love with the land of my childhood. The fight against heat and the worry about my new baby seeped out of me and I felt myself yielding to this place and to my new life.

Then, sometime toward the end of February's oppressive humidity, the mild buzz of what felt like permanent, low-grade malaria morphed into serious, recurring malaria. Fever abutted fever until at last I had an unending dose of tropical malaise. One night in March, a fortnight or so before my twenty-fifth birthday, riding a collapsing wave of infection, it occurred to me that I was probably dying. I could feel the parasites exploding in my blood, flooding my organs, clouding my brain. I woke Charlie up. "I don't think I can hold on," I told him.

Charlie leaned over me. "Bummer," he said.

I remember the outrageous instinct of laughter. *Bummer! Bummer?* I'm dying, and that's it? But I didn't have the energy to laugh. And anyway, it seemed a perfectly reasonable response. Charlie's love for me was waning—I'd been a disappointment, it was obvious—but I was still his wife and the mother of his child; there still remained a residue of dutiful love in sickness and in health. After all, isn't that what we had signed up for? Isn't that what the Polish priest had warned us we were in for? Charlie was the mate I had chosen, and he had chosen me. Marriage was a contract: you could hope it would be for better, but it might also be for worse. In any case, we had the baby now. There was no going back from how much we both loved her.

I turned my head, and by the light of the silver moon I looked at Sarah, asleep next to me. I ached to put my hands on her face, to trace the milky luminosity of her skin, but I couldn't make my arms move. Instead I stared at her with all that was left of my focus, imprinting her onto my soul: the silky cloud of blonde hair, the huge, bruised-looking eyelids, the red stain of her birth still evident on her forehead as if the scarification of her delivery from my body into this world would be with her always. I willed her to know that I loved her and that if there was a capacity for love beyond this life, I would go on loving her always. Then I closed my eyes and felt something darker and deeper than sleep pull me away.

Afterward, Charlie would sometimes say that we left Zambia to save me from the seemingly permanent malaria I had contracted, to save my life. But that was only half true; we had already decided to leave the country. Months after arriving in Livingstone, we had begun to send boxes with my books and our clothes and Charlie's African curios to Wyoming. We found prospective homes for our animals. We started to look at flights. By March, by the time of my full-blown almost constant malaria, we were already half gone.

The whole truth is that we left Zambia not only because I had almost died of malaria but also because the reality of the country had not matched Charlie's vision of how it should have been and he wasn't prepared to beach up against the reality of the place in the manner of Grand'Mere and my parents and any number of other hanging-in-there settlers and their descendants. Romance isn't everything. In fact, romance is what gets you killed if you get too enveloped by it. Charlie had choices, and he was going to make the right one.

Westerners came to Zambia and felt an inexplicable sense of connection in part because back then in the early 1990s, the country still had much of what the developed world had destroyed: vast pockets of roadless land; wild rivers; sizable herds of charismatic and sometimes dangerous animals. But our south-central African beauty wasn't as unspoiled as it looked, and we Zambians weren't as innocent and uncomplicated as we first appeared. Most Zambians I knew would pick air-conditioning over virgin forests; a car over a bicycle; antidepressants over despair. The purity that foreign visitors elected to see in many of us—so friendly, so earthy, so naïve— was partly a glitch in translation and partly a willing suspension of disbelief.

Charlie shook me and said my name, and when I did not respond he pulled me from under the mosquito net, draped my weight over his arms, hurried across the garden and into the cottage. He made his way through the dark, stifling sitting room and through our tiny bedroom into the bathroom. He hoisted me against his chest and switched on the light—a single electric bulb sizzling from beneath its banana-leaf-woven lampshade. Then he lowered me into the bathtub, still full of cool boiled river water from Sarah's bath earlier that evening. I woke up startled to find myself wet. Charlie held my head and my back. My cotton nightie stuck to my belly and hips.

"There you are," Charlie said.

"I think so," I replied.

Charlie made some milky, sweet tea, and I kept it down. Then I took some aspirin and another dose of chloroquine, and Charlie helped me out of the bath and into dry clothes. The next morning after Charlie left for work, I drove myself to a clinic in Zimbabwe. The doctor looked at a slide of my blood under a microscope and said he was surprised I was walking. He wanted to admit me to the hospital and hook me up to an IV, but I thought of how reminiscent of southern African boarding schools that would be—hot, antiseptic-smelling wards overseen by fierce matrons—and I said I felt fine, relatively. So he put me on a course of oral antibiotics and quinine. "It'll seem as if your head is stuffed with cotton wool," he warned.

"That'll be an improvement," I said.

The doctor didn't laugh. "There will be a bitter taste in your mouth, you could be nauseous, your hearing might get a bit fuzzy." He looked at Sarah and then added, "And you'll have to stop breast-feeding. Quinine can cause hemorrhaging in the baby's mouth." He was a kind man, overwhelmed by the sheer numbers at his door, perpetually dealing with near death. He put his hand around Sarah's thighs and gave them a squeeze. "You've done well," he said. Then he asked the orderly to bring me tea and hurried back into his office.

So I sat outside the clinic under a mango tree for an hour,

drinking tea and watching Sarah nurse for the last time. Then I swallowed two quinine tablets and drove to Jay's Supermarket to buy baby formula and bottles. I figured I had three hours in this heat before Sarah would be thirsty again. So I hurried across the border back into Zambia—baboons seething over the roofs of vehicles in pursuit of Zimbabwean groceries—willing the officials to stamp our passports quickly and let us through customs without a prolonged car search. Then I rushed through Livingstone, turning at the Anglican church onto the road to Quiet Waters, making short shrift of the twenty or so miles to the rocky little farm. For the rest of the day I lay under the mosquito net in the garden, weak and bilious, spilling rivulets of quinine-poisoned breast milk onto facecloths and listening to Sarah's angry confusion as Josephine—who had taken the baby out of my sight but not out of earshot—tried to persuade her to take the bottle.

At four, Mildred brought a tray of afternoon tea, and Josephine brought Sarah back under the mosquito net. The three of us sat up in the bed and watched the sleeping baby. She was blotchy from crying, her cheeks tearstained, the edges of her mouth pale with dried formula. Seeing her made my breasts ache worse than before. "This hurts," I complained.

"I know," Josephine said.

"Oh, Josephine!" I was aghast. "I'm so sorry."

"It's okay," Josephine said. She put a strong, expert hand above my nipple and pushed. Milk gushed between her fingers. "It will get worse and then it will get better," she assured me.

I got tears then, but Josephine looked away and chewed her lower lip angrily. This country could turn everyone a little extreme—everyday unhappiness greeted with impatience, or sometimes even a kind of terrible laughter, and then years of stoicism giving way to the visceral anguish of the ululating women on their way to the too little graves of the village's children. My mother had told me over and over, "Save your tears for the big stuff, Bobo." Sometimes I fancied I could see the strain of all that containment in the sinew-drawn necks of the women, their bunched jaws, the sad spokes of worry at the edges of their eyes.

A month or so later, just as the mornings were finally turning brisk with winter wind, I walked for the last time to the stand of fever trees at the bend in the river and touched four of them, superstitiously and ritually, as if they were the walls of a house to which I wished to return. I said farewell to Jamie and Mildred. Josephine and I embraced, the baby sandwiched between us for a final time. Then the Charlie Ross party of three left Livingstone and flew to the United States.

It had been decided then: our marriage wasn't going to be about nearly dying, and violent beauty, and unpredictability. Our union was going to be about sticking it out, sensible decisions, college funds, mortgages, and car payments. Maybe it wouldn't be the seductive edges of terror and madness. But we would have medical insurance and a retirement plan. We would have reliable electricity and running water and refrigeration. Our lives would be good and ordinary and sane.

MAD BEANS, TIME,
AND GHOSTS

The United States came as a relief and a puzzle both. We built a small house in a new subdivision at the foothills of the Big Hole Mountains in eastern Idaho. We had a view of the Tetons and of a valley of farmland, although almost everywhere we looked, new houses and developments were spreading out where once there had been potato fields, and before that willow bottoms and sage meadows. A crippled-up cowboy whose cousin had sold the land on which we now lived told me that when he was a boy, seventy years earlier, this place was still three-quarters wild: bears and wolves, herds of elk and mule deer, the odd remnant bison. "It's too bad memory doesn't reset once a decade so you can't tell what you're losing," he said, and he sounded lonely and regretful in the way of an elderly person whose relatives and friends have died and who is no longer visited by his children.

I thought then of the collective memory of land, of the ways in which people and animals and geological events cannot help but leave scars, sculpt wonders, and weave stories onto its cover. And I thought too of how I had inherited my understanding of land both from southern Africans for whom there was no separation of soil and soul and from European settlers for whom land was a commodity, even if it was a commodity with which they had fallen so violently in love that they had forgotten both the ungodliness of the original acquisition and the godliness of soil. "Stand unshod upon it for the ground is holy, being even as it came from the Creator," Alan Paton wrote. "Keep it, guard it, care for it, for it keeps men, guards men, cares for men. Destroy it and man is destroyed."[4]

But from a commodity perspective, standing unshod upon the earth is less an act of reverence than a symptom of insanity, wasted time as well as a way to burn or freeze or dirty your feet. So most of us spend our lives creating buffers between us and ever having to feel the ground. We shield ourselves with comfort, dogmas, committees, and half-acre lawns. We put as much space as we can between the scary instructions of the spirit and our transactional selves. It doesn't matter that Alan Paton and thousands before him had arrived at this truth: the way we treat land, and the ghosts of our land, is the way we will treat everything including ourselves. People who are careless of the land and of the creatures and spirits with which we share it are careless of themselves.

But if I knew any of this back then, I didn't yet have the vocabulary for that knowledge. And perhaps because of that, without intending to do so, I had continued the pattern of some of the men, and most of the women, in my family, reaching as far back as we had memory. We were careless, and shiftless, and unthinking. We left our ancestral homes, we birthed and sometimes buried our children in far-flung places, and we started afresh over and over. We cared for land, but too often it wasn't our land to care for.

---

4. Alan Paton, *Cry the Beloved Country* (1948).

I suppose in some instinctive way, I believed that Charlie would be the route back to something more solid and enduring. After all, inasmuch as settlers of anywhere could be, he was of this nation; too many generations to count back how long his people had been here. Our children would be able to stand unabashedly unshod upon this soil, they would sense their ancestors, they would feel a belonging. I didn't want to know or believe that this land had been as violently stolen as our southern African land had been. And it would take years for me to understand spray-painted signs I once saw on a sidewalk in Michigan: "You Are Standing On Native Ground."

The United States seemed so settled to me, so resolved, so tamed. Even the wild bits seemed wild in an insistently domesticated way. Americans were not expected to encounter unexpected, surprising hazards. "Be Bear Aware," signs advised in Grand Teton National Park. And in Yellowstone, "Warning: Many Visitors Have Been Gored by Buffalo." Mile markers along trails reminded us how far we had walked, and how far it was back to our car. There were frequent watering stations and places for people to eat, to stop and apply sunscreen, to rest. It was like being in the constant company of a kindly, sandwich-toting, risk-averse aunt.

Growing up in Africa, we had never carried water, food, and spare socks with us on a walk or on our rides. Moreover, we never knew when we set out if we would be gone an hour, a morning, or the entire day. I can't now imagine what stubborn idiocy drove us to such unnecessary measures of discomfort. "A bit of thirst never hurt a person," Dad always said, but being thirsty did hurt in my experience. So did hunger and blisters. "You're getting soft," Dad insisted. "You don't need the bloody kitchen sink every time you step two inches away from the front door."

But now, from the magnifying distance of the United

States, my family was beginning to seem even more careless, unbalanced, and mad than they had when we'd all been in Africa. Meantime, close up, Charlie's family looked saner than I had believed it possible any family could be. For one thing, his Main Line Philadelphians turned out not to be heroin addicts at all. At least not many of them, and certainly not in the way I imagined. In fact, aside from a cousin's brother by a failed marriage who shot his inheritance up his veins and died from a flesh-eating bacterial infection, Charlie's people were heroically reticent and moderate. They buried generations in a single cemetery; they thought about their legacies in concrete and protective ways; they were not squanderers of life and money and health.

And from what I could see, when anyone in Charlie's family did do anything at all out of the ordinary—running away to Woodstock at the age of fourteen as a brother had done, disappearing to Thailand to become a Buddhist monk as a cousin had done, or taking up extreme river guiding as Charlie had done—it was viewed as a lark, an experiment, a brief expression of the unconventional. No one expected anything like that to last forever, and mostly it didn't. Sooner or later, his people returned to the mean, reverted more or less conventional. They seemed to follow uninterrupted, undismaying covenants. Their dead seemed to take their earthly desires, passions, secrets, and complications with them; names and dates were carved into stone, their inconvenient or immoderate impulses were immobilized, their legacies were entrusted as if time went only forward.

Until I came to the States, I believed I knew without any doubt that time could be linear only if you counted it not by the moon, or by a sundial, or even by a watch, but by the loneliness of your own relentless trudge toward death, as if yours was the only life to live and time was something to be endured until you had worn it out. "Time is only as heavy as the thoughts you have to push through it," Dad told me in Malawi when I was fourteen and had been hit by buffalo bean at the lake and had to sit motionless for a couple of hours. "The less you have to think about, the less time matters." By which I now know he meant that the demons, doubts, and guilt we carry fluster time and make it take on an unnatural, constructed weight.

It's a wondrous plant, buffalo bean—*Mucuna pruriens,* or as Mozambiquans call it, feijão maluco, the mad bean. It has a cascade of purple blooms in the spring, and in the winter it carries seedpods with long golden beans covered in shimmering tiny hairs. The hairs contain a chemical, serotonin, that causes unbearable itching when they lodge in the skin. Local healers had long understood that the very plant that has the capacity to drive you crazy in one manifestation would almost necessarily have the capacity to heal madness in another. The healers dried the leaves; smoked, it settled the mind. They crushed and prepared the seeds; consumed, it calmed the spirit.

But if the hairs hit you, it was very important to stay willfully calm. Scratching and movement only served to spread the chemical and resulted in worse itching. To get caught in a current of windborne hairs, or to brush up against it, was to be sent into an involuntary crash course in conscious immobility. A person had to empty her mind of the possibility of relief. Suffer calmly. "Sit still, Chookies," Dad said when I came crying out of the lake where hairs from the plant had landed on the surface, worked their way into my bathing suit, leaving no part of my body untouched. "You're not alone."

My suffering did not make me unique, it made me belong. The gust that had brought my maddening misery had not discriminated. When I looked along the lake's beach that late windy, sunny afternoon, I saw a dozen fishermen and several other women and children sitting as stock-still as I was supposed to, only they were seeming to stare placidly into the wind-whipped water whereas I squirmed and resisted. Also, no one tended to them. Meantime, Mum fed me antihistamines and Dad brought me tea.

"A couple of hours is all," he said. "And anyway, it's all relative."

Dad was a fan of throwing away watches. He always said time was something we invented to make people into money. Clock in, clock out. On the farm, Dad didn't have punch cards. Work started at dawn and ended when it got too hot for plants, animals, or humans to endure movement. Then everyone slept in the middle of the day, dreaming through the stupefying heat. And in the late afternoon, when the sun loosened its grip, work started again until impending darkness finished the day's business.

"Do you know how to empty your mind?" Dad asked.

I shook my head.

Dad sat next to me. "Well," he said. "It helps if you smoke a pipe. There's no definite end, and there's no fresh start with a pipe, properly smoked. It's all the same; the beginning, the end." Then he lit a cigarette. "Not so much a cigarette," he said, looking at the tip of his Benson and Hedges. "A cigarette comes to an end. You throw it away. Then you have to light another one. After that, all you have is a habit."

"Are you drunk?" I asked, not unreasonably I felt.

"A little," he admitted. So for a while we looked at the lake, the waves coming in and going out, the sun striking everything yellow and pale with its heat. The water appeared infinite here, disappearing into nothing, touching shores in Mozambique eventually, lapping back to us in time. I tried to take my mind off my itching, which had the effect of putting it more terribly onto it. Dad smoked, and other than lifting a cigarette to his lips he sat utterly motionless too, as if he had been covered in searing hairs also. He had been hit by buffalo bean often in the war; the Himalayas behind our house in Rhodesia were smothered in the legume. "But a little itching doesn't matter so much when you're worried about getting stonked," Dad said.

I knew without being told that this wasn't the worst suffering in the world. Not by a very, very long shot. And it wasn't even close to the worst suffering I had ever felt. But it was the only suffering I had come across that required you to remain utterly still in its presence and do nothing else except be there, feeling it.

The sun slid down toward the lake. The chemical fire on my skin lifted. Now I could feel where the sun had scorched the back of my neck. Along the beach, the fishermen were beginning to move again. The women picked up their baskets of mangoes and fish and gathered their children around their skirts. Egrets billowed white over the hills behind the lake. Cooking fires shimmered orange from the villages. "Everything ends if you let it," Dad said. "Good and bad."

What I didn't know then, but what I understand now, is that my father was giving me a mini crash course—a crammer—in time, suffering, and relativity. In some ways he had become like the rural southern Africans alongside whom he had worked for so many years; his beliefs had become less solid and certain over time, and therefore more fluid and fearlessly unsupportable. From them he had learned that if you wait long enough, time will circle back to you, and that to attempt to quash or deny trauma was to make a monument of suffering. Dad got to his feet and helped me to mine. "I always think it's worth remembering," he said. "Tobacco's a fourteen-month crop."

|||||||||||

Time was the first thing I noticed about the United States. There seemed to be so little of it, and its unaccustomed short supply panicked me in grocery checkout lines, during meals, and at traffic lights. I fumbled with my checkbook, I was unsure how to use credit card readers, I sat a beat too long at the intersection when red changed to green. I found time was jealously guarded too, as if to share any of it, or to take up someone else's allocation, was the greatest crime. Ironically, it seemed obvious that most Americans had more time than almost any other humans in the history of the earth; they lived longer and more luxurious lives than had ever been lived before. And yet instead of slowing down to fill all the space of their extra years, they sped up and up and up.

In Africa, we filled up all available time busily doing not much, and then we wasted the rest. We didn't bother trying to hoard what could not be safeguarded, restrained, and stored. Sometimes things got all urgent and life tore through us, whether we wanted it to or not. And sometimes the rain wouldn't come, or the heat would not abate, and there was nothing to do but wait. As a result we were emotional spend-thrifts, feeling and living as much as was required from moment to moment, using time carelessly. But from what I could tell, most Americans—at least the people I met—were emotional conservatives, using time and their feelings frugally, selfishly. They believed time belonged to an individual. "Don't waste *my* time," they said.

True, I had been raised with my father's impatience—"Don't just stand there, do something!" he admonished frequently—but southern African time had nonetheless always seemed to me to stretch the distance of the sun, the length between seasons, the availability of light. Until now I had spent most of my life among people who dwelt in time, as if it were as unaccountable as air, or sunshine, or the wind, something that allowed life but that didn't belong to anyone in particular.

Of course I changed and sped up. And in time, Africa changed and sped up too. Almost anywhere you go on the continent, synapses have quickened to accommodate communicating in 140 characters or fewer, to click efficiently through the hundreds of channels on television, to instantly like or dislike some fresh input, to endure the momentary flicker between e-mails sending and receiving. Even the churning slowness of the Internet during Zambia's steamy rainy season is quick enough to allow Vanessa to bash off e-mails late at night so that they arrive in the middle of my afternoon, appearing as time-lapsed conversations, off by a whole season, and by half a bottle of wine. "Huzzit Al-Bo. It's stinking HOT. We're like in a Hoven in here. The kids have SPOTS from the heat. Need more rain like a cat on a hot tin roof. Lots of love, and hugs Van xoxoxox"

Most of all, coming to America, I didn't understand the culture of where I had landed. When I opened my mouth, people knew I wasn't from the United States, but I was white-skinned and blonde, and in every other way appeared to be what people considered a normal-looking, nonminority U.S. citizen. The truth is, though, as much as I spoke English with a noticeable southern African accent, I behaved with an invisible southern African accent. I didn't understand the luxurious entitlement of choice; I couldn't see the point of Saran Wrap, I was baffled by garbage-can liners, I was amazed by the idea of heated driveways and roofs.

Also, I had never been anywhere with a community so disconcertingly vigorous and restless as the western side of the Teton Mountains in the early 1990s. People we knew got sick, of course, there were a few deaths—a five-year-old girl whose anesthesia had been botched, a young mother lost to breast cancer, a climber swept to his death in an avalanche—and I knew there were ill, old people because I volunteered for Meals on Wheels in our valley, but such tragedies and misfortunes were an unintegrated intrusion. It was as if anyone not vibrant and relentlessly healthy was sequestered or quarantined into some shuffling sideline.

"What's been the defining tragedy of your life so far?" I asked Charlie one night after we had put Sarah to bed.

He seemed impatient with the question. "What do you mean?" he wanted to know.

"The worst thing that's happened to you," I said.

Charlie shook his head. "I don't know." And then, "Why would you ask such a thing?"

I couldn't tell him at the time. Only long afterward, I realized perhaps I really wanted to know what had happened in my husband's past, and to his people, because I believed that unless we are vigilant and aware, we are destined to repeat ourselves, generation after generation, more or less distilling the habits and accidents and triumphs of our predecessors and drip-feeding them forward. I wanted to know his family's eddying sadness, their inescapable patterns not only because I cared about what Charlie's history had been but also because I was curious about what our future might bring. Although when I saw where he had grown up—in Pennsylvania, with his gentile parents, their pleasant neighborhood, their understated ways, and on his grandmother's ranch in Wyoming with its beaver ponds, and charming log cabins, and private access to world-class trout fishing—Charlie seemed the textbook recipient of white, male, middle-class American privilege. Nothing bad had happened to him. Nothing bad would happen to him. He would always be okay.

It took me two decades to realize that Charlie's family had endured more than their fair share of troubles; they just chose not to exploit, exude, and air them. They were the most silent people I had ever encountered, artfully uncommunicative, deeply stilled, as if they had all taken a pact not to leak emotion—pleasant or not—or divulge their motivations. Even after years of acquaintance, it would be hard for an outsider to know that anything at all bad had ever happened in this family, now or in any generation. It was as if the Rosses had figured out the secret to the impossible alchemic wish expressed by the crippled-up Idaho cowboy: they had worked out how to reset their memories every ten years, to erase pointless nostalgia, to relentlessly pursue the future.

This was utterly foreign to me. Even glimpsing us Fullers very briefly and from a great distance, a person would realize we had encountered worlds of pain and we still wore that pain, as if we had swum in an ocean of it and had forgotten afterward to towel off the emotional kelp and the eccentric boas of woebegone seaweed. There was the immoderation, of course, the excessive insouciance, the unbridled bonhomie—all a tip-off that stick around long enough and hilarity would likely end in tears. It's true that we had been raised to maintain a stiff upper lip, and sometimes we did. But also, perhaps because there were so few condemning witnesses to our behavior, it didn't matter if we spectacularly dissolved.

Like most drinking families, we usually aired our feelings late at night. It was when someone sighed and warned the others, "Oh, careful now, Bobo's getting tired and emotional." It was when Dad sometimes leapt on the dining room table and roared, "Music, maestro! Music!" It was when Mum admitted, "Oh dear, rather too much excitement, I'm afraid," and gestured that her legs no longer worked. And it was when Vanessa reached behind her and started to fling bottles at whoever was standing in the way, declaring in a voice of deadly calm, "Okay, that's it. I've had enough."

Charlie's family didn't seem to get drunk, and they certainly didn't speak of their losses and tragedies. They didn't roar and battle and laugh, but neither did they harangue and confess and sob. It was as if they were terrified of losing control, but I could not imagine of what. And when they did speak of their deepest grief, they did so with such a civil overlay of commanding restraint, I couldn't hear them. I didn't hear them. Perhaps I willfully *wouldn't* hear them.

In southern and central Africa, tragedy roared at us, and we roared back. We shared our dramas publicly, bled them on the corridors of hospitals, laid our corpses on the beds of neighbors, held our sorrows up in full light. We were volume ten about our madness and disorder, even if we were also resilient and enduring and tough. We survived magnificently, and pretended to qualities of stoicism, but actually, even the most silent of us shouted the disordered history of our lives in our bodies and habits.

On the other hand, Charlie's inherited sorrows were spoken so softly and so reluctantly, I didn't register them as ongoing torments. I barely registered them at all. It took me longer than it should have before I finally understood that his family too had had children carried off by disease, they too had had fatal accidents, they too had known the living waste of drunkenness. Most astonishingly, it took me longer than a decade before I realized that his family had endured a tragedy of such moment, it set the standard for such tragedies: Charlie's great-great-uncle had been the victim of the first kidnapping for ransom in the United States.

On July 1, 1874, little Charles Brewster Ross, aged four, and his eight-year-old brother Walter were snatched from the front yard of their home in Germantown, Pennsylvania.

Walter managed to get free and find his way home, but as far as anyone knows—and at least as far as the Ross family is concerned—little Charley was never seen again. Little Charley's father, Christian K. Ross, was thought to be very wealthy, but he had been nearly bankrupted by the stock market crash of 1873, and the exorbitant ransom demanded by the kidnappers in a series of semiliterate notes was well beyond his reach. His friends offered to take up a collection to meet the kidnappers' demands, but Christian refused, having been advised by the authorities that paying the ransom would encourage other would-be kidnappers to follow suit with other families.

Initially, having no precedent for such a crime, the Philadelphia police told little Charley's distraught father that drunks had likely snatched away the child, and would return him as soon as they sobered up. When it became apparent it was not a drunken lark, but rather a kidnapping for ransom, the case became a national sensation, precipitating one of the largest manhunts of the nineteenth century. Seven hundred thousand flyers were distributed with a sketch of little Charley and a detailed description that reads as the agonized longing of a mother who has kissed and breathed every inch of her lost child's skin. "He is about four years old; his body and his limbs are straight and well formed; he has a full, round face: small chin with noticeable dimple; very regular and pretty dimpled hands; small well-formed neck . . ."

Three weeks after the kidnapping, the mayor of Philadelphia announced a $20,000 reward for information that would lead to either the lost child or his captors. Telegraphs spread the word across the country, and pandemonium ensued. Impostors, do-gooders, spiritualists, and conspiracy theorists clamored to offer intelligence and their services. Parents dressed their children up—girls as well as boys, of every age—in the hope they would pass as little Charley and become absorbed into this illustrious and respectable family.

In December 1874, little Charley's kidnappers were shot while attempting a burglary. One of them died instantly, but the other confessed to the abduction on his deathbed although he would not give the child's whereabouts. "The boy will get home all right," the kidnapper is reported to have said. Christian spent the rest of his life, and the remainder of whatever money had survived the 1873 stock market crash, traveling the world, searching in vain for his lost son. He died of heart failure in 1897. Thereafter, little Charley's mother, Sarah Ann, took up the search until her death, also of heart failure, in 1912.

The kidnapping became the Ross family's most enduring personal secret, to the degree that anything so glaringly public could remain under wraps. After the ransom notes, missing for over a century, were unaccountably and accidentally discovered in the basement of a school librarian's house in northwestern Pennsylvania in March 2012, little Charley's grandnephew, Chris Ross, a nine-term Pennsylvania state representative, said that his parents' generation didn't speak of the disappearance. It was, he said, a forbidden subject. He also said he had no interest in purchasing the ransom notes when they came up for auction. They had, he claimed, caused his family much sadness and trouble and harm.[5] It seemed he would prefer the whole affair forgotten.

But a family's withdrawal, grief, and reticence do not stop a public's participation, curiosity, and prurience. In the years after the crime, until it was torn down, the Ross mansion—a grand Victorian Italianate set back from the road—was one of Philadelphia's most visited tourist destinations. "This high

---

5. Carrie Hagen, "Past Imperfect: The Story Behind the First Ransom Note in American History," *The Smithsonian*, December 9, 2013.

old standing home on Washington Lane has melancholy interest all its own," one contemporary wrote in *Ladies' Home Journal*. "It is preeminently Philadelphia's House of Sorrow."[6]

Songs were written, "Bring Back Our Darling" and "I Want to See Mama Once More." Dozens of articles and books were written about the case: Carrie Hagen's *We Is Got Him: The Kidnapping That Changed America* and Norman Zierold's *Little Charley Ross: The Shocking Story of America's First Kidnapping for Ransom*. In the summer of 2000, for an article in the journal *Pennsylvania History*, Thomas Everly wrote, "Journalists, dime store novelists, mystery writers, amateur historians and crime anthropologists all re-told the narrative in periodicals such as *The Daily Graphic* and *Headline Detective* and books entitled *Mysteries of the Missing* and *The Snatch Racket*."

But most harrowing and heartbreaking was the 1876 best seller, written in the desperate hope that one day little Charley would read it, recognize his own story, and make himself known to his family: *The Father's Story of Charley Ross the Kidnapped Child: Containing a Full and Complete Account of the Abduction of Charles Brewster Ross from the Home of His Parents in Germantown, with the Pursuit of the Abductors and Their Tragic Death; the Various Incidents Connected with the Search of the Lost Boy, the Discovery of Other Lost Children, Etc. Etc. With Fac-Similes of Letter from the Abductors. The Whole Carefully Prepared from His Own Notes and Memoranda and from Information Obtained from the Detective Police and Others Engaged in the Search. By Christian K. Ross of Germantown (Philadelphia).*

It's the longest subtitle I've ever read, and certainly the most agonized. It was as if, from the outset, Christian could not contain the urgency and insistence of his paternal grief,

---

6. Thomas Everly, "Searching for Charley Ross," *Pennsylvania History* 67, no. 3 (Summer 2000): 376–96.

his "bereavement sharper than death," as the introduction to the book would have it. But although little Charley's siblings, the five remaining Ross children, continued to receive claims for decades—thousands of boys, teenagers, and, eventually, men all professing to be the kidnapped child—none of them checked out to any satisfaction.

The only witness to little Charley's kidnapping, his older brother Walter Ross, grew up and eventually married a beautiful socialite, Julia Peabody Chandler, with whom he had five children. The eldest son was named after himself, Walter Lewis. The second son bore two-thirds of the name of his lost brother, Charles Chandler Ross. It was this Charles Chandler for whom my husband was named, as if the family could not quite give up the memory of little Charley, but was reluctant to impose the full title of the lost child—Charles Brewster Ross—on anyone.

In spite of his early and enduring tragedy, or perhaps because of the morality tale of his father's lost wealth, Walter Ross was a roaring success by any standard. In 1899, he bought a seat on the New York Stock Exchange for a then record sum of $29,000. In 1927, avoiding by two years a repeat of his father's experience with a stock market crash, he sold it for another record sum of $270,000. Walter and his wife were listed in the Social Register and were members of the Germantown Cricket Club; they had a luxurious home on Chestnut Hill and a summer escape on Saranac Lake.

But in spite of all the social attainments and the cushioning consequence of affluence, it was as if tragedy, having settled on the Rosses, found comfort there and stayed one generation into the next. Julia and Walter's eldest son, Walter Jr., was all set to become every bit as successful as his father. He married well and had two sons; he showed himself to have inherited astute business acumen. Then, on the night of

November 29, 1931, as he and his wife were driving across Campbell's Bridge near Philadelphia, the steel girders buckled, left their concrete moorings, and the vehicle plunged into Neshaminy Creek thirty-five feet below. Walter Jr. died instantly. His wife survived, my Charlie's indomitable grandmother, Margaretta Sharpless Ross. She was left with two very young sons: my father-in-law and his older brother.

A few years later, perhaps to recover from her heartbreak, or perhaps to provide her sons with an unequivocally masculine influence, Margaretta Ross took her young boys out west to Wyoming, to spend the summer at the famous Bar B C dude ranch in the shadow of the Teton Mountains. There she fell in love with the co-owner of the ranch, Irving Corse, and eventually married him. When Irving shot himself in 1953 after years of enduring excruciating arthritis, Margaretta took over management of the ranch until her own health declined in the mid-1980s. When I met Charlie in 1991, his grandmother had been dead only three years. "She wasn't easy," he said. "I think she was afraid of people taking advantage of her."

Years later, I boarded my horse on a ranch owned by an elderly woman who had known Margaretta as a younger woman. The elderly woman told me Margaretta was the most difficult person she had ever known, which was really saying something, because the elderly woman was quite difficult herself; hard-drinking, chain-smoking, cantankerous. "When I heard the story about that bridge collapsing, I figured it was about right," she told me. "If you had met her, you'd know it would take more than a collapsing bridge to kill that tough old cow. God, she was difficult."

Upon Margaretta's death in 1988, a life estate negotiated in 1929 by her late husband, Irving Corse, terminated and the Bar B C became part of Grand Teton National Park. From a ranch auction, Charlie acquired a couple of rickety pine beds, a few rough chairs, a dining room table that had been raked by the claws of a marauding black bear, and a cowhide sofa dried to the point of such fragility that one of our guests eventually fell right through it. Charlie also kept his step-grandfather's cowboy saddle, on the back of which was still the name, written in clear, if fading, white letters: CORSE. It seemed a bad-luck saddle to me, given Irving's tragic end. The suicide wasn't much spoken about, of course, but it seemed all the louder to me because of it—the dreadful, conclusive loneliness of that final self-inflicted shot.

|||||||||

The case of little missing Charley Ross dragged on well into living memory. In 1939, a sixty-nine-year-old retired carpenter named Gustave Blair sued Walter Ross, now aged seventy, in an Arizona civil court. He claimed to be the little Charley Ross and wanted a share of his father's estate, although Walter vehemently denied the existence of any trust. Gustave's story was as convoluted as it was tragic, but having heard evidence of his fantastical and harrowing tale—the child was allegedly hidden in a cave in Pennsylvania to begin with, and thereafter led a restless, threatened life—the Phoenix judge ruled that the retired carpenter was the "only and original" Charley Ross. But Walter, wary of imposters, worn out by a lifetime of false claims and dashed hopes, ignored the ruling.

Gustave then requested a jury verdict, and on May 8, 1939, after only eight minutes of deliberation, a jury of twelve men issued on their verdict in the civil action *Blair v. Ross*. Gustave Blair was, they declared, the lost boy, legally entitled to change his name to Charles Brewster Ross. But Walter continued to refuse to accept the court's decision. "Blair is evidently just another one of those cranks who have been bothering us for the last sixty-five years," he told the Associated Press. "The idea that my brother is still alive is not only absurd but the man's story seems unconvincing." When Gustave made plans to see Walter in Philadelphia, Walter bolted to his summer cabin on Saranac Lake.

Undeterred by his supposed brother's reluctance to acknowledge him, Gustave legally changed his name to Charles Brewster Ross. A few months later, he traveled to Pennsylvania with his second wife, Cora, in an attempt to remarry under his freshly retrieved identity in the church that now sat on the site of his old family home. However, given the Ross family's refusal to recognize the man as their lost brother, the pastor refused the couple's request. "If my older brother lives for five years, he'll seek me out and admit kinship," the latter Charley Brewster Ross declared.

Four years later, in July 1943, Walter died. He was buried in St. Thomas's Episcopal Church outside Philadelphia. "Above all, he had not allowed his father's obsession to become his own," wrote Thomas Everly. "In order to live, he let Charley Ross die."[7] Six months later, the last man claiming to be Walter's lost brother died of influenza in a Phoenix hospital. But the lingering memory, the nagging doubts about little Charley Ross, meant that he remained stitched into the family's thinking and soul. He was silently but persistently everywhere.

As a child, my Charlie Ross—Charles Chandler Ross II, named in part for his family's most enduring tragedy, as had been his great-uncle before him—was taunted by his older brothers. "You'll get kidnapped," they predicted. "No one will ever find you again." But if such taunts terrified Charlie at the time, he not did not later cite them as the source of his hypervigilance against the world's injustice, or his

7. Everly, "Searching for Charley Ross."

amorphous but persistent sense that he was not living the life to which he had been entitled. In any case, the taunts were nothing compared to the threats his brothers delivered to throw him from the third-story window of their house, and their subsequent denials of any such behavior.

"It was just what brothers do," he said.

"Is that code for something?" I asked.

Charlie looked blank. "Code for what?"

And when in 1997 Charlie suggested naming our son Charles Ross, it didn't apparently occur to him, and certainly not to me, until someone else pointed it out, that we were keeping alive the name of the missing child. So on and on the missing went, well after little Charley could possibly have still been alive, as if the itch of him yearned to be uncovered. "Fear them not therefore: for there is nothing covered, that shall not be revealed; and hid, that shall not be known."

|||||||||||

There is no loneliness quite like the loneliness that comes from living without ancestors, without the constant, lively accompaniment of the dead. And it was true, the people I knew on the farms and ranches of my youth accepted their dead relatives into their houses and bodies, not in the way Christians might accept the Eucharist—a weekly ritual—but in vivid daydreams, in the conception, birth, and rearing of their children, in the ingestion of every meal. The dead, disentangled from the prison of their flesh, were expected to engage in a busy, even mischievous afterlife, affecting weather, health, and fertility. They did not disappear, and freeze or desiccate beneath a slab of stone, or in some vault. They did not leave wealth or reliable inheritances of property for their successors. Nor did they rest in peace.

THE RIVER RUNNER

AND THE RAT RACE

When we first arrived in the United States, I got a job five days a week as a river guide in Jackson, Wyoming. I wasn't very good at it, but I earned twenty dollars a trip, and other than cracking my chin open on a rock, no one got hurt on my raft. Three evenings and one lunch shift a week, I waitressed at a high-end restaurant in town. I wasn't very good at that either, but it was busy season, help was hard to find, and no one at my tables actually starved to death. On good nights, I could earn a couple of hundred dollars in tips. It seemed like a small fortune until Charlie told me it wasn't enough. He explained that a house was very expensive. Childcare was very expensive. Health insurance was very expensive. Then I realized my unskilled labor wouldn't be worth anything in the winter. In September, when the cold weather came, river operations would shut down and the restaurant would close for the off-season, and then where would I be?

I hadn't thought it through, to be honest. It's not that I wasn't familiar with seasons. Growing up on farms in southern Africa, I was very aware that we had cooler dry seasons and hotter rainy seasons. We'd reaped and we'd sowed. But regardless of whether crops were going into the ground or coming out of it, we had always seemed more or less short of money. "We're on the bones of our arses," Dad would say. But he said it in a way that suggested being poor wasn't a bad thing; if anything it was a jokey thing.

On the other hand, when Charlie showed me our budget and presented a list of numbers that would not zero out, it was not a jokey thing. I didn't really understand the accounts, nor did I understand the words that were coming out of his mouth, but what he told me with his body, his quietly contagious anxiety, made me nearly dizzy with panic. I picked up an extra shift at the restaurant. Then summer ended, and I found part-time office work at just above minimum wage. Meantime, I woke up at four in the morning and worked on a novel about a lonely, unhappy Zimbabwean housewife whose husband ignores her and never laughs at her jokes until she runs off with an aid worker woman and opens a florist called the Placid Lily. Charlie looked for a job—but not just any job. He wanted to earn a *real* wage, he said. I said I thought all wages were real; what was surreal, I told him, was the cost of everything here.

Then Charlie came home one day and announced that he was going to be an estate agent in Jackson. To begin with, I didn't understand what he was telling me. And then when I did, I reacted poorly. I burst into tears and said it would kill his soul to sell houses here and to develop land. This, after all, was the earth he loved above all else: this was where he had planted himself as a seventeen-year-old; these rivers had taught him to read water; these were the snow-peaked mountains he had dreamed of on hot nights in Zambia. Charlie got angry and asked me if I had any better ideas. I said I had

dozens: we could move back to southern Africa and live in a
hut; we could move into a teepee and wait for one of my books
to get published; we could sell our bodies to science. I said
there had to be something that Charlie could do that didn't
involve the murder of his spirit.

It took Charlie more than a year to sell his first property.
In the course of those long, worrying months, he was tired all
the time and felt nonspecifically unwell. Eventually he was
diagnosed with having profound environmental allergies:
sagebrush, aspen, grasses, dust. Charlie's body had turned his
treasured, chosen world against him. I took books out of the
library and read everything I could find on allergies and
autoimmune disorders. "You're fighting against yourself," I
told Charlie. "You need to find work that fulfills you." But
bills piled up faster than I could imagine our way back to a
simpler life; a life in which our means exceeded our wants; a
life in which we could explore what it was that we were born
to do, rather than what we needed to do.

Feeling complicit in Charlie's fatigue and ill health, I
made myself busier than ever. I was still working three days a
week, taking care of Sarah on my days off, cooking, cleaning,
and waking up early every morning to write. I had moved on
to a new novel, the first one unsurprisingly having been
rejected by publishing houses everywhere. Then my second
novel got unsurprisingly rejected too. It seemed to me, our
safe, sane American lives weren't any easier than our crazy,
diseased African ones. Charlie talked about the way things
used to be when he lived here in the seventies and eighties. I
invited his friends over and tried to recast his nostalgia in the
present tense. But it wasn't ever going to be enough; I couldn't
rewind the clock back to those happier, simpler times. I suffered from bouts of depression and I missed Zambia.

But I was losing much of what had made me southern

African; our toughness, our humor, our hardiness—these didn't translate easily in a culture that had made comfort the primary goal, and challenging that comfort something we did on weekends, for fun in the mountains, on the ends of ropes, or on bikes and horses. Also, identity is easily corruptible. As soon as we mistake our ease for our security, our conveniences for our human rights, our luxuries for our entitlements, we aren't culturally distinct anymore. Then we're part of someone else's corporate plan, we're a predictable, fulfilled expectation; we're a black dot on a bottom line. Retaining culture takes effort and persistence and discipline. It's a commitment, not a flag. You can't just pull it out and wave it about when it's convenient.

At last Charlie had some real estate deals—the sound of nail guns echoed in frenetic new subdivisions in the forests all around us—and suddenly there was some extra cash around. I felt guiltily relieved. I no longer had to add up each item in my grocery cart to make sure I wouldn't go over our modest budget. We sold our house in Idaho and moved to Jackson. But Charlie didn't seem happier—if anything I was even more aware of the multiple ways I was failing to be the person he expected me to be.

"What do you want from me?" I'd ask.

"What do you want from *me*?" he would echo.

Then sometimes on a summer day Charlie would announce time off from work and he would take Sarah and me down the scenic section of the Snake River, or we would hike up in the mountains, or kayak into a remote campground in Yellowstone. In those sunstruck hours, Charlie would recall how he had been riotously happy near here fifteen years or a decade ago, how he had thrown famously raucous parties in those days, how he had been soul-connected to this land back then. But he said it as if that experience was now an unreachable fantasy, as if the past were a foreign land and the present was a regrettable chore. I understood then that no matter what we did, we could never recapture those hallowed times. The best we could aim for were weeks or months of grinding slog, with these brief intervals of relief as compensation. Unbridled joy was not a realistic—or necessarily worthwhile and commendable—goal.

I got pregnant again, and in early March 1997, Mum flew over for the delivery, arriving in the same spring blizzard that pressure-dropped the baby into my pelvis. Labor came like a train shunting back and forth over the same piece of railway track. Charlie sat by the television nursing a swollen foot brought on by an attack of gout, while I screamed and screamed. Nothing would budge. Mum pronounced herself impressed and shocked all in the same sentence. "It's all very nice and shiny in this hospital," she said. "Lovely views of the mountains, and they do seem to like their appliances and beeping things, but where are all the nurses and helpful people? There are no helpful people here."

Nine hours of screaming and still the baby was no closer to being born, and I was becoming overwrought with pain and with the terror of the next contraction. "For God's sake," Mum said at last. She hauled me out of the bed and marched me down the empty corridors. "A walk will do you good," she said as I continued howling in protests of awful agony. "Oh, this is inhuman," Mum muttered. "We'll all go deaf." She elbowed her way into an empty bathroom and filled the tub. "See if you can get in there," she said. "Honestly, how hard can it be to have some Epsom salts on hand?"

Much later, Mum found a nurse and insisted the doctor be summoned. "You can't just leave us like this," she pointed out. "It's been going on all day. Knock her out at least." Then she took the nurse outside and I don't know what else she said, but there was suddenly a small cluster of nurses around my bed, and Charlie hobbled down to the nurses' station to wait for the doctor, and then the baby started to come, although his head was far too large for the space allowed, and by the time he arrived he was all limp with exhaustion and needed to be taken from me into the bright gadgetry of an incubator in another room. "He'll be all right," Mum said. "Babies are as tough as cockroaches, really." Then she peered unhopefully under the sheets. "Although you won't be getting back in the saddle anytime soon."

I quit my menial office job to take care of the children. I cooked and cleaned and I still woke up at four in the morning to write. My third novel was rejected, as was a fourth and a fifth. But Charlie was selling more land and more houses. We commissioned an architect to design a mountain home for us, with hardwood floors and cherry cabinets. We bought nicer furniture, newer cars, a Labrador puppy. To pay for it all, Charlie went into the office earlier and returned home later; he brought back piles of paperwork and sat late into the night worrying numbers into columns.

There didn't seem to be any way for me to repay Charlie for all the work he was doing to make our material lives possible. I wrote, and raised the children, and kept house, and almost every evening I welcomed Charlie home with painstakingly prepared meals, wine, and overeager chatter that too often became a list of demands. I needed Charlie to bring back with him from the world beyond our children and the housework news and ideas and conversation. He didn't have to slay dragons, but a few shiny scales from the fight would have been diverting. "Oh, just make something up if it was a boring day," I implored. But Charlie complained of ever-increasing exhaustion. He grew more silent and withdrawn. Sometimes I got drunk and railed, "You seem so unhappy.

What are we doing this all for?" Charlie would look embarrassed on my behalf and in the mornings I would wake up dry-mouthed and repentant.

Growing up, I could measure my father's stress by the length of the cigarette ash on the veranda in the morning where I found him at dawn after those uneasy nights, hands hovering over a game of solitaire, a cigarette shelved into a groove on his lower lip, a cup of tea at his elbow. "Top of the morning, Chookies," he'd say. "Sleep okay?" And then I knew the yields weren't matching up to expectations, or the price of fuel and fertilizer had just surged, or the government had suddenly decided to raise the minimum wage by fifty percent. "Well, I tried worrying about it all night," he said, slapping cards down on the coffee table. "And it didn't change a bloody thing. You'd think I'd have learned by now, wouldn't you?"

Years later, I stumbled in an accidental way on some of the works of the desert mothers and fathers, the ascetic, hermitic holy people who lived in the deserts of Egypt starting around the third century AD. I liked their names to begin with: Sarah of the Desert, Paul the Simple, John the Eunuch. And then I liked their teachings: know who you are; know where you are; know what is happening. Surrender anyway. One of the instructions of peace given by the desert father Moses seemed to me to trump all else: "The monk must die to everything before leaving the body, in order not to harm anyone."[8]

But I think really to live with even a small degree of that deliberately careless wisdom requires the precondition of fearlessness, trust in oneself, and belief in one's own personal culture. My father had taught me one kind of fearlessness and

---

8. Benedicta Ward, trans., *The Sayings of the Desert Fathers: The Alphabetical Collection* (Kalamazoo, MI: Liturgical Press, 1984).

trust. He had taught me how to get from one end of a bit of land to the other; he had taught me endurance; he had shown me what an unrestrained life looked like. But a more cautious life—one without geographical markers, a life of bills and bank statements—was foreign to me, and I could not catch up to it. Work, in some unexplained, inexplicable way, seemed to be the key to such a cautious life. Work, work, work, as if it were the modern equivalent of decades in the desert.

I took another menial part-time office job, and continued to get up at four in the morning to write. My sixth, seventh, and eighth novels were rejected. I submitted a ninth novel. My agent didn't even bother to shop it around; instead she wrote back to me saying that she felt it was a waste of my time to continue writing, and a waste of her time to represent me. "You may have some talent," she offered cautiously. "But you don't have a story."

So with nothing left to lose, I wrote the truth. I wrote about growing up in Rhodesia during the war, about the deaths of three of my siblings, about my crazy-wonderful parents. Into those pages went all my loneliness of my new life, all my love for the land that had raised me, all the pain of having left it. The pages seemed different from what I had written before—nonfiction instead of fiction, obviously—but also *of* me, eccentric, mordant, irreverent. I found a new agent and she sold it within a few days to publishers in New York and Europe. Suddenly I had a public voice and another full, distinct life from the one I had shared with Charlie. For the first time since falling in love with him, I could imagine myself as a separate being from him. And because of that, our arguments became more damaging; there would be tears, rages, threats, and afterward neither of us would sleep.

In the next couple of years, I traveled back to southern Africa and wrote a troubling book about soldiers from the war I had grown up in. Charlie grew tired of the way I seemed to need to peel back the scabs on old wounds and explore the painful bloody parts of my vicious history. I told him I was compelled to dig into the world in this way. He said it was unnatural and unhealthy and made of me a terrifying wife. I said he would do well to explore his own demons and sadness and that I could stand for him to get a little more terrifying.

"I'm perfectly fine," he said.

"Then why don't you laugh at my jokes?" I asked, half joking even as I said it.

"Because your jokes aren't funny. They're unkind."

I fell in love—or imagined myself to have fallen in love—with a backcountry explorer who lived two and a half thousand miles away. I felt unrestrainedly, disturbingly hungry for the sort of scant attention he could offer. I waited until we were driving, the car holding us in unambiguous confining coupledom, before I told Charlie, "I think our marriage is in trouble." And then I said that I was at least tempted by the idea of falling in love with someone else. Charlie stared through the windshield, tight-lipped, silent. Miles clocked by. I said, "Please say something."

He said, "You're married. You're my wife."

I said, "I know." I looked out the window and watched the way the farmland slumped and rose in ripped contours along here. Every spring when the farmers plowed these fields, topsoil picked up in the wind and blew west, sometimes in such a thick cloud that the road was closed for hours or days at a time. "This can't go on," I said.

"No," Charlie agreed.

After that, he started to read my e-mails, check the phone records for unfamiliar numbers, and he started to see affairs where there were none. He would confront me. There would be more fights and tears. I said, "Don't check up on me.

Check in with me." I thumped my chest and burst into tears. "I'm right here, for God's sake." But I wasn't. Neither of us was there. We were between mother ships, struggling to stay buoyed. The signal flag Kilo is a rectangle of yellow next to a rectangle of blue. It means, "I wish to communicate with you."

We separated—a trial separation we said, as if to lessen the blow. We told the kids that nothing would change which, looking back, was not only a lie, but also a terrible threat. The whole point of the separation was that everything needed to change. We couldn't carry on in the stagnant-feeling deadlock of our relationship without putting ourselves into a kind of living death. I rented a one-room cabin in a friend's back garden, Charlie kept the house, and he continued to keep track of the finances and pay the bills. I felt as if I had left home as a sort of silly, unsustainable experiment, more like a teenager practicing living alone than a woman in charge of her destiny.

After six months we crashed back toward one another, unable to tolerate the unaccustomed anxiety of ourselves alone and the children's bewildered sorrow. And perhaps we remained desperate to heal not only the old wounds we carried from our own families and histories but also the fresher wounds we had made in one another. We decided to stay married. And once again I convinced myself that a deep, nurturing connection coupled with the vigorous defense of each other's freedom was a false expectation, something that happened so rarely between two people that it was a completely unrealistic goal. It was better, I decided, to have the sort of marriage the bedrock of which was a complicit agreement to say nothing of real substance to one another.

We shared a bed, a bathroom, a closet, our meals, and the gift of our children. We phoned one another through the day and had the sort of mundane exchanges overheard in public places everywhere. Sometimes, we reached reflexively for one another in the middle of the night. But in every real way, we steered assiduously away from one another.

Charlie continued to sell real estate, manage our finances, and plan adventures abroad. To keep himself in adrenaline, he took up polo again, playing in the summers at the little club in Jackson with patrons, mostly from Texas. He bought four ponies and an old four-horse trailer and his Wednesdays and Saturdays were taken up with chukkas. It was a far cry from Prince Charles and Nacho Figueras, but it was a big step up from the dust-gusted pitches of Lusaka, and even though Charlie's was a mismatched string—ranging from Big Boy, a towering thoroughbred of over sixteen hands, to a tough little Argentinean criollo—the whole idea of polo with its flashy, champagne-and-cigar and private-plane implications didn't seem to fit with Charlie's continuing concerns about our never-enough bank accounts.

Polo seemed a grand, extravagant, incongruent gesture that was not of a piece with how Charlie did anything else. He had budgets and constraints and columns of numbers and a preoccupation about those columns of numbers that became the weather system of our home, building and swirling regardless of how much we worked or played or loved. Sometimes Charlie talked about retiring early—he would travel the world, fishing and skiing and running rivers, he said— but I didn't see where I could ever fit in with that plan. For one thing, I always wanted to write, and I couldn't imagine a time when I would want to stop. For another thing, I couldn't see the point of living a piecemeal, disparate, unfulfilling life now with the expectation of something glorious to come. It was the biblical promise of a future reward for current slog writ in material, pointless, selfish miniature.

The grand, extravagant, incongruent gesture was much

more my territory: it was of a piece with the way my parents had raised us and done everything else. On the rare occasions we had money, my father slammed his fist on the bar. "Round's on me!" And when money ran out, conspicuous, exaggerated destitution was part of our family vaudeville act. For example, during the long unhelpful stretch when the ancient Peugeot 403 took to stalling and we couldn't afford the spare part to fix this problem, Vanessa and I had to jump out at traffic lights in Umtali and push the car through the intersections when the lights changed to green. "Come on girls, don't just stand there!" Dad yelled while Mum wept with laughter in the passenger seat. "Put some vim into it."

For a while, in that same Peugeot, it was possible to watch the road whip by as we drove, dust billowing up into the backseat in a reddish film until Mum put bits of cardboard down where the floorboards had rusted through. She painted sunsets, giraffes, and flowers on the cardboard, and signed her name in the corners with a flourish. "Like the Sistine Chapel, only not the ceiling," she said. "Although I wouldn't stand on it if I were you, or you'll plop right out." Which served to prove to me from an early age that imminent danger and innovative beauty were often closely linked.

When Mum and Dad finally did get their hands on a stack of money from the sale of the English farm on which I had been born—"Bloody stockbroker paid a fortune for a barn and a soggy field," Dad said in incredulous delight—we lived like tycoons for a time. "Well, there's no guarantee we'll be around to enjoy it later," Dad said. "And anyway, who wants to retire and die of bloody boredom?" Money was put aside for Vanessa and me to be educated overseas—Vanessa to finishing school and art college, me to university. Dad bought an old diesel Mercedes-Benz, spray-painted a remaindered peach. "The nipple-pink baby," he called it. Then he invested in some horses off Zimbabwe's racetracks—"Pukka things, these," Dad promised. "Four legs, the lot"—so we could play polo and Mum could show jump. "Marvelous way to shake up the liver," Dad said. And finally he took Mum on a once-in-a-lifetime holiday to New York, the West Indies, and England.

After a while, Vanessa and I left home, the money dried up, and my parents were back to starvation rations. "We seem to have taken another inadvertent vow of poverty," Dad said. But they kept the horses, and the Benz, and they held on to the memories of the large times. To this day, Dad recalls the name of the taxi driver who took them under his wing and showed them around Montserrat. "Winthrop," he says. And then he sings in his botched West Indian accent, "Goat water, goat water, good for ya' daughter." And Mum still recounts how people in New York mistook Dad for Crocodile Dundee. "That wonderful film had just come out, and of course Americans are very impressed with anyone who can wrestle alligators or play with snakes." But she never fails to act as if it is my personal fault that the difference between an Australian drawl and my father's impeccable English enunciation was lost on an entire nation. "Dad's sunburn must have confused them," she says regretfully. "I suppose they expect all their Englishmen to be pink."

|||||||||||

Charlie and I had another baby. And for over a year, while I breast-fed her, a familiar tranquility washed over me. I was more or less permanently contented and mildly exhausted, my blood awash with the mellowing agents of oxytocin and prolactin. For those long blissed-out months, I spent my days moving through the rhythm of the baby's needs: her baths, her feedings, walks by the river. I cooked, I cleaned, I wrote, and at night I fell asleep with Cecily pressed against my skin, her breath innocent with the charmed, milky scents of babyhood.

"If they could bottle these hormones and make them into pills, my marriage would last forever," I told a friend.

"They do," she said. "Valium, Prozac, Xanax."

I laughed. "If I ever have to be tranquilized to stay in my marriage, it's really over."

At fourteen months, the baby grew out of breast-feeding and I took an assignment following pilgrim Mexican cowboys in Guanajuato, then I signed a contract to write a book about the effects of a natural-gas boom on a small cowboy town in southwestern Wyoming. There was talk, and increasing evidence, of air and water going bad where hydrofracturing was occurring. The safety practices of the drilling and oil companies were blatantly shoddy and the willful carelessness of Wyoming's legislators seemed directly linked to their obeisance to the industry.

Now I worked hard not out of fear but out of outrage. I wrote letters to editors of local newspapers and op-eds for national publications, I went to Cheyenne to testify in front of the Wyoming House Judiciary Committee, I attended meetings about declining air quality and unsatisfactory working conditions. I lodged complaints. I knew my noise was unlikely to change anything, but I didn't feel it was responsible of me to shut up now, of all times.

Then I helped organize a tiny protest right on the oil patch of the Upper Green River Valley: a few cowboys, ranchers, hunters, and residents from the area, a local rancher's son driving a tractor, a few friends who didn't particularly care about the issue but wanted to show their support of my cause, the way we all gave money to one another's favorite local charity at Christmas. Charlie joined me and brought the horses and the children. Mum and Dad were visiting and came along too.

"Peace protest," Dad said doubtfully. "You know I'm deadly allergic to hippies." But there were no hippies, only a rather inadvertent Burmese Buddhist monk in orange robes whose presence was more than offset by the very intentional cop who had come to monitor the event. Mum's eyes lit up when she saw a man in uniform. "Oh," she said. "What fun. A bulletproof vest *and* a holster. Very satisfactory." I steered her toward a difficult horse.

Dad clamped his pipe in his mouth, held his hands behind his back, and performed what amounted to a field inspection of the cop's weaponry, stalking circles around the rig, puffing fragrant clouds of tobacco in his wake. Then, when he had satisfied himself that he had never seen so much firepower in the possession of one man in his life, he removed his pipe and addressed the cop in tones of regretful apology. "Look, I'm terribly sorry," he said. "We've been trying to shut her up for forty years ourselves. Maybe a dart gun would do the job?"

Photographs of Charlie and me from around this time show us seeming-happy: I was fulfilled by my work, and Charlie was doing well in his; we were both rewarded by parenthood. Yet no matter how committed I was to our unit—this beautiful family I had been complicit in creating—I remained unsettled. I felt as if we were living half a lie, or perhaps the greater part of a lie. "There is a sense of discrepancy between what we do and what we are, between appearance and reality, that is the motive force that impels us to seek unity," Justus George Lawler wrote in an essay entitled "The Two Great Sadnesses."

But instead of either of us slowing down to address my misgivings, we plowed on, out of habit, out of expediency, out of fear, and out of denial. Once, elbow deep in bubbles at the children's bath time, I suddenly found myself praying in a kind of panic that nothing would ever change. "It never has to get better than this," I remember thinking. "We can do this forever. Just like this." But the mere fact of my thinking it was a kind of acknowledgment that this couldn't last, neither the equitable moment of our marriage nor the shaky American dream in which it had been conceived.

Because seen in a certain light—the flat, hot light of a summer afternoon, for example—that promising dream has a depressing, thrill-ride quality about it, hurdy-gurdy with brightness, loud and distracting. And however much fun people seem to be having, however endless the music and gaiety seem, soon the ride will be over and then there are the carnies all jittery with meth, and there is the dust and the heat and the desolation. The truth is the American dream had never been an innocent, harmless way to make a living. "It's incredible," Dad kept saying when he came to visit. "Who's paying for all this lot?" Then I saw him make mental calculations. "Well, bloody nearly free petrol helps, doesn't it?"

I remember exactly where I was and what I was doing when Charlie knew that our good, ordinary, sane lives had proved to be risky, expensive, untruthful gambles. It was the summer of 2008: gas prices had just peaked at their highest level in history, and there seemed to be no end to what was beginning to look like a war on Wyoming's open spaces. Drilling rigs were going up near tributaries of the Colorado River; wildlife roadkill collected off the oil patch was stacked next to Highway 191 and reached the length of a football field and three animals deep. I was up in my office, writing. Charlie came upstairs—which he hardly ever did—and said, "The real estate market has crashed." A long silence settled into the tiny space.

"Good," I said at last.

Charlie looked at me, like I had no idea what I had just said. He said, "Things are going to get tough for a long time."

"Good," I said again. I thought about the pile of papers next to me: the OSHA reports of dead natural-gas rig workers; the accumulation of evidence of contaminated groundwater near natural-gas wells in the state; the plummeting air quality in sparsely populated mountain communities; the reports of melting glaciers in the Wind River Range; evidence of crashing whitebark pine tree populations; the ways in which this boom was never sustainable, not for the communities that hosted it, nor for the wildlife populations that bore its most immediate and brutal brunt, nor for the state or ourselves and our children. I thought of the wars we were in over power and resources, the ways in which Wyoming children were being recruited straight out of school—into the armed forces and onto the rigs—to feed our appetite for cheap energy. But it was as if morality had been turned on its head by the promise of corporate profits—it was our moral imperative, it seemed, to make money now. It was morally questionable to call for caution, restraint, and breathable air. It was an outrage to ask about tomorrow.

Charlie said, "I'll have to sell the polo ponies."

I said, "Well, they should be worth a bit more than our souls were."

There was a long, silent standoff. Then Charlie said, "I am a decent, good person, Bo."

"I know," I said. "I'm sorry." I pushed away from my desk and folded myself into his arms. "I'm sorry," I said. "I didn't mean it."

In the following months, Charlie showed me columns of figures representing our situation, and even with my limited financial literacy I could see how they marched away from each other impossibly. There didn't seem to be a way to work our way out of our unwise investments, out of our unreasonable cost of living, out of our belief that the economy could keep on growing and growing. Charlie became ever more silent and worried. I worried too.

Over the next two years, Charlie's work dried up, and in an effort to keep us afloat, I accepted every magazine assignment I was offered, I took every speaking engagement possible, I wrote proposals and book reviews and taught workshops and said yes, yes, yes. But every check I brought home and delivered to Charlie only seemed to make him more desolate. "It's not enough," he said. So I slept less and wrote more. Deadlines touched tails with deadlines.

Then I went to Dallas and gave the talk that finally made me acknowledge that I wasn't African anymore, not especially. And two weeks later, when I lay in bed coughing and fevered, I believed I could remember the woman who had made me sick, because however hard we work to isolate ourselves from one another and to shore ourselves up against discomfort, we are not immune from one another. There is no way to shut the doors against our contagions, to ward off the effects of our collective stupidity and greed and violence. Those who have an understanding of the mhondoro ceremony were correct when they told me that all beings in a community are connected, that the madness of one is the madness of everyone, that there is no separation of minds and bodies between people. It was true when they said the wickedness and carelessness and avarice of one would bring pestilence on the whole. Your sickness is mine. My sickness is yours.

Our houses were falling, falling, fallen.

What Charlie and I did was not uncommon. We had taken ourselves hostage, plowed ourselves under with debt, and then battled to pay for our freedom. Still, neither of us understood our lives in that way. Even less did we figure out that we were compelled toward one another not just because of some inexplicable passion, but also because we must have recognized in one another wounds of unresolved and repeating tragedy. We had glommed on to one another in happy unconscious relief, as if the inherited and accumulated wounds in each of us had recognized their matches, their balms, and their ends. But neither of us had been able to get beyond ourselves to reach the other, and perhaps we'd never had the will to try.

I have heard it said there are at least two ways of living, at least two levels of awareness. One is the obvious way: the groceries and bank accounts and routines that allow life, as we know it, to churn along in its solid-seeming myth of continuity. The other is the hidden way: the soul-searching and epiphanies and insights that allow soul, or what we suppose of it, to manifest and direct us. To have one without the other is to live dangerously and blindly and violently. But how few of us even know the language of the other way of life; how few of us ever surrender, even briefly, to the sacred terror and beauty of the other way.

Charlie and I may have initially connected over a sacred terror and beauty, but we had become ensnared in accounts, in transactions and a kind of economic allegiance to one another. It was like we had made a tiny most-favored-nation treaty with one another, but we were separated by a border fence that didn't allow for breaches of security: I couldn't break through Charlie's silence; he could not penetrate my noise. It was a more or less peaceful standoff on which our securities, welfares, and identities depended. But it wasn't a partnership, it was a power struggle, and like all power struggles it wasn't sustainable.

FORTUNE TELLER FISH

In the end, at least in *this* end, the world beyond me and the world that was inside me could no longer exist in the same place and I broke. Or at least the way in which I had been functioning as wife and mother broke. Perhaps that is the definition of madness, but madness, if that is what it was, didn't happen the way I imagined it would. Witnessing madness, I had always assumed it came with a snapping sound, followed by some kind of definite, momentous impact. If I were to go mad, I assumed I would no longer be familiar to myself. People would pass me in the street and I'd be unknowable to them too. My children would veer from the very scent of me.

I knew this because on the several occasions that Mum went truly mad she stopped behaving in ways that were recognizable as her at all. It was as if her mind had been whisked away and the body we knew of as my mother's had been left in the possession of some other entity, which did not much care for it. This manifestation of my mother wasn't vain, or splendid, or capable. It did not bother with any of the usual biological needs: it drank to heroic excess, it refused to bathe or eat or exercise, it lost weight, it lost control of itself, and it went deaf to everyone and everything.

But that is not what happened to me when I went mad. I still felt a connection between my mind and body. And I never stopped caring about ordinary, sane things: I wanted normalcy for my children. I didn't want us to go broke. I ate right and exercised. And yet at the same time, I felt I was in the process of becoming two people—the person I had been, and the person I was becoming. I couldn't sleep, I'd lost my appetite, I had two glasses of wine every night and then poured a third even though I knew it was contributing to the sleeplessness and a general feeling of daily malaise. "Oh Al, it's probably just your midlife crisis," Vanessa said when I phoned her shortly after returning from Zambia. "Next thing, you'll grow a mustache and cry all the time."

"Don't be ridiculous," I said. "I'm far too young for that."

"All I'm saying is don't say I didn't tell you. And whatever you do, don't get a perm."

"What are you even talking about?"

Vanessa sighed, as if I had missed the key moment in a movie's plot. "Don't you know, people always do something drastic to their hair when they're having their midlife crisis?"

In the second week in October, Charlie called me from his safari in Zambia. I was in a hotel room in Minnesota. The disconnection between us could not have been more vivid if I had bought myself a one-way seat on a rocket to the moon and he had sunk himself to the bottom of the sea in a submarine. It didn't feel as if we were breathing the same air, speaking the same language, living in the same world.

"I was almost eaten by a lion last night," he said.

My hotel room overlooked a parking garage. Beyond that,

I could see the metallic thread of an interstate. It was night, but the city threw off a yellow glow like the light in a sick-room. I said, "Oh."

"Two of them. I was stalked. They followed me into camp." And then Charlie told me how he had been walking from his tent when his flashlight caught the reflection of the lions' eyes, or maybe he hadn't seen the spoor until morning, either way, at some point he noticed he had been followed. And perhaps there was more to the story than that, but none of it seemed to matter then because the fact of Charlie having been stalked by lions changed nothing. He sounded no more alive, or grateful, or excited for having been nearly dead. And his inability to get hurt by animals had long ago ceased to impress me.

What would have impressed me now was Charlie finding work that paid, Charlie asking me how I was, Charlie allow-ing me a full night's sleep, Charlie laughing at my jokes, Char-lie laughing at all. What would have impressed me was if he'd admitted that we were broken and needed to tear ourselves open and start again, from the ground. I wanted him to say we'd made dreary, intractable mistakes and now we needed to make the sort of mistakes that would jolt us awake and make us unstuck. I closed my eyes. "Look," I said. "It's really late here. I have to go to bed." I could hear Charlie's disappoint-ment, and I could feel my own. "I'm sorry," I said. We hung up, then I lay on the hotel bed fully clothed and counted the number of hours and airplane flights before I would be home with the children. "How do people do this?" I wondered.

For the first time in my life, I was conscious of this thought: I believed in what I was doing—in my children, in my work, in my reading—I just no longer believed in the per-son who was doing it. I had come to the Midwest to speak at an event that promoted literacy for Africa. I had spoken about how literacy saved lives; I had said how it was important to have the vocabulary for what was happening to you. I said that when there is tyranny and war and censorship, our ability to possess—to truly own and occupy—our own words might be all that's left of us. I said, "In Zimbabwean culture, it is taboo to name the genitals. So when rape is used as a weapon of political intimidation it is doubly silencing. Not only is there the act of violence, but there is also the prohibition against naming what has happened to you. You are not allowed to say 'vagina,' 'penis,' 'testicles.'"

I realized it wasn't the talk people wanted to hear, and although I couldn't blame them, I kept talking anyway. There is nothing feel-good about rape camps, about women being taken out of their villages by the score and assaulted along with their six-year-old, ten-year-old, thirteen-year-old daughters. But this is why literacy matters, I was saying. Words count. "Hear this," I said. "Women must be able to read the labels on medicine bottles after they contract HIV from the soldiers who have raped them. And they must be able to read their human rights, and they must be able to speak and write about the atrocities to their bodies and to the bodies of their daughters." And then I felt alarmed by a low-level cloud of disillusionment from the audience, so I stopped talking and stood in silence while they waited for me to say something uplifting.

Afterward, while I signed books for a trickle of readers, an elderly Zimbabwean man approached me and told me in a low, calm voice, "You are not a good daughter of Africa." He gestured to the room. "You said those words with my wife present. I am offended. Don't you know better?" I knew the man, or at least I knew his type. He was polite, educated, urbane, and unused to challenge, and he had some academic post at a small university where his eloquence and his beautiful manners overrode this benign brand of chauvinism.

"Don't you?" I asked. "When was the last time you were home? Have you not seen?" And suddenly there was a large and growing pool of silence around us, and everyone was embarrassed. The room was too hot—the building's thermostat apparently had been set for winter in spite of an unseasonably warm fall, and now no one could readjust it. Both the elderly Zimbabwean man and I were sweating. I let my shoulders sink. I said, "You're right. I am not a good daughter of Africa."

The truth is, I wasn't only not a good daughter of Africa, I was not a good daughter of anywhere, nor was I a good wife or a good mother. I was a woman on the brink of free fall, and it was hard to be a good, acceptable woman in any language or in any place when simultaneously contemplating becoming undone. For the first time, I was beginning to see that for a woman to speak her mind in any clear, unassailable, unapologetic way, she must first possess it.

||||||||||

When he came back from not being eaten by a lion in Zambia, Charlie and I put the house on the market. Then all through the winter and into the early spring of 2011, we acted as if we could still be a couple and as if we could still hold together a family. We acted as if we were more than the home we had built, as if we were the duo that could survive the loss of our house, and as if there was reason for the children to believe that things would always be okay. But each night Charlie and I faced one another as if we were drained adversaries, admonishing one another to get up one more time, to keep fighting.

In April I flew to New York to work further on the frustratingly out-of-reach screenplay with a director who had half a dozen other ideas in the fire. In the end, as much as I wrote draft after draft, the screenplay didn't happen, but other things did in that intimate, intoxicating city. For one thing, my already chronic insomnia crashed up against the relentless rush of noise outside my window, and meant that I was now utterly without sleep. For another thing, someone who had been until then a friend suddenly seemed to turn sideways and the light shifted on him differently and I fell into him, as if into the rainbow cast by a prism.

As affairs go, it was short but catastrophically intense, more like a physical accident than anything amorous, as if I'd slipped my own moorings completely and was cast adrift in someone else's shipping lane. "Everyone needs a place," wrote the poet Richard Siken. "It shouldn't be inside of someone else." I left his apartment one morning—a narrow series of three cramped rooms in which I already felt too untidy and too noisy, too much as if I was off course—and went back to the place I had been staying and was suddenly violently sick. Later, dizzy with the implications of the affair and over-whelmed by the ways in which it is possible to betray oneself and the people to whom one is supposed to be undyingly loyal, I took myself to the Guggenheim Museum, hopeful that the tranquility of a muffled public space would soothe me, and allow space and quiet.

Off the main rotunda, I found a series of darkened rooms featuring video installations of eleven different artists. A sign explained, "Found in Translation." There were places to sit, but there was nowhere to rest until I found a bench in front of what looked like home-movie footage of a homely elderly woman with a pudding-bowl haircut. She was reciting Bertolt Brecht. "And I always thought: the very simplest words must be enough. When I say what things are like / Everyone's heart must be torn to shreds. That you'll go down if you don't stand up for yourself— / Surely you see that." I sat and waited for the piece of footage to replay, and then I waited to hear it again, and again, and again.

After that I flew home to Charlie and asked for a divorce.

"We can't," he said. "We can't afford to."

"We can't afford not to," I said.

Charlie shook his head. "You don't understand. The timing could not be worse."

I stared at him for a long time, wondering if there was something worse that he wasn't telling me. Worse than the fact that the house could not sell for what we needed to meet the debt we had on it, worse than the fact that I was having an affair, worse than the unbearable loneliness of being in this marriage. I said, "Don't you think you'd be better without me?"

Charlie said, "We can't get a divorce now."

I said, "I mean, don't you feel as if we've done the best we can?"

Charlie said, "This can't end now. We'll go completely broke. We have to stick it out."

But to me, it was like the end of the dry season in southern Africa, when the sun has swallowed all the obvious water— the lakes and rivers and streams—and somewhere else, as if rumored, there exists the promise of rain. Every year, animals stir toward that promise however dangerous and unlikely-seeming, however instinctive and potentially unfounded. The Germans have a word for this, *Zugunruhe*, meaning "migration restlessness" or "the stirring before moving." From the wrong perspective, it would be easy to mistake *Zugunruhe* for something destructive, mad even. Who in their right mind travels hundreds of miles in the dry season, when rain is nothing more than an idea? Why not hunker down and wait to see if things improve? Who goes anywhere on empty?

|||||||||||

May in the Rockies is a time of collision, winter crashing against summer. The Snake River becomes a pale, boiling green torrent with glacial melt. Elk herds begin dispersing out of their man-made winter feed-grounds where they have been fed alfalfa for the season, and revert wild in the cottonwood forests. Ski bums pack up their gear and make for the beach. Snowbirds flee southern heat and begin arriving at their second homes. The off-season is about to turn on.

One Wednesday in the middle of this colliding time of year, in the middle of my usual biweekly exercise class, I suddenly found myself unable to keep track of where I ended and the gym's mirrors began. Just as suddenly I felt as if I could no longer move my appendages, as if I could make only grand flopping gestures like one of those red plastic Fortune Teller Miracle Fish. Curls Up Entirely—Passionate. Turns Over—False. Motionless—Dead One.

The class finished, and I faltered out into the parking lot. For a while I sat in my car waiting for myself to return from wherever I had gone. Then I phoned Charlie. "I'm so sorry. I think I am having some sort of breakdown," I said. I closed my eyes and thought of the children getting out of school about now. I thought about bus stops and dinner and laundry. "I probably shouldn't drive," I said.

It was as if Charlie had been waiting a decade for that phone call. He arrived in minutes, hurried me into his car, and drove me to his doctor's office. "You'll be okay," he kept saying.

"Thanks," I said. Now that someone else was taking my collapse, or whatever it was, so seriously, I didn't think I was necessarily suffering an emergency, although I knew I was in the throes of at least a smallish crisis. "I'm probably just overtired," I said. But then I noticed the meadows by the side of the road weren't keeping up with the speed at which we were driving. Or perhaps it was my brain, going too fast.

I'd always known my mind could hop logic and bypass tedious necessities. I was good at instinctively knowing when to dive for cover, and when to leap to my feet. I wasn't afraid of doing things other people would have thought crazy, illogical, or risky. Of course, I realized that I simply had a higher than usual tolerance for eccentricity, but I also hoped I would know when I had crossed into madness. When I crossed into madness, I trusted it wouldn't be my usual brand of inspiration. "A queer, divine dissatisfaction," as Martha Graham would have had it. "A blessed unrest that keeps us marching and makes us more alive than others." When I finally and profoundly slipped my mental moorings, I believed it would manifest as an accursed wreck with me crumpled and undone at its center.

Charlie helped me into the examination room and stayed with me while I told his doctor what was happening: I hadn't slept for some time, I was in some kind of mild existential extremis, I'd had an affair, I'd been drinking too much, I felt as if I was leaving my body, I thought my brain might be going a little quickly. The doctor didn't look at me much. He stared at his computer screen and scrolled through a list of questions. Did I have a family history of mental illness and alcoholism? Did I sometimes feel hopeless and despairing? Had I ever had thoughts of suicide?

"Who doesn't? Who hasn't?" I said.

The doctor offered me a couple of choices. "You're either a sociopath, or you have bipolar disorder."

"Really?" I said. "Those are my only choices?"

The doctor was grave. "Look," he said. "Normal people don't lie, or think about suicide, or have affairs."

I wanted to say, "I think normal people who are unhappily married might do all three in a single day." Instead I said, "Okay then, I'll go with the bipolar."

Charlie drove me home. I had a hot bath and swallowed some pills as directed. Then I got into bed and suddenly a profound exhaustion overcame me, as if my arteries had been filled with lead. I tried to read the small print on the pharmacy printout. "Listen to this. Fainting, dizziness, fatal inability to swallow," I said. "Good God, what's in these things?"

"They have to say that," Charlie reassured me. "It always sounds bad when you read the side effects."

"Am I drooling yet?"

Charlie phoned my closest friends and assured them I was in good hands, I would be fine now, I was on the drugs I needed. But I didn't feel fine. My tongue was the size and consistency of a mattress. Words floated to the top of my brain and reassembled into gibberish before a sentence could form. I couldn't make my eyes focus on words anymore. Then I passed out and slept for eighteen hours without moving. When I woke up the next morning, I found a line from a U2 song had floated into my head and eddied out there. The words looped over and over. I felt a little hungover—as if I'd taken a sleeping pill with wine on top of jet lag—but also as if everything in me was back in place, like iron filings realigned on a magnet. "Maybe all I needed was a decent night's sleep," I said.

On such little evidence, I wasn't convinced I was completely sane. But I was absolutely certain I didn't have the luxury to lie around in a tranquilized state. From what Charlie had kept telling me in the past months and weeks, we weren't going to get any less in debt, the house wasn't going to get any less repossessed, something had to be done. I got out of bed and pulled on my clothes. "Time to shake a leg," I said. But Charlie didn't smile at my father's old instruction. I said, "We're going to be okay. It's going to be okay, right?"

But I had no idea what okay might look like, because for reasons that had long ago trickled out of my grasp, I had never fully, or even partially understood whole parts of our life. Beyond the certainty that we were in dire straits, financially, I wasn't sure exactly what that meant. I didn't know how or when our taxes were due, or even how we could still owe taxes in our current financial state. I didn't know what a second mortgage was, or why we had one. I couldn't imagine the figures Charlie told me. How did people go about getting so powerfully in debt to begin with?

It wasn't at all obvious. True, we had a house, a cabin, some investments, but it turned out we didn't own any of the roofs over our heads, the bank did. We had three horses on some pasture in Idaho, those were ours, but Charlie said we'd have to sell them too, not because they were worth anything, but because we could no longer afford to feed them, we couldn't pay the vet for their annual checkups. We didn't have fancy cars or expensive art. I owned no good jewelry, nor did I desire it. Neither of us had much in the way of an extravagant wardrobe. We didn't eat out often, or go on luxurious vacations although in retrospect we had clearly traveled more than we could afford. Sometimes Charlie frowned at my grocery bills—did I need to buy organic food? he wanted to know—and I disliked his habit of buying three cheap things instead of one decent thing. But I didn't see how we could have spent ourselves into such a dead end.

"How did this happen?" I asked.

Charlie was defensive. "I've tried to explain. You won't listen."

My brain spun. "It's not that I won't listen. It's that I can't understand what you're saying."

Charlie had taken control of the money side of my business from the very start. When checks arrived from my agents, they went straight to him. I didn't have a credit card in my own name; there was nothing under my own Social Security number. When I thought about it, in all ways except for putting my name to the words I wrote, I didn't even own Alexandra Fuller. She had become a Ross—she had taken Charlie's name, his nationality, his advice. It was as if we had taken laws from a century before and folded them into our modern lives. "A man and wife are one person in law; the wife loses all her rights as a single woman and her existence is entirely absorbed into that of her husband." "A wife's chattels real become her husband's by some act to appropriate them." "Money earned by a woman belongs absolutely to her husband."[9]

It wasn't as if Charlie was a misogynist, or old-fashioned, or malicious. He was none of those things. For the most part, he was gentle and current and kind. I had been so subsumed by Charlie and by his identity, not on purpose or through any deliberate intent, but because we had fallen into those roles through necessity and expediency and now we were so far into them that getting out felt like it would take an act of God. "Until you make the unconscious conscious," Carl Jung said, "it will direct your life and you will call it fate."

---

9. Barbara Leigh Smith Bodichon, *A Brief Summary in Plain Language of the Most Important Laws Concerning Women; Together with a Few Observations Thereon* (1854).

FALLING

A month later, in less time than it takes to read these words, everything changed forever. That's what they say, of course. In the blink of the eye, in a single heartbeat, in one distracted moment, all the life we've got mapped out—however messy and uncertain—becomes certainly uncertain. And that's not divorce, which is like a pot sitting forever on the stove suddenly coming to the boil. Nor is it children leaving home, the way they grow up and then for the last time go down the end of the driveway and disappear into their own lives. It's not even the phone call from Vanessa saying Dad will be dead in a week. Those events still allow for denial and pretense, as if time is an open door between two rooms and we can still choose between now and the period in which we want to stay. But the blink, the heartbeat, the moment—that is the thing from which there is no coming back, that is the thing beyond which there is no reminiscing.

For months after the accident, this was the image that came to me when I closed my eyes for any length of time: the last of Charlie's polo ponies, Big Boy, was upside down and he appeared winded or wounded or both. His legs batted the air; his great black hooves sliced first the sky, then the sagebrush. His neck lunged sideways and I could see his eyes rolling white. I could see the saddle with Charlie's step-grandfather's name across the back of its seat appearing and disappearing like code for something imperative: CORSE, CORSE, CORSE.

Underneath the horse, still improbably in the saddle, I could see Charlie. Mostly, I could see his agonized face, his straining neck. The rest of his body—legs, torso, chest—was covered and in the process of being crushed. Mint-colored dust, powdered sage, and earth surrounded the scene. Two minutes before, when decisions still felt reversible and the world was still right side up, I'd dismounted to open and close a makeshift concertina gate. Then, before I was able to put the loop over the top of the gate's pole, I'd heard a soft commotion behind me, turned around, and seen the impossible horror of the flipped-over horse.

An animal sense of impending slaughter prevailed; there was nothing to be done or said; nothing to be undone or unsaid, either. Charlie was going to die, of that I was certain. I dropped the gate I was in the process of closing, I dropped Sunday's reins too and she wandered off, unconcerned, to graze. Dilly hurried anxiously between the huge, thrashing horse and me, as if trying to convey the horrifying urgency of the situation to someone who could fix it.

The seconds swelled and grew and burst; fat drops of very distinct time. Big Boy made an effort to right himself, pitching over sideways time and time again. I glimpsed Charlie's crumpled body, free of the horse, but then Big Boy, unable to rectify himself, rolled back onto him again. It seemed like several more minutes before Big Boy at last found purchase, his hooves connecting with the ground. Slowly he heaved himself up. Then he stood next to Charlie's body, head hanging, flanks pumping, legs quivering. A thick thread of blood dribbled from his nose and there was a gash on his knee. The ground around him was flattened; sagebrush folded down on itself, grass mashed into the earth.

I thought, "It's not supposed to happen *this* way." This was supposed to be our calm, reasonable, reasoned way out of the marriage. We were supposed to be out for a quiet Saturday afternoon ride to discuss how we could end our stalemate. It was five days after our nineteenth wedding anniversary; Charlie had spent it alone in Wyoming, and I had spent it surrounded by two hundred Lakota Sioux on a magazine assignment near the Black Hills. Charlie was planning to leave the next day to accompany our son on a school-sponsored trip to Washington, D.C. I was planning to leave in a week back to the Pine Ridge Indian Reservation.

I suppose we thought we didn't have much time. And we were wary of being in the house together, of arguing in front of the kids. But I don't know why we had decided to go riding. For one thing, there's something unthinking and unseemly about getting on a horse to talk about divorce. In some cultures it's expressly taboo to ride in an altered state of mind, without clear and benevolent intention. "Even into battle," a Lakota elder told me afterward, and then amended that to, "Especially into battle." For another thing, I'd just ridden more than a hundred miles from Fort Robison, Nebraska, to the Pine Ridge Indian Reservation in South Dakota. A few hundred Lakota take part in the ride annually to commemorate the murder, in 1877, of their leader, Crazy Horse. "Today is a good day to die," he is supposed to have said on the morning of his death. "For all the things of my life are present."

I had found the Lakota were fearless horsemen—skilled and tough and careless. Most had forsworn saddles, and a few had little more than a strap of leather or halter rope between them and their mount's mouth. Some of the horses were barely green-broke. Even before the ride started, one horse bolted around the perimeter of the field where we had gathered at dawn, bucking wildly and dumping its rider hard on the June-verdant grass. No one helped the fallen rider to his feet. "Hey, you been hanging around the fort too long?" someone yelled. "Have you been shot at, or what?" someone else asked. "Camera wasn't rollin'. Go again." There was a lot of laughter.

But Charlie had pointed out that we would always have a reason to postpone this conversation. Also, we would soon have to get rid of our horses, sell their pasture, give up that life. We should ride while we still could, he argued. Besides, he reminded me, we needed to figure out the financial mess we were in sooner rather than later. Then the fighting started. Me saying again that I didn't understand our investments; that I had trusted him not to get us here in the first place. Him saying that he had been trying to tell me all along things hadn't worked out so well for us; that I had been an active participant in our economic demise.

||||||||||

"Easy there," I told Big Boy, taking his reins and moving him away from Charlie. Then I crouched down next to Charlie. He was still alive, but he was lying utterly motionless, and was strangely bloodless, by which I mean not only was he not bleeding—and it seemed as if he should have been—but all blood appeared to have left his body: his face was gray, his lips were slack and colorless, his eyes were open but unfocused. I thought it couldn't be long before a breath left his lips and no new breath came in.

"Hang on," I told him. "Please hang on."

I didn't tell him, "It's going to be all right," because I knew that would be a lie, and I knew if Charlie could hear me, he wouldn't want me to say something pointless and untrue. "I love you," I said. "I'll be right back." And then I spun down the trail we had just ridden up, back toward some mountain bikers we had seen earlier, and I was shouting as loudly as I could. But even as I came tearing down the road toward help, that single word pouring out of my mouth, I couldn't make the world do what I wanted it to do. The two men and the woman in their mud-spattered Lycra remained fixed in place against the tailgate of their car, a still life of bemusement. And Charlie remained on the trail in the hills, dead or dying alone.

I managed to say what it was I needed to say: Charlie had been crushed by an eighteen-hundred-pound horse, and he was in grave if not critical condition. My mind attached to the definition of those words, as if the accuracy of what I was saying was now somehow linked to Charlie's odds of survival. "Extremely critical," I said. Someone had the sense to dial 911, but it wasn't me. Afterward, I read in a *Harper's* magazine's "Findings" that African Americans are more likely to call a friend in a crisis than they are to call emergency services. That was my instinct too, perhaps because growing up I had never known a single person who had been in an ambulance, or really even believed in them. In the countries of my youth—Zimbabwe, Malawi, Zambia—we rescued ourselves and went to each other's aid. If you waited for official help, you'd die waiting.

When I got back to him, Charlie was sitting up, supported by one of the mountain bikers. He wasn't able to talk—pain and shortness of wind prohibited—but he could respond enough for us to know he had remained conscious for the entire ordeal. "It's going to be okay," one of the men told me. "He's all right." But I had seen the accident, and I knew enough about the overriding effects of adrenaline to feel a discomforting wave of doubt. I took off my sweater and put it over Charlie's shoulders. "Just keep breathing," I said. "An ambulance is on the way."

By the time we got to the hospital, news of the accident had sizzled up and down lines of communication and friends were waiting for us in the emergency room. The doctor arrived and inspected Charlie. He had the cursory bedside manner of a man used to dealing with thrown cowboys, tractor-crushed farmers, and smashed-up bullriders. In the room next door, a man who had turned his four-wheeler onto himself was shouting in distress. The doctor sighed and told us we'd be there for a while.

Charlie phoned his doctor in Wyoming and his parents in Pennsylvania. He told everyone he was sore, but he didn't think he was in any real danger. He was hoping the doctor would just order him bandaged up and send him on his way. He phoned our son and said he'd be on the plane to D.C. the next day, no matter what. One of our friends went to fetch food, an impromptu summer picnic in an unlikely setting. Someone else made Dilly comfortable in the back of a car. Another friend wondered aloud if anyone other than himself would benefit from the calming effects of a Pabst Blue Ribbon. The mood lifted a little. Everyone kept saying, "It's going to be okay now, Bobo."

It was an hour or two before the nurses wheeled Charlie out for an MRI. Then we had to wait for the results. "We don't read them here," the doctor said, by way of not much explanation. "They're interpreted by a person in Australia or India or somewhere." Another hour or two passed. Charlie got restlessly agitated. He was on the same stretcher the ambulance crew had loaded him onto at the scene of the accident hours earlier and the back of his head hurt where it had been strapped down tightly to the inflexible board. Could they not just loosen the strap a bit? Why couldn't they just wrap his ribs and let him go home? And he was terribly thirsty, but he was still not allowed to drink. Instead, we could give him rations from a small sponge on a stick dipped into a cup of water. His lips were cracked. We smeared them with Vaseline.

Then the doctor reappeared. "The news isn't good," he said. Charlie had a ruptured spleen, it was possible a lung had been punctured, and it looked as if his liver and lower intestine had been perforated. It had been four and a half hours since the accident and we didn't have time to waste, we needed to get to a level two trauma hospital fast. The man who had turned the four-wheeler over on himself was in the only ambulance being raced to Idaho Falls as we spoke. The doctor would order a life flight out of here.

I went into the corridor outside the emergency room and slid down the wall onto my haunches. I called the kids and told them everything was going to be okay, but we needed to get Daddy to a bigger hospital and I was going with him. I told them they should be brave and cook supper and have their baths. I called Bryan, who has always felt like my one-phone-call friend, the person I'd call from jail, maybe because he was a lawyer and has an analytical mind, or maybe because he's now an investigative reporter and nothing surprises him. He said, "Do you need me there?" And I thought yes, but I said no.

Then I began to negotiate with everyone I could find. What could we do to make Charlie more comfortable? When would the helicopter be here? And what did I have to do to get on it? The doctor said the helicopter would be here in twenty minutes. And the pilot would have to make the decision about whether or not I could go with Charlie. Air ambulance crews were worried about patients' wives getting airsick or hysterical, he said. I'd been in some lesser version of this place a time or two before. This was not, as they say, my first rodeo.

"Well, I bet it's your worst horse wreck," he said, as if he took personal pride in the probability.

"Hands down," I agreed.

|||||||||

When I was ten, I had been scraped off my bolting horse and smashed into the dry-season earth about a mile from the house. As I lay on the ground, breathless and in pain, the horse came back, as horses are supposed not to do, and stomped on my back and kicked me in the head. Then for a long time after that, I lay facedown in the pasture first waiting for air to come back into my lungs, and then for some help to arrive. Finally, a farm worker on his way back to the compound from his morning shift at the barn was made curious by my thin cries and walked over to where I lay. I recognized the man from the workshop.

"Help," I said. Mr. Chagonda seemed embarrassed by my condition. He stood over me, waiting for me to help myself. "I can't walk," I explained. So he hauled me up from my armpits unintentionally roughly, and a pain of such awfulness tore through my neck and back that my vision went into black pools and my ears started hearing screams. And after that I could not make any sense of my body. "Please," I told Mr. Chagonda, barely able to make the word. "Please."

When Mum saw me cradled limply in Mr. Chagonda's arms, she had him put me on her bed. She shone a flashlight in my eyes and pricked my feet with needles and said, "You need to buck up, Bobo." Then she sent a runner with a message to the top of the farm where Dad was vaccinating cattle.

After that, I drifted around on Mum and Dad's bedspread in a sea of agony until Dad came into the room smelling of cattle dip, manure, and cigarettes. He put a steadying hand on my forehead and said, "Dismounting without permission. Against regulations, you know." Then he radioed the police station and asked for an army escort into town.

We drove at speed, not because of the condition I was in, but because of the condition the country was in. We were at war, and slow-moving vehicles were easy targets. Still, from my perspective, the risk of getting ambushed seemed a worth-it trade-off. Going around corners fast made pain wash to the places where my spine had been crushed. I screamed and I shouted and I begged for help. I cried for the car to slow down. Then I began to vomit and Dad said, "Hold on tight, Chookies."

At the hospital the orthopedic surgeon was furious with Mum, as if the accident had been her fault. "Don't you know we've got a bloody war on?" he shouted. And he gestured to the bays outside the hospital entrance where Rhodesian government army trucks pulled in several times every day carrying wounded soldiers from the front, their limbs and bodies shattered by mortars and bullets and land mines. "And you bring me this! A horse riding accident? Where do you think we are? The bloody English home counties?"

I spent some lonely time stationary in a hospital bed in the children's ward with its faded murals of Mickey Mouse and Donald Duck and Goofy. The pain was terrible, and no one wanted to waste precious morphine on someone who still had all their limbs, but eventually the shock of the accident wore off and I could move my arms and legs. Then I was released and told to take it easy, although that advice seemed redundant, since for a year or so afterward I couldn't do much more than walk, and if I lifted my hands above my head, pain shot through the center of whatever was holding me up. Also, much of the time it felt like armies of ants in tiny fiery boots were marching up and down my legs through my spine and into my neck.

"All things are relative," Dad said whenever I complained. "It could be worse." And it was true. We knew scores of southern Africans who had been convulsed with malaria, trampled by wildlife, bitten by snakes, shot, burned, assaulted. The stories of their misadventures reverberated around bars and campfires for a time until someone else's disaster eclipsed theirs, usually in short order. But there were never sirens in these stories, and often hospitals didn't feature, although sometimes funerals did.

This was going to be different though. This was now, and here. Soon we were going to be in a helicopter carrying us swiftly to a reasonably sized, properly equipped, state-of-the-art hospital. I had been wrong to think things looked worse than they were. Charlie was in good hands and he wasn't going to die. He wasn't even going to be uncomfortable for much longer. I thought, "You've gotten soft living here. There's no need to panic as if this were Africa. This is the States. The end can be delayed and delayed and delayed." *Of course* Charlie wasn't going to die. People here had accidents and survived. Then they spent the rest of their lives showing off their scars and making dinner conversation more tedious.

||||||||||

Charlie's stretcher was lifted into place and I was strapped into a jump seat next to him. Then the helicopter shuddered to life and floated upward into the night sky. I put my hand on Charlie's arm and looked out the window. The moon was waxing gibbous and by its burning silver light I could trace our passage over the Big Hole Mountains, into Swan Valley, and along the South Fork of the Snake River to the farmlands south of Idaho Falls. Then we were coasting above the ponderous porcelain-white arms of energy-generating windmills on the outskirts of the city. It was surreal and serene and coordinated. "What an amazing country," I thought. "God bless America."

Our helicopter landed, and before the rotor blades had even calmed to a stop, a team of medics swarmed out of the emergency room and whisked Charlie into the hospital for another X-ray, an MRI, a CT scan. Meantime, I told the team of attending physicians the story of what had happened: the horse going down, the painful but mercifully short ambulance ride, the helicopter flight, the fact that Charlie had not lost consciousness for a moment, the suspicion that he'd sustained numerous internal injuries and had definitely broken several ribs.

"A rough day," one of the nurses said.

"Pretty rotten," I agreed.

Then I called Charlie's parents to give them an update. Charlie's father had gone to bed, but his mother was waiting up. "It's late there," I said. "Why don't you try to get some sleep? I'll let you know how he's getting on tomorrow." But I was thinking, "What can go wrong?" If anything, it seemed like overkill to me. "He's got an army taking care of him," I said. Charlie would be attended by a surgeon, a doctor, an anesthesiologist, a few nurses. Half a dozen people, it looked like to me.

Nothing like Zambia: in recent memory, Mum had had an emergency abdominal operation and they'd chopped her open without knocking her out properly. She was awake enough to feel and know what was going on, but paralyzed and unable to complain about her situation. "It was a Congolese doctor, and a Rwandan assistant—they were very good if you don't count the bit where they didn't give me enough anesthesia—and they were jabbering away to each other in French the whole time. Very uncomfortable *and* I couldn't even understand what they were saying." She gave me a dark look. "Schoolgirl French will only get you so far, and these central Africans have quite difficult accents, you know."

It was nearly eleven by the time Charlie was taken into surgery, roughly seven hours after Big Boy had reversed the natural order of the world and fallen backward onto him. I was shown to a lonely waiting room, beige with the indifferent anonymity of sad public spaces, whirring with the accumulated energy of other people's anxiety, grief, and hope. I had been told the operation would take sixty minutes, so I stationed myself in front of the clock and looked at its hands nudge time slowly beyond now, and now, and now. An hour passed, and then another. And then it had been three hours.

I phoned friends, waking them up. I said, "Do you think something's gone wrong?" My friends made reassuring noises. I told them I thought it was what I had said before the ride—"I don't want to be married to you"—that had brought the horse down. Bryan said, "Look, sunshine, it was an accident." But he knew me, and he knew too well the old broken place in me where responsibility settled and festered into self-blame and guilt. "It was an accident," he said again.

At last the surgeon came down to the waiting room. He told me everything was going to be fine, better than expected, in fact. In spite of what we'd been told in Driggs, Charlie's lungs, liver, and stomach were uninjured. True, the spleen was beyond repair and the surgeon had been forced to remove it, but this was cowboy country and plenty of people burst their spleens one way or the other and got along just fine without one. Also, there was nothing anyone could do about the broken ribs except wait, but that was pretty common too. "You can have your husband back home by Wednesday," the surgeon said. "Thursday at the latest."

Then I was shown up to a room where Charlie lay grog-gily in a bed with pipes and tubes running in and out of him. There were beeping monitors, the breathing sound of the blood pressure cuff, the occasional alarmed-bird chirp of the morphine IV kicking in. "There you are," I said.

"I think so," Charlie said.

"Dismounting without permission," I said.

There was a chair next to the bed. I sat on it and took Charlie's hand, stroking the chapped knuckles, the bitten nails, the tennis-racket calluses. Just before dawn, Charlie's breathing finally settled down and I could tell he was asleep. I put some blankets on the floor next to the bed, curled up, and tried to sleep myself. But when I closed my eyes the vision of Charlie trapped under Big Boy's enormous, upturned body came vividly back to me and I had to open them again and stare at the yellow glow of the night lights on the wall.

Eventually I got up, pulled the blinds back from the win-dow, and watched the sun break over town. The panic and fear of the long, waiting night drained out of me. I thought if Dad were here he would have brought me a cup of tea and a cigarette by now. Or better yet, his more drastic remedy of a medicinal quantity of brandy. If Mum were here, she would have brought me a calming pill. But my parents were beyond reach in some little hotel near the Sacré-Coeur on their last tango to Paris. "Mum and I are going to misspend my youth," Dad reminded me the last time I phoned home. "It's going to be a full-time job from now on." And I could hear Mum in the background warbling tunelessly, "Non, je ne regrette rien!"

Then the morning nurse came in. She woke up Charlie

and the business of morphine and antinausea medication and checking the dressing began. Charlie's incision from the splenectomy was nearly a foot long, all the way up his belly, held together with large steel staples. A slab of contusions covered the skin over the contours of his broken ribs. His groin was a mottled black apron of insulted flesh. The nurse asked him where his pain was on a scale from one to ten and Charlie said, "Six."

I said, "That's about a twenty-six for most people."

Then Charlie started to vomit—agonized unproductive heaves—and it was late morning before he was able to rest comfortably again, eyes closed, morphine raining into his veins. He looked disappointed, and a little angry, in repose. A dry frost of salt-and-pepper stubble covered his chin and cheeks and upper lip; the insistent process of his body's regeneration didn't seem to understand priorities. "Fix his injuries first," I silently instructed it. I thought of corpses, whose hair and nails are supposed to continue growing after death. How poorly we communicate, even the most drastic messages, even to ourselves.

I perched next to Charlie and stroked his forehead. When he got sick or hurt as a kid, Charlie had once told me, his father had done this. In turn, we did it for our children or, more and more rarely, for one another. Then, when Charlie appeared to be sleeping, I closed my eyes and rested my forehead on the corner of his pillow.

I wanted to take back everything I had ever said to hurt Charlie, to spool the pointless words from the air and ravel them back into my mouth. I wanted to press my lips over his, to feel the warm rush of relief of his lips pressing back on mine. I wanted that unreliable, occasional anesthesia of feeling as if we belonged together. I lifted my head. "I'm so sorry," I told my sleeping husband. And I thought, "What is wrong with me? I should have been quicker with the gate. I should have let cattle run riot. We shouldn't have been on horses."

|||||||||||

Incredibly, by late afternoon Charlie was ready to try walking a bit. So I helped him out of bed and he shuffled down the corridor, pushing his IV pole, his hand on my shoulder. He wanted to see mountains, he said. We found a window and looked out at the city, and at the spread of farmland to the north. In the distance we could see the rim of the snow-peaked Centennial Mountains, a light cloud sinking off its shoulders.

"I wonder if I'll ever get on a horse again," Charlie said.

"Of course you will," I said. "Don't be silly."

Then Charlie said he would like to wash. So we slowly walked back to the room and I undressed him, peeling away the hospital gown, stripping off his shorts, removing his tangle of tubes. Then he stood up in the shower and I sponged him gingerly with warm water. I knew this body better than I knew my own. The long, perfectly muscled legs; the broad back with the scar halfway down the spine; the slight paunch of his belly with the fresh, livid slice down its middle; the ribs rising like whale bones below the chest; arms still powerful from years of rowing a boat.

I had the nurse change Charlie's sheets and then both of us climbed into the bed. The nurse reattached the IVs and replaced the monitors. I found a position where I wouldn't hurt Charlie's ribs or squash any tubes, and he put his arm around me. We turned on the television and watched a Wimbledon rerun on the tennis channel; Björn Borg versus John McEnroe. The early eighties looked a simpler time—the big hair, the little shorts, the silly shirt lapels. The game ended and I switched off the television. Then we lay together in silence, with the huffing and beeping of the medical equipment.

I waited through supper. Then we watched some somnolent golf on the sports channel and Charlie dozed off to the polite patter applause of spectators on a course in Georgia or Florida. I kept my eye on the clock, digital numbers changing one red stripe at a time: a five morphing into a six, a six squaring into a seven, a seven into an eight, an eight to a nine. In the no-time of permanent lights and the round-the-clock nature of illnesses and broken bodies, clocks were the clearest way to mark the passage of day into night and of night's slow creep into dawn.

It was late by the time I left the hospital and found a motel. Then I read for a while until I was sure I was tired enough to sleep. But as soon as I shut off the light and closed my eyes, the vision of Charlie's accident returned, so I switched on the light and stared at the ceiling. The Snake River ran past my room near here. I could hear it racing west contained by banks of concrete. At last I got up, dressed, let myself out of the room, and walked along the river, watching streetlights bounce off the oily water on either side of the place where it had been abruptly broken by the imitation waterfall.

Early the next morning, I did an interview with a journalist from Colorado for my new book. My editor had offered to cancel any publicity until things settled down again, but I welcomed the distraction of work, the chance to talk about writing—this was my everyday world and the ordinariness of it comforted me. While the journalist and I were talking, another call came through. I looked at my phone and said, "I'm sorry I have to cut this short. I think that's my husband on the other line. He's in the hospital."

"Nothing serious, I hope," the journalist said.

"Oh no," I said. "He's going to be fine. A horse accident is all."

But when I returned Charlie's call he said he felt confused. "I can't get my . . ." He paused. "My brain is . . ." There was another pause. "Can you come?"

I hurried to the hospital. Charlie looked baffled and fretful. "I'm mixed up . . ." He pressed his lips together in an effort. "My head . . . I can't remember how to . . ." I called for the nurse and she called the doctor and he administered tests of the sort commonly depicted on afternoon soaps when someone comes out of a conveniently amnesic coma and has to prove their identity. Could Charlie say his name? What year was this? Who was the president? Did he know what had happened to him and where he was? Could he hold his thumbs and little fingers together? Could he touch his nose with first one forefinger and then the other?

Charlie answered all the questions correctly and managed all the physical tests, but he seemed uncharacteristically irritable and he was having trouble telling us what was going on in his brain. "What I want . . . ," he said, but he couldn't tell us what he wanted. "There are . . . ," he said. "Oh, I'm brain broken . . ." His hands went into the air and he conducted his remaining, unspoken words in the ensuing silence.

I pulled the physician into the corridor outside Charlie's room. "What's happening?"

The doctor was calm. "He's on some pretty strong medication. It's scrambling things a little, that's all." He smiled at me conspiratorially, as if Charlie were on a magical, drug-induced trip that we would all be so lucky to experience. Then he looked at his watch. "We'll keep an eye on him," he assured me, and then he hurried away. I phoned Charlie's doctor in Wyoming and he reiterated that pain and painkillers might cause confusion; it was nothing to worry about. I called another doctor, a friend of Charlie's. She said, "Are there any recreational drugs he might be withdrawing from?"

I felt as if I alone were watching an accident unfold in slow motion, Charlie falling silently off a cliff, his body plummeting through the sky. I felt as if I alone was shouting in alarm, "Look! Fetch a safety net!" But it seemed as if everyone else was purposefully ignoring him, admiring the blueness of the sky, the steepness of the cliffs, the incidental brightness of a bird flapping past Charlie's tumbling body. And I was an annoyance to them, a meddlesome woman saying the same things over and over, distracting them from an otherwise pleasantly normal day.

By early afternoon, there was no denying the severity of Charlie's condition. He understood what was expected of him—a horror of frustrated effort burned from his eyes—but when the doctor asked him to repeat certain phrases, he managed only exhausted, preemptive moans. And when the doctor asked him to touch his nose, or lift a foot, his movements were hard-won and approximate. The doctor ordered more tests, summoned a neurologist, agreed with me that things were worrisome.

While Charlie was being taken down for an MRI, I phoned his brother, a psychologist in New York. He has the soothing, unhurried delivery of one accustomed to dealing with the seriously unhinged. "Please, you've got to come out here," I said. But I couldn't bring myself to say what I really thought, which was that in a few hours Charlie might not be here anymore. Or that if he was here, he would be so far removed from a familiar version of himself that he would be unrecognizable. Charlie, as we had known him, was dying. A body remained that resembled Charlie's, but it had none of Charlie's acuity and power. Charlie's mind—that predictable thing so certain and in control two days ago—had slipped its coils and was now beyond the bounds of ordinary reach.

I called Bryan. "Things are getting weird," I said.

I could hear Bryan measuring my words. He said, "Are you okay? Have you slept yet? Or eaten?"

"Well, yeah," I said.

"Your voice just went up an octave," Bryan said. "Where do I fly into?"

At three o'clock the neurologist—a visiting physician from out of town, avuncular and undismayed—confirmed that Charlie had suffered a shower of strokes, for no really good reason that he could tell. Then he said he would order a course of intravenous blood thinners right away and that we shouldn't worry: rehabilitation would take care of Charlie's failed faculties; people had strokes all the time; Charlie was relatively young and very fit. So Charlie was hooked up to more medication, and then the nurses and doctors filtered out of the room and we were left alone in the surreal new reality of that word, *strokes*. I kissed Charlie's sagging cheek and pressed his inert hand. "Please hang on," I told him. And then I lied for the first time since the accident: "Everything's going to be okay."

Five hours later—seventy-six hours after the accident—the threads that were holding Charlie to his life were snapping fast. He had lost words and the use of his limbs, he was unable to hold his lips firmly against his teeth, his eyelids were sagging and his jaw was becoming slack. The doctor and nurses began to speak of him in the third person and I could tell it wouldn't be too much of a jump for them to begin referring to him in the past tense. But I knew Charlie was in there. I knew he could hear us. And I assumed that he would want me to fight for his life, harder than I would want him to fight for mine if the circumstances were reversed.

I had always told Charlie and the kids, "Pull the plug on me for anything worse than a bad head cold or a stubbed toe." I didn't think I could take the indignities, the beyond-ten-on-the-smiley-face-scale pain, the pools of bodily fluids, and the bags of excrement. That kind of fighting, that kind of life seems as if it takes courage and a depth of resources I'm certain I don't have. But I knew Charlie had those qualities in spades. I knew he was tolerant of pain, that he would take physical anguish over emotional turmoil any day, and that he valued life differently—not better or worse—but differently than I did.

In the back of my mind, I also knew there was a good chance I could end up fighting too hard, that I could fight beyond what was reasonable and not allow Charlie the dignity of a simple death. I knew that Charlie in a permanently vegetative state was not something he wanted. But there's a lot of room between vegetative and the way-he-was, or the way he could tolerate being. Too late, I needed to ask him, "Show me how hard you want me to fight." Too late, I needed to know what an acceptable life might mean to him. Too late, I needed to understand what a good death might look like.

"You always take things too far," Charlie repeatedly told me in one version of our frequent arguments. But there seemed to be nothing for it. If I didn't risk taking things too far, Charlie would die. Of that I was certain. So I pushed, and made calls and pushed harder, and when the neurologist could not be found, nor could he be made to answer his cell phone, I insisted we move Charlie to Salt Lake City, to a proper hospital, to a place with a neurological ICU.

"It's very risky to move him," the doctor said.

"It's very risky to keep him here," I replied, and I felt not angry, but something akin to that emotion that allowed me to speak in clear, whole sentences, paragraphs of persuasive, quiet outrage.

Then everything suddenly started to move quickly, time taking on a shocked, jumping quality. I signed papers authorizing Charlie's removal from this hospital and his transfer on a life flight to the next. The nurses began to prepare Charlie for an ambulance ride to the airport, attaching his monitors, IV bags, and medical equipment to mobile units, moving him onto a gurney. He was breathing, but beyond that, he had stopped existing in any way I could recognize. I kissed him. "Hang in there," I told him.

Our medevac airplane took off from Idaho Falls at midnight. The darkened cabin contained Charlie, two nurses at his head, and me on a small jump seat at his feet. In the dark, I strained against my harness and wrapped my hand around the high arch of Charlie's left foot, the only piece of him I could reach. "I love you. I'm sorry. Forgive me," I thought, over and over. *"I love you. I love you. I love you. I'm sorry. Forgive me."*

Charlie and I had let the sun set on our anger too many nights, too many months, too many years in a row. We had brought each other our defenses, not our vulnerabilities; we had attacked one another with our strengths instead of shoring one another up with them; we had been disloyal to one another and to ourselves. We had allowed old, unrelated wounds to become the battle scars of our marriage. We had been so careless, so arrogant, so heartless, always assuming there would be another day, another chance, another way to fix ourselves, to forgive one another, to see and be seen. "One of the most widespread adult illusions," John Berger wrote in his 1967 biography of a country doctor, *A Fortunate Man,* "is the belief in second chances." Charlie and I had used up all our illusory second chances, and now we were here.

BROKEN

As soon as the ambulance deposited us at the doors of the hospital in Salt Lake City, Charlie was taken away for scans and tests. Meanwhile, a brain surgeon put the images I had brought from Idaho Falls on a screen. He pointed to two dark places on the monitor where Charlie's neck connected to his head. "These are bilateral dissected carotid arteries," he said. He went on to explain that carotid artery dissection was not an uncommon injury associated with severe whiplash but that it was very rare for both arteries to be dissected. It was even more rare for someone to survive this eventuality. The surgeon didn't look at me. "There's not enough blood getting to his brain to support normal life," he said. Then he excused himself and hurried away into the rest of the dark hospital.

The definition of hell has been the same forever, or at least since Dante's *Inferno*. The beginning of pain, the moment at which it is instinctive to flinch away, is simply that. It's the beginning, it's not where we get to stay, in mediocre discomfort: "But the stars that marked our starting fall away. We must go deeper into greater pain, for it is not permitted that we stay." The ICU was an eerily static place, pale fluorescent lights whirring into echoing spaces. There were beds taken up with bodies collided into silence by strokes, vehicle accidents, and system collapse. Monitors beeped from one room to the next like electronic insect-creatures trying to locate one another in the humming, weird, no-night hospital. It seemed a terrible place to have come to, the sort of place you don't come back from.

Charlie's room was still empty; a tiled floor held the space into which his gurney would be wheeled. I propped myself up in the corner of the room where the walls could support my shoulders. I dug my phone out of my bag and called a friend with medical training. He was someone I could trust to tell me the truth. Then I phoned Vanessa in Zambia. I told her I needed to speak to Mum and Dad. I said, "There's been an accident. I think Charlie's dying."

Vanessa said, "Oh Al, I'll get Rich."

Richard came on the line and told me the name of a hotel in Paris. He said he thought my parents were staying there and gave me a number. When Dad answered the phone, I started to cry. I told him everything: the ambulances and helicopter, the airplane ride, the strokes. There was a pause, then Dad said, "That's a lot of roaring about." And I could see him weighing up the cost of all that fuel against the odds of Charlie's ultimate survival and I was suddenly furious with the people who had raised me. Their crazy courage no longer seemed charming and life-affirming and more or less innocent, it felt deliberately distancing and brutal.

"I can't do this alone," I said. I was trying not to shout, and surges of resentment I didn't even know I harbored came flooding up. Why could no one from my family be with me now? What calamity could shift them?

Dad was saying, "It doesn't sound like I can get there in time, Bobo."

"Please, Dad."

"What can an old madala do, that you can't?"

I imagined Dad in an inexpensive little hotel near the Sacré-Coeur, sitting on the edge of a small single bed with the phone against his ear, his pipe cupped in the palm of his hand, fingers pressed against his chin, a cloud of tobacco smoke around his head. I imagined Mum on the other bed, her feet up, an open book next to her. I knew she had been rereading George Orwell's *Down and Out in Paris and London* in preparation for this trip: "It is a feeling of relief, almost of pleasure, at knowing yourself at last genuinely down and out. You have talked so often of going to the dogs—and well, here are the dogs, and you have reached them, and you can stand it. It takes off a lot of anxiety."

"I'm so frightened," I said.

There was a long pause, and then Dad said, "You already know everything there is to know, Bobo. You've been here before."

I hung up and hugged my knees and the ways in which loneliness surrounded me became its own weather system. Dad never apologized for not being there, but months afterward he said to me, "Sometimes you can give a person just enough help to sink them." And I thought back to those days of Charlie's accident and how it felt a lot like being alone on a crowded boat and that if anyone from either of our families had swooped down and made my loneliness feel less profound, I might have been able to carry on as we had been, and everything might have been worse in the long run. "Letting other people row their own boat to shore," Dad said. "That's the tricky bit."

About an hour passed. At last Charlie was brought back to the room and he was hooked up to monitors, and IVs, and a catheter. The nurse said, "Does your husband have a living will?" And then I noticed that the pupil in one of Charlie's eyes had frozen into a wide black dilation. I knew there was a name for this: fixed dilated pupil. And because of this, I knew too that Charlie's condition had plummeted from extremely critical to whatever came next. I squeezed Charlie's hand and he squeezed back. "The company of six is reduced to two," Dante wrote. "By another way the wise guide leads me, out from the quiet, into the air that trembles, and I come into a region where is nothing that can give light."

The surgeon returned and said there was nothing more they could do for Charlie in this hospital. He seemed matter-of-fact in his delivery of this bad news. What else could he be? I knew he was just doing his job, grinding away through another shift, paying the mortgage or a car payment or for his family's vacation. To him, Charlie was a body making its way through their system. But to me he was Charlie Ross, father of my children, my dream-relinquished spouse. "Then we'll move him to a hospital that can," I said. I kept touching Charlie's arm, so he would know I was near.

The doctor shrugged. I asked him to make the necessary phone calls now, I didn't care that it was three in the morning. I knew that every minute we waited, every minute no matter what, Charlie was sinking further and further beyond the reach of any help. I could only imagine his torment, to be mentally alive and alert and aware, but trapped inside a dying body. It was Jean-Dominique Bauby's short but beautiful memoir after his stroke: "Paralyzed from head to toe, the patient, his mind intact, is imprisoned inside his own body, unable to speak or move."[10] It was Michel de Montaigne's

---

10. Jean-Dominique Bauby, *The Diving Bell and the Butterfly: A Memoir of Life in Death* (New York: Vintage, 1998).

reminisce after his near-fatal riding accident: "I can think of no state more horrifying or more intolerable for me than to have my Soul alive and afflicted but with no means of expressing herself. I would say the same of those who are sent to be executed with their tongues cut out."[11]

At first light Charlie was wheeled out to a tiny translucent-bellied helicopter on the tarmac outside the hospital. I kissed his forehead. "I love you," I told him. His eyes were open, his mouth slack, as if agog with horror. "Hang in there," I told him. "Please hang in there." The sun appeared suddenly, unapologetically bright behind the Wasatch Range. The sky raged pink with dawn. "Look, the sunrise," I said, as if that was something that might give Charlie hope. Wasn't there a statistic that most people died before dawn, not after? If he'd made it this far, he could make it for the rest of the day and all he needed was this day, today, now. The orderlies loaded Charlie onto the helicopter, and two nurses climbed in next to him. Those of us left on the ground ducked and turned our backs against the turbulence of the blades as the helicopter lifted into the perfect June morning.

|||||||||

I had a map of everyone's whereabouts in my head. Charlie's parents were hurtling through the unimaginable space between their home and this hospital. His brothers were on their respective ways from New Jersey and California. His sister was staying put in Washington State. Vanessa was at home in Kafue. Mum and Dad were in Paris. Bryan had left Philadelphia and would be landing in Salt Lake in the early

---

11. Michel de Montaigne, *The Complete Essays*, translated by M. A. Screech (New York: Penguin Classics,), 421.

afternoon. The kids were home, taking care of themselves and the dog and the horses. My friends were checking in every few hours; some had taken the children food, some had driven my car down from Idaho, yet others had offered to track down Charlie's living will if I thought he might need it. "I have no idea what it says," I admitted. "I have no idea how much he wants to live." It was appalling. How had Charlie and I come this far without knowing even this about one another?

I spent the hours of Charlie's surgery alone, bent over a chair in the waiting room of the neurological ICU at the University of Utah hospital, bargaining with every power I could summon in the universe. "Let him be able to feed himself, let him be able to bathe alone, let him be able to speak," I prayed. Sometimes I added, "Let him be able to walk in the mountains again, let him be able to row a boat, let him be able to play tennis." I cradled my phone in my lap, waiting for a call from the outside, as if there was a power beyond these walls that could reach me now, as if the gods could literally check in and let me know how things were going to pan out.

At noon, a team of surgeons and specialists came to tell me that the procedure had gone miraculously well. One of the surgeons actually used that word, *miracle*. They had inserted a stent in Charlie's right carotid artery. His left carotid artery remained dissected, but blood was flowing to the brain. "Are you here alone?" someone asked. Someone else brought a warm blanket to put over my shoulders, and asked if I had eaten or had anything to drink, which seemed so beside the point. Then I was taken to Charlie's room.

He was barely conscious, strapped to his bed with wide belts at the head and thighs and feet. He looked like a medical experiment, or a dangerously mad person, or like someone being prepared for lethal injection. I wasn't prepared for how little of Charlie's mind appeared to have made it back from my image of who he would be now. I'd expected a miracle to be more obvious, more flashily impressive, which is just one of the problems of thinking about miracles in biblical terms. One of the surgeons tucked his finger under the straps experimentally, the way we did when we didn't want the raft to fly off the trailer. He explained, "It's very important the patient be kept completely still. We noticed there's a blood clot in his groin and we don't want that coming loose."

I stared at the surgeon. "Meaning?"

"Well, if that got into his lungs, or his brain . . . That's fatal."

I wanted to protest, to declare a truce. Charlie's body seemed to know endless ways of fighting against its own recovery. I pulled a chair up to his bed and put both my arms over his thighs. "He won't move," I promised. The surgical team left and now it was just the two of us, me silently willing Charlie to consciousness, he battling whatever internal force was keeping him under. He would wash awake, speak a few mumbling words, only to get flooded back before his eyes could completely clear. Sometimes he moaned and thrashed, indicating he wanted the straps made loose. I pressed down hard on his legs. "Please don't," I begged. "Please be still."

Then suddenly, a little over two hours after being wheeled up from surgery, Charlie opened his eyes and asked, in a clear, lucid voice, for water. I dipped a sponge in a cup and held it to his lips. To my joy, his mouth closed obediently around the sponge. He sucked and swallowed. That simple act—pushing a few drops of water down his throat—now seemed a wondrously complicated achievement. "You're going to be okay," I said. I kissed the edge of his chapped lips. "Oh, thank God, you're going to be okay."

CRY FOR A WHOLE PEOPLE

Life doesn't stop just because life as we know it has ended. Charlie spent four weeks in hospital. When he came home, he slept a lot, and then he spent almost every waking moment on the phone either on hold or with insurance agents and doctors. His pain ebbed and flowed: it was soothed by a quiet, dark room; it escalated with tension and stress. The equation was simple: we needed more quiet darkness, less tense stress. You'd think the bluntness of this message, if not the fact of one of us nearly dying, would be enough of the lesson we needed to slow down and pay attention to how we were living. But it was harder than you'd think it should be to get away from the ways our lives were inextricably knotted in systems designed to keep us churning ahead.

Insurance claims and bills piled up next to the bed. Charlie sifted through the envelopes, e-mails flooded his inbox, and I could hear him clicking replies. Then his head pounded with headaches of such blinding severity that they took up all his energy, and he lay still with a facecloth over his eyes breathing into the pain. Doctors told Charlie the headaches were likely a result of the strokes, but no one could tell him how long they would last, or if they would ever diminish. "We don't know anyone who has survived what you went through," they explained. "Or if they did, they can't talk."

There seemed very little I could do for Charlie except stay out of his way. I had deadlines to meet. I didn't sleep much, worried into wakefulness by everything that had happened and everything that still needed to happen or that might happen. The house would still have to go, to the bank if no one else, and we would have to work out how to survive. And we would also have to work on the end of our marriage. "But we can stay together until you're better," I said. "I can be here for you."

He said, "Will you work on the relationship then?"

I knew what that meant: it meant Charlie wanted me to work on myself, to journey away from the bits of me of which he disapproved and to arrive at a place he liked and understood and to stay there, as that fixed and dependable person. Then we would be okay. I would be unchallenging and calm in this manifestation. I would not read books that would unspin my mind from where it had been; I would not fall in love with strangers and their strange ideas; I would not have unfixed and unappeasable ideas that made me stay awake half the night. "No," I said. "I'm done working on the relationship."

Charlie's face clouded. "Then we're done."

Friends and acquaintances came round with meatloaf and casseroles—the meals of catastrophe—and some of them offered sympathy and advice. A few said they hoped Charlie and I would stay married now, as if the accident had been an alarm that had required everyone to get belowdecks and stay there in hunkered endurance. But after all that terror and pain and fighting I knew I loved Charlie deeply and reflexively. I knew he was brave and enduring and stoic. I knew too that if I had to again, I would do everything in my power to save his life. Of course I would; that went without saying. But I also knew I couldn't change myself into the solid thing he needed me to be and because of that I couldn't save our marriage. *We* couldn't save our marriage. Not with all the power in the world. The knot had tightened and loosened, and for the last time, it had untied. I do. We did. It was done.

Even now, broken in obvious and not so obvious ways, it seemed not only possible but also probable that Charlie would be better off without me and that I might be better off without him. It wasn't so much that we weren't right for one another, but rather the ways in which we were wrong were so intractable and damaging that nothing—however profoundly accidental or deeply deliberate—could fix us. His flaws and my flaws didn't weave together or tear us apart; they enmeshed us. We had loved one another into an eddy in which one or both of us would eventually drown, because accidents frequently happen at the liminal line between the world's innate chaos and the belief that your own skill and sanity can save you.

There is a perfect angle at which to break through an eddy line. Charlie understood that pure mathematical moment, the exact place at which to slice a raft from an eddy into the current. When he had first taken me whitewater rafting, I'd been amazed by his code-breaking abilities, his understanding of the language of rivers. Above us the world's largest sheet of falling water, Victoria Falls, plunged into an intimidating recycling pool. It was infamously difficult to get out of that eddy—the Boiling Pot, they called it—but with almost casual ease, Charlie edged our raft into the current. The nose of the raft caught the current, we spun, Charlie calmly put his oars into the water and pulled back powerfully. We surged into the current and plunged headlong into the roar of the Zambezi. "This is a man who will never get stuck," I thought.

The local paper ran a front-page story, "Ross Knows Wife Saved Him: 52-Year Old Makes Remarkable Recovery from Medical Nightmare After Horseback Accident."[12] People I barely knew stopped me in the grocery store and in the post office and repeated reported truths and half-true bits of gossip back to me, as if I was no longer a participant in my own life but an actress in someone else's version of a life, someone who had forgotten her lines. "But he's alive, that's the main thing," they said, as if Charlie's accident was something more imperative than his purpose. "Well, it's *a* thing," I said. I started to avoid public places.

I lay awake night after night mulling the same question over and over, but the answer was always the same. Charlie's accident was not an excuse or a reason to continue an ongoing misadventure. "Thoroughly unprepared, we take the step into the afternoon of life," Jung wrote. "Worse still, we take this step with the false presupposition that our truths and our ideals will serve us as hitherto. But we cannot live in the afternoon of life according to the program of life's morning, for what was great in the morning will be little at evening and what in the morning was true, at evening will have become a lie."

Time and place circled. After a few days at home, Charlie went back to the office in the mornings, and then rested at home in the afternoons. The brown velvet curtains billowed into the bedroom. A hushed, sour atmosphere prevailed in the house. Sarah and Fuller got summer jobs in town. Sometimes they ferried messages from the other side, condolences and support from the community. My friends pooled together

---

12. *Jackson Hole News and Guide,* July 20, 2011.

and paid a caterer to bring meals every evening. "No more of these nosy people dropping by with a dish," my Utah-raised friend said with final authority. "I grew up Mormon. I know what your fridge will look like in a month."

Weeks passed. Charlie's insurance paid for him to get physical therapy, although the therapist could find little wrong with his coordination. He started to take walks along the river, and planned for when he might play tennis again. He put on weight, and his appetite returned. He slept better at night, and needed less sleep during the day. We undid our lives.

||||||||||

The house didn't lift off its foundation, but we could not find a way to keep it, and it went to another family. Charlie built a new house and furnished it along clean, modern lines; I found a condominium in the middle of town and called it the "Paris Flat," because there was mildew on the inside of the windows and that first winter the plumbing froze solid. The kids split their time between us. Dilly moved in with me, mostly. A cowboy who said he didn't mind Big Boy's unpredictability took him off our hands; a friend offered to board Sunday and the children's horse.

I used my restored name to open a bank account and get a credit card. For a few frozen Tuesday afternoons that first winter I met with other women who were financially illiterate, and together we learned to read the numbers that had for so long frightened and confused us. The women were a lot like me—they had been raised by people who had taught them how to ride a horse, shoot a gun, and endure, but had somehow forgotten to teach them how to count. "Holy crap, this is certainly easier than cooking breakfast for twelve men at four in the morning," one of the women said, when the numbers fell into place for her. "No wonder they kept it a secret."

The divorce got difficult and antagonistic in all the usual ways. Charlie and I both felt betrayed and wronged and misunderstood. Nevertheless, long after the divorce was final, and I had sat with that decree on my lap for a full afternoon feeling immovably weighted with grief, I experienced his removal like the earth itself had been taken from under my feet. You can be the perpetrator of your own emptiness, it can be the very thing you need, and it can still undo you.

Recently I caught a glimpse of Charlie in the grocery store. I saw him before he saw me and I wondered at how well and how happy he looked. He still has his athlete's command of the earth, he walks casually and covers ground easily, he looks fit in that way of people who live in mountain towns. His left carotid artery spontaneously reconnected, which so amazed the doctors they were helpless to explain how or why. The kids tell me his headaches are almost gone. He skis, he plays tennis, he fishes, he goes whitewater rafting. He's even taken the children's horse and his old saddle with its CORSE written across the seat and ridden in the hills around his summer cabin.

It's not anyone's job to make another person happy, but the truth is, people can either be very happy or very unhappy together. Happiness or unhappiness isn't a measure of their love. You can have an intense connection to someone without being a good lifelong mate for him. Love is complicated and difficult that way.

|||||||||

I went back to Zambia in May. It is my favorite time of year on the farm, the end of the rainy season, but before the bush grows dry and brittle and the fires start in the valley. The second week of my visit, Dad and I walked down to the river and sat on an old dugout canoe upturned in front of the pub at the bottom of the farm. The Zambezi is wide as a lake just here, interrupted by a long, blond bar of sand at the tip of which a small crocodile was basking. Behind us, evening was happening, and the jesse bush around the pub was chattering with weavers and thrushes and chats.

It had been two years since Dad had threatened his biblical death. In that time, he'd stopped joking about his threescore years and ten and he had given up the idea of misspending his youth. Something about the Paris trip with Mum had sobered him. "Well, Bobo," he said. "Paris will always be Paris. But I suppose I am getting a bit long in the tooth for it all." Also, he was starting to talk about the possibility of selling the farm. "You don't want it, do you?" he asked.

"No thanks," I said, but I knew it wasn't really a serious offer. I'd already made a life elsewhere, and whatever else I was going to do, I wasn't going to leave my children, or bring them here. In any case, southern Africa had changed so much in the twenty years since I'd left, it was no longer reflexively familiar to me. It wasn't just the pace of development but also the rate of loss that had estranged me. Our forests, which had been my deepest memory of Zambia's essence, were vanishing so fast it was like seeing someone in the unstoppable course of a disease. It was likely that elephants and lions would no longer exist in the wild here well within my lifetime. Roads hurried out of the city center to uranium mines all over the country. This was industry with heat, poverty, and dust. And it was relentless.

"I don't think I could handle the snakes," I said. "And the rabid dogs." I pointed to the sandbar, to the crocodile soaking up the last of the day's sun. "Or the crocs."

Dad considered the crocodile silently for a while. Then he grunted. "Hm. Been there all week, that fellow. Patient things, those." Then there was the business of restocking his pipe, and the several matches flaring before it was finally lit. A puff of smoke enveloped our heads. Dad cleared his throat. "Yes, well, I suppose I always thought there would be time for one more farm. I thought I'd have time to go back to cattle. A small ranch somewhere near Choma, you know?" He shook his head. "And then one day I realized this is it. We're not going anywhere. This is the last farm. You always think there will be more time and then suddenly there isn't. You know how it is. You have to leave before the rains come, or it's too late."

For a long time after that, Dad and I sat in silence. In time a flock of egrets came up the river to roost. I thought about Charlie on this water twenty-two years earlier, how he'd seemed to know its submerged, invisible secrets. We'd camped a mile or two south of here on the second night of our first date, that same canoe trip when we'd been mock-charged by the elephant and I'd thought that this Charlie Ross, *my* Charlie Ross, was invincible. I'd never thought then to be sitting on the banks of this river again, exactly here, now, or that my parents would have left the plateau and made a farm out of a scrub of land in this valley.

"I always thought I'd leave you a bit of land," Dad said at last.

"It's okay," I said, which it mostly was.

"Oh, that reminds me," Dad said. "I nearly forgot. I got that ring for you."

"You did?" I was amazed. Around the time I was getting my name back, I had asked my father if I could have a copy of his family's signet ring.

"It's only for sons," Dad said. "Properly speaking."

"How about improperly speaking?" I asked.

The Fuller crest is a rampant lion holding a ball. Where my father's ring has rubbed against guns and fences and tools, the lion and the ball have almost worn off, and the gold has become tenuously thin. Still, it seemed something magical to me, a talisman handed down through the generations, like a distant assurance that you were at least somewhat deliberate, potentially worthy, acknowledged as heir.

"Well, I suppose times have changed," Dad said, but he didn't sound as if he thought it was a good idea to change with them. So I resigned myself to the reality that I was a daughter, and in my father's eyes, that excluded Vanessa and me from the automatic stamp of approval that would have been afforded his sons. Then, without my knowing anything about it, over the next couple of years Dad had put signet rings together for Vanessa and me. He found the gold in South Africa, he had the rings made in Zambia, and then he had sent them to England to be engraved. Now he fished around in his pocket. "Here you go, Bobo. Here's yours."

I found a finger that fit the ring. "It's perfect," I said. "It'll be good to have when things get tough."

"Yep." Dad messed with his pipe some more. Then he lit it and a cloud of smoke wafted over me. "Although it's worth remembering it isn't supposed to be easy," Dad said. "I'm not sure who came up with that load of old bollocks. Easy is just another way of knowing you aren't doing much in the way of your life." More smoke came my way. "But you're doing it, Bobo."

"Sometimes," I said.

There was a long silence. Then Dad said, "I should have probably warned you from the start. Living your own life can be bloody frightening, and you will be lost half the time. But if I had told you that, you might not have set out in the first place, and that would have been a terrible waste."

"I know," I said.

Then mosquitoes lifted in a thirsty cloud off the ground and misted off the edges of the river, so Dad and I stood up and walked back toward the noise of the camp, where Mum, Vanessa, and Richard were sitting around the coffee table and my nieces were playing cards. A fire in front of the camp chugged woodsmoke and the singe of cooking meat. The dogs were curled up at people's feet. It was deeply comforting and familiar, and yet I knew I no longer really belonged here. At least, I had lost my unequivocal sense of belonging. I'd fledged too hard, flown too urgently from the nest, been carried off by stronger trade winds than I could fight against. And now I was solo, truly. And it was okay.

A long time ago in Malawi, Dad had bought a Mirror dinghy from a neighboring farmer and rigged it up on the lake. He showed me the basics. "Bottom is wet, top is dry," he said. "If that changes, you've capsized." Vanessa asked if she could have my cassette player if I drowned. Mum warbled Frank Sinatra's "Red Sails in the Sunset" at me. Dad gave me a shove, and I was off skimming across the top of the water, the sound of the sails clacking in the wind. Things went well until I accidentally went about and the boom swung around and smacked me in the mouth. But even after that, with my fat lip and gappy smile, the taste of freedom had felt worth it.

I learned this then: sometimes the wind lulled and there was nothing to do but wait it out in the tiny patch of shade afforded by the sail. And sometimes the wind got gusty and unpredictable, and then whatever line I pulled, things didn't make sense and the boat seemed to get a mind of her own. But there was a feeling of emancipation too, the way I had sometimes felt on a horse, as if nothing malevolent could touch me. As if for once I wasn't my gender, or my powerlessness. As if for those hours, I was enough.